# DYNAMICS OF FAITH AND CONFESSION

## Charles Capps

# W.O.F. PUBLICATIONS
### DALLAS, TEXAS

**All Scripture quotations
from the *King James Version*
of the Bible unless otherwise stated**

**ISBN 0-914307-05-3**

**Printed in the United States of America
Copyright©1983 W.O.F. Publications
Published by W.O.F. Publications
The Publishing Division of Word of Faith
World Outreach Center
P.O. Box 819000, Dallas, Texas 75381
All Rights Reserved
No Reproduction Without Permission
Second Printing 1985
Third Printing 1985**
Cover Photo by Lauren Schunn — WORD OF FAITH

# Table of Contents

*There are many truths in the Bible that never come to light unless you look at them from a specific angle. This is what I endeavor to do concerning faith and confession.*

*This book is dedicated to the body of Christ to help clear up much misunderstanding about these principles of faith and confession. Read it prayerfully. Have an open mind to the scriptures. Take the time to research other scriptures that are not covered in this book. Be honest with yourself and God, even though you may have been taught contrary to these principles. Allow the Holy Spirit to reveal these things to you personally. Then let your decision as to how you can put these principles to work in your life be based on what the Holy Spirit reveals to you.*

**Charles Capps**

# INTRODUCTION

Much has been said about faith and confession. Much has been taught, but many things have been misunderstood about it.

In this book I will share with you the practical application of God's Word regarding faith and confession. It will clarify much misunderstanding on the subject.

I want you to understand there is a balance in the faith message. Balance is not a bad word. Sometimes people get disturbed when they hear the word *"balance."* They think I mean mix faith with some unbelief. But that is not what I mean.

When I say *"balance,"* I am talking about not going so far in one direction until you run in the ditch on the right or left. But keep it balanced by all of God's Word.

As we study faith and confession, we are going to dig up some things and say some things **which have been left unsaid** regarding the faith message. We will talk about how to apply the principles of faith, and how to operate in faith according to the Word of God.

When we deal with faith, a few people run off with the message. They thought they heard. But they understood only part of it. Some of them run off in the ditch on the right hand side of the road saying, *"All you have to do is have faith. Have faith, and you won't ever have any troubles."*

But I don't know anyone who has ever lived in this world without having troubles. You are going to have some troubles and some problems in life. But God has given us a way to walk victorious through the problems of life.

I want to teach you the **principles** of faith and the **principles** of confession, **not just a formula.** Many people have just gotten the formula. If you get the

3

formula without the principle, then you are going to get in trouble.

I am going to say some things which have been left unsaid. I think sometimes we have been guilty of just saying the good part and not telling all of the other things that go along with it.

I want to admonish you who are going into the ministry to pay particular attention to what I say. Be careful in the way you present faith and confession. Proverbs states it this way: *"The sweetness of the lips increaseth learning."* (Proverbs 16:21)

I have seen many young people and young ministers who have gotten hold of the faith message and had a good message to deliver. But their attitude, their arrogance, and the way they presented it turned people off so they did not want to hear it at all.

There wasn't a thing wrong with what they said. **It was the way they said it.** It isn't just what you say, it's also the way you say it. You can be so dogmatic about a truth that you turn everyone off so that no one will want to hear it.

You must guard yourself against getting dogmatic about anything and making it so strong for people that they can't handle it. You have to minister to people on the level where they are. Deal with people where they are and get them developed in their faith.

Certainly there are some stronger things that you can say to people later on in their development. And there are ways of saying things. You can say almost anything to people while teaching them, if you say it in love. Say it as Proverbs says, with sweetness of the lips.

## DON'T RUB THE CAT THE WRONG WAY

When you rub the cat the wrong way, the fur is going to fly. And irritated people will not listen to you, even though what you say is right. Even though what

4

you are preaching is the truth, you must have an attitude of humility to teach the Word of God in love so that people can receive it. **No matter how great the truths you teach, if they are not received, you have failed.**

I want to say one other thing by way of introduction. Don't ever take **a truth** and try to make it the whole truth.

Many people have done that. Perhaps all of us have done that in time past. We have taken a simple truth which is **a truth** and tried to make **the whole truth** out of it. People have tried to do that about confession and they get in trouble. They say, *"Well, all you have to do is confess it. All you have to do is confess what you want, and it will happen."*

Then somebody said, *"Well, the Bible says all you have to do is say it. When you say it, you are going to have it."*

## DON'T MAKE A TRUTH THE TRUTH

Well, that is **a truth.** But it's not the whole truth. So don't ever take **a truth** and make it **the truth.** There is more to faith than just saying it.

These are some of the things I want to point out. I want you to take note of these things as I teach and give you illustrations.

Learn to relate to people on their level. If you can't relate to people on their level, then you have missed it. You have to reach them where they are. For if you are not careful, you can get a lot of people turned on to faith and confession, and they are like a man who wants to build a third story on a vacant lot. But you can't do that. You have to start with the foundation.

# Chapter One

# GOSPEL
# IS THE POWER OF GOD

*So, as much as in me is, I am ready to preach the gospel to you that are at Rome also.*

*For I am not ashamed of the gospel of Christ: for it is the power of God unto salvation to every one that believeth; to the Jew first, and also to the Greek.*                    *(Romans 1:15-16)*

Notice what the apostle Paul said here. He said, *"I am not ashamed of the gospel."* You know, we shouldn't be ashamed of the gospel.

You know what the word *"gospel"* means. We all know what it means. But sometimes we forget. **Gospel means good news.**

Paul said, *"I am not ashamed of the good news."* But I have seen people who were ashamed of the good news. Part of the reason was that they had heard someone who was arrogant about their faith, and about teaching it. They taught it in such a manner that people just didn't want to hear it.

## DON'T BE ASHAMED OF GOOD NEWS

I have heard people say, *"I tell you, I've heard all of this faith business I want to hear."*

Well if you have, you have heard all of the Word of God you want to hear, for God's Word is filled with faith. If you teach God's Words, you will be teaching faith.

That isn't really what those critics meant. They meant they didn't like the attitude with which some people delivered a message of faith.

If you are going to reach people, you must reach them where they are. And the message must be presented in an attitude of love.

The same is true of the prosperity message. Some people got turned off by the prosperity message because of the ways it was presented. I also know that the individuals who taught it didn't mean for it to sound that way.

## CHECK UP ON YOURSELF

**It helps us speakers to go back and listen to our own tapes sometimes to see how our message is coming over.** We need to check up on ourselves. Sometimes things come over to the congregation or audience in a way that we didn't even realize, and they misunderstand it.

Unless you are careful with your words, people think you are just bragging on yourself.

Paul said, *"I am not ashamed of the good news, for it is the power of God."* Good news is the power of God. It is the Gospel. And the gospel, of course, is faith, and it is prosperity, and it is healing. All of these are involved in salvation.

When Paul said that, he was telling us the power of God is in the Word of God. The Bible says He upholds all things by the Word of His power.

Then the gospel is the good news. It is the power of God unto salvation — which means deliverance, preservation, healing, soundness, and prosperity.

If you preach it the way the Word says it, and with the right attitude, people will believe it. But you can turn people off by saying things the wrong way. Don't take the Bible and beat people over the head with it. Sure, they are bound in religious tradition. You were too when you first heard it. I know you were, because we all were. We were all in the same boat. We were bound by religious tradition.

8

Then because we were set free from it, sometimes we would like to say, *"No, you're wrong. Here's the way it ought to be."*

## BE RIGHT SCRIPTURALLY AND IN ATTITUDE

Any time you teach something with an attitude people won't receive, I don't care if you are right scripturally, you are wrong in attitude; you have missed it. Understand what I'm saying here.

*"The sweetness of the lips increaseth learning."* Paul said the gospel, the good news, is the power of God.

Paul didn't say it was bad news. Sometimes people take good news and turn it into bad news. It's amazing to me that ministers can take good news and when they get through with it, it is bad news.

They can take a scripture that actually is one of the great healing scriptures and then turn it into bad news. As an example, I think of what Jesus said to the apostle Paul when he prayed asking to be delivered from the thorn in the flesh. Jesus said, *"My grace is sufficient for thee."* (II Corinthians 12:9)

## RIGHTLY DIVIDE THE WORD

I have heard people take that verse and, because of religious tradition and lack of understanding, say, *"Well, God wouldn't heal Paul."* But, Jesus said *"Paul, My grace is sufficient for you."*

**Grace is God's willingness.** That scripture is one of the most powerful scriptures in the Bible for healing and for deliverance.

First, you must understand Paul's thorn in the flesh wasn't sickness. The scripture plainly calls it a messenger of Satan.

*And lest I should be exalted above measure through the abundance of the revelations, there*

9

*was given to me a thorn in the flesh, **the messenger of Satan to buffet me,** lest I should be exalted above measure.*

*For this thing I besought the Lord thrice, that it might depart from me.*

*And he said unto me, My grace is sufficient for thee: for my strength is made perfect in weakness. Most gladly therefore will I rather glory in my infirmities (weaknesses), that the power of Christ may rest upon me.*

*Therefore I take pleasure in infirmities (weaknesses), in reproaches, in necessities, in persecutions, in distresses for Christ's sake: for when I am weak, then am I strong.*

*(II Corinthians 12:7-10)*

The Lord said to him, *"Depend on My grace, Paul."* He had to tell that to Paul three times before Paul got it. He finally understood it.

But God wasn't going to remove it. He just wasn't going to do it. It was up to Paul. He had to act on that grace. He had to resist the devil. And then he did get rid of the thorn in the flesh. Read the last two verses in the book of Acts.

You see, the gospel is the power of God. It's the good news. Some people take it and make bad news out of it, or are ashamed of it. I have seen some who were ashamed of the prosperity message.

But we are declaring the **principles** of the Bible. God's Word is full of prosperity. Prosperity is involved in salvation.

Now here is the point I wanted to get to in this scripture. Paul said the gospel, the good news, is the power of God unto salvation. The word *"salvation"* there is the Greek word *"sozo,"* which means deliverance, preservation, healing, soundness. The idea encompassed in it is total prosperity for spirit, soul, and body. That's all involved in this word *"salvation."*

10

# FAITH IS SUBSTANCE - HOPE IS GOALSETTER

The apostle Paul said that the good news is the power of God.

With that in mind, let's go to Hebrews 11:1.

*Now faith is the substance of things hoped for, the evidence of things not seen.*     *(Hebrews 11:1)*

Paul says **now faith is.** Notice that there is a present tense word on both sides of the word *"faith."* Now faith is. Somebody said, *"Faith is the substance of. . . ,"* but the Bible says, *"**Now** faith is the substance of. . ."* If it's not **now** faith, it's not faith at all. Faith is in the now.

**Hope is always out in the future.**

Many people miss it here. They confuse hope and faith. They say, *"well, I believe God **is going to** do this **sometime.**"*

But God has done all He is ever going to do about your healing. He has done all He will ever do about your finances. He has done all He will ever do about the devil until the end times.

The promise of God is already spoken. God's Will is in His Book — the Bible. It is the will of God. It is God's purpose. It is Jesus' last will and testament. He has already said *"yes"* to it. It's not a matter of what God is going to do someday. **It's a matter of us receiving what He has already done,** and then bringing it into manifestation through the spiritual force called faith.

God could have created the world any way He wanted it. He could have created this earth and said, *"We are going to have a 'feel like' world."* Then, when you get up in the morning, however you feel, that's just the way it will be.

We would really be in a mess, wouldn't we? We would have gotten up some mornings not feeling saved. Then we'd have to get born again once again.

11

Whether or not you feel saved, if you have acted on the Word of God and if you have done what the Word says, **then you are saved.**

## LAW OF FAITH

God has established some laws, including the law of faith. Faith is a law. It's a law of God. The apostle Paul talks about that in Romans 3.

> *Where is boasting then? It is excluded. By what law? of works? Nay: but by **the law of faith.***
>
> *(Romans 3:27)*

Paul was talking about being brought into Christ by faith. He was talking about receiving Jesus by faith and entering into the provisions by faith. He says you can't boast about it, you can't boast about the fact that your sins are gone, because it is something you have received by faith.

He said, *"Where is boasting then?"* It is excluded. By what law? Works? No. By the law of faith.

See, the old law was a law of works. But now he says it's by the law of faith. So he could actually say this, **that faith is the law of the new covenant.**

Under the old law, people went by the law. In other words, their works made them righteous. But under the new covenant, righteousness is not works at all. It comes by faith. Righteousness comes through the law of faith.

> *Do we then make void the law through faith? God forbid: yea, **we establish the law.*** *(Romans 3:31)*

What law are we establishing? The law of faith. This law of faith Paul is talking about is the same law the apostle Paul refers to in Romans 8.

> *For to be carnally minded is death; but to be spiritually minded is life and peace.*

12

*Because the carnal mind is enmity against God: for it is not subject to **the law of God,** neither indeed can be.*                    *(Romans 8:6-7)*

The carnal mind cannot operate in the law of God. The law of God he is referring to is **faith.** You see, faith is a law, just like any other law.

It is just like God's law of gravity. It works. Whether or not you believe it, it works. The law of gravity works all the time. God's law of faith works. It works all the time.

The problem is that **some people don't work it.**

The law of gravity is going to work. It's mandatory. This law of faith is optional. God tells us how to operate it. It is a law. It will work whenever it is applied properly. It will not work whenever we fail to work it the way God said to work it.

## FAITH IN HEART

Notice in Romans 8:7, the carnal mind is enmity against God and not subject to the law of God; neither indeed can it be. The carnal mind can't operate in God's law of faith.

Faith works in the heart (spirit). We need to understand that faith is a spiritual force. It works in the spirit of man. It works in the heart of man.

It doesn't work in the head. Mental assent works in the head. Some mistake it for faith. But mental assent is not faith.

Mental assent working in the head says, *"Yes, that's in the Bible, so I believe it."* But they really don't believe it. If it's only in the head, you don't really believe it. Mental assent says, *"Yes, it's truth, because it's the Bible."*

**But is it truth in your life?**

13

*"Well, no, it hasn't come true in my life."*

Then it's not in your spirit yet.

If you get the faith of God in you, it will produce the reality of that thing. But it has to get in the spirit (heart). It won't work in the head.

## FAITH WON'T WORK IN THE HEAD

This is where so many people get into trouble. They try to operate faith out of the head. They think all they have to do is say it. They say, *"Mark 11:23 says that I can have what I say, so I'm just going to start saying all these things I want."*

Here is an example of what I am saying. A certain man said to a friend of mine, *"I'll tell you, this faith confession stuff doesn't work."*

He replied, *"Oh, why do you say that?"*

He said, *"I confessed three hundred times in one day that I had a new car, and I didn't get it."*

You can see **all he had was the formula.** He thought it was just some magic formula or something — you say it and the car appears the next morning in the garage.

No, that is not what the Bible says. That is not the application of scriptural faith. All he had was the formula, or mental assent. He totally missed the principle.

You see, faith will work, but you have to develop yourself in it.

Here is something that many have never understood. When you teach this, you need to teach it this way from the beginning, and then fewer people will misunderstand.

Just because you believe the scripture is in the Bible does not mean the promise in the scripture is going to be true in your life. **You must develop yourself in faith regarding that promise.** Again, just finding something

14

in the Bible doesn't mean you have faith to believe it, or to believe for it. Just saying, *"I believe the scriptures,"* doesn't make it come true in your life.

*"Now faith is the substance of things hoped for."* You **hope** for that promise to be true for you. That's what everyone **hopes for.** We all **hope for** the promises of the Word of God to become true in our personal life for healing or financial prosperity or spiritual gifts. We **hope for** that to become true in our life.

But hope will not get it done. Yet, **hope is needful.**

**Without hope you would have nothing for faith to give substance to.**

People come to be prayed for in a ministry line, **hoping** to be healed. Hope will not heal them, because there is no substance of healing in hope. Yet, if they didn't have hope, they wouldn't have come.

Reading this, you **hope** to learn something. If you lacked hope of learning something you wouldn't be reading this.

**Faith is the substance** of things **hoped for.** Hope will not bring it to pass, but without hope you wouldn't even be there. Many lose hope, then they have nothing for faith to give substance to. They give up too quickly.

## DEVELOP YOURSELF - IT TAKES TIME

I'm a pilot. I have been flying planes for over thirty years. I didn't just wake up one morning and say, *"I believe in airplanes. I guess I can fly one."*

I had to learn to fly airplanes. I didn't just go out there one morning and say, *"Well, yes, I believe that airplanes will fly. I can fly one."*

**I had to develop myself.** I had to try. In fact, it's trial and error. And I made a few errors. But I had an instructor with me. He helped me along. I learned what will work and what will not work.

I don't care who you are, when you start developing your faith, you will have to grow and develop as I developed as a pilot.

**You start where you are in faith and develop from there.**

You have to develop yourself. Over a period of time, you will learn what works and what doesn't work. You will learn what will short out your faith and what will make it work faster. We are sharing some of those things in this book.

## FAITH COMETH

There are not many shortcuts. However, there are a few avenues which will cause faith to come more quickly to you as an individual. If you will use them, that spiritual force within you will build more quickly.

Here is the specific thing I am referring to. **If you speak God's Word out of your own mouth, faith will come more quickly.**

*So then faith cometh by hearing, and hearing by the word of God.* (Romans 10:17)

The Holy Ghost, through Paul, is talking about faith in God and in His Word. He says faith comes by hearing God's Word. Now, that being true, it has to be spoken in order to be heard. You can't hear something that isn't spoken.

I am convinced that the apostle Paul is referring to you hearing your own voice and hearing your own words repeating what God said. For you have more faith in what you say than in what anyone else says. At least you should.

That is the way God designed us. He designed us to like what we say more than what anyone else says.

Again, you must start where you are. The way that faith comes is by hearing.

Hebrews 11:1 says faith is the substance of things. Notice that faith is the substance of things hoped for. Faith is the evidence of **things not seen.**

We have assumed that you use your faith on **things which you can see. That is directly contrary to what the Bible said.**

The problem is that in religious tradition, for years we have drifted over into this area. I don't know if we were taught that way or if we just ended up thinking that way because we didn't have the right teaching on it.

## FAITH SEES THROUGH THE STORM

You know the old saying that seeing is believing. Well, that's not really true. **The Bible says that believing is seeing.**

Somebody said, *"Well, now, old brother so-in-so, he just had blind faith."*

But true faith is not blind. Faith always knows. Faith always sees. Faith is able to look through the storm and see the end results.

**Faith will always talk the end results, instead of what is.**

Faith is like the radar in an airplane. If it is turned on when you are approaching a thunderstorm area, it will paint those storm cells on a screen that's like a little TV screen. You can tell exactly where the cells are. That radar can see through that storm and show you exactly how many miles it is to the other side, and exactly what turns you have to make to miss the heavy rain cells.

I have flown through widespread thunderstorm areas. Covering a large area. I couldn't go around them, but I picked my way through them. It looked like a solid line to me, but my radar could see through the storm. I have picked my way through the clouds when I couldn't see anything outside the windshield of the airplane; I have gone right through the storm without getting into the heavy cells of rain.

## FAITH KNOWS

That's what faith does, and that's not blind faith. Faith always sees and faith always knows. Faith is not blind. What some people call blind faith is presumption — and presumption is blind. With it, you will end up in the ditch. **What some people call faith is not faith at all. It is foolishness** or presumption. They just presume that something will happen, but not because they had faith in God's Word.

Some of you have done things acting in what you thought was faith, because someone else did it. *"Well, brother so-in-so gave his car away and he got a new one. I'm going to give mine away."*

Yes, and you may walk for ten months.

**Don't ever base your faith on what someone else did. Don't ever base what you are doing on someone else's faith.**

## ACT ON GOD'S WORD, NOT OTHERS' FAITH

**You** have to hear from God. You see, God may have told brother so-in-so to do what he did. But did He tell you to do that? When you check up on some things, sometimes you will find out why so many have what they call faith failures. **It wasn't faith at all. They just did it because someone else did it,** or because somebody else got blessed. You see, it makes a difference when you do things because of the Word of God. You need to do it because of the Word of God, and not because of what someone else did.

If God makes the Word come alive to you in a certain area, and impresses in your spirit that this is what you are to do, it will work out. You will know.

18

Faith always sees. **Like radar, faith sees right through the storm.** It knows what the end results will be. It always knows.

*"Believing is seeing."* This is a scripturally correct statement.

*"Faith is the substance of **things.**"* Some get uptight when you start talking about things. They say, *"Well, you're just teaching people to get things."*

God had lots to say about things. Especially things that He had given us.

> *According as his divine power hath given unto us* ***all things*** *that pertain unto life and godliness, through the knowledge of him that hath called us to glory and virtue.* (II Peter 1:3)

## DON'T LEAVE ANYTHING UNSAID

You wouldn't think that people would be this foolish, but some man said this. *"Well, the Bible said that God has given us all things, then I'm just taking what's mine. I'm not really stealing, I'm just taking what's mine. Paul said, 'all things are yours.' So if all things are mine, I'll just go get it; I don't have to pay for it."*

Now, you wonder about people like that. You shouldn't have to say these things, but you do. You who are going into the ministry to teach this will have to deal with some people who think like that. You shouldn't have to say some things, but you must not leave anything unsaid.

We sometimes assume that people understand what we are saying. But don't ever assume anything. You must cover every avenue. Say it so many ways they can't miss it. Cover all areas, and repeat what you covered.

Faith is the substance of things. It is the evidence of things not seen. You use your faith on something you don't see. Let me give you a simple illustration. Let's

19

use a clear plastic or plexiglass podium as an example. The person who built it didn't create it. It was made of soybeans, or petroleum, and other substances.

Well, the podium exists. It is in the natural realm. We can see it. It's clear, so it's a little hard to see sometimes, but it is in the natural realm. I don't have to use my faith to believe it's here. I can look away and still touch it. When I slap it, I can hear it. By the realm of the five senses I know it's here. There is no need for me to use my faith to believe it's here. Why would I want to use my faith, when I can see it? It's in the natural realm. I know it's there, you know it's there. Everyone who sees it knows it's there. There is no need to use faith on it.

## GOD DOES NO CREDIT BUSINESS

**You use faith on things you can't see;** things which are not manifest.

But somebody said, *"I'm going to believe it when I see it."*

Well, God doesn't do any credit business. You have to believe it first. You have to pay cash up front to get things from God.

You have to believe it first. You have to believe it before you see it with the natural eye. That's what faith is about. Faith is the title deed. In other words, faith is of the same value as the thing hoped for.

Faith is right now. Faith is seeing in the Spirit what the Word promised, when it is not yet manifest in the natural.

> *Therefore I say unto you, What things soever ye desire, **when ye pray,** believe that ye receive them, and ye shall have them.* (Mark 11:24)

What *"them"* is he talking about? *"Them"* things you prayed. The things you prayed is what you believe that you receive.

20

If you prayed the Word of God, that will increase your faith. If you pray the words of the devil, or if you pray the problem, it will decrease your faith and cause fear to come.

You see, if we are going to operate under the principle of faith, if we are going to follow these things, we have to believe some things that we can't see in the natural.

The best way to get the image of the thing hoped for in you is by **your words.** You must speak words of faith. You must speak the word of promise. God has given to us all things that pertain to life and godliness. (II Peter 1:3)

It's not a matter of God doing anything about it. Often we say that we believe God is **going to** do this, referring to a promise. But that is really not the right way to state it, for God is really not **going to** do it. **God has already done it.**

We need to acquire the substance of things and cause the manifestation of the thing.

God gave us that faith and that power and that creative ability in His Word. His Word is filled with faith. There is enough faith in every promise of God to cause it to come true in your life and in the life of every person on the face of the earth. And still there would be as much faith in it as when you started.

That's why Paul said the gospel is the power of God. It's the good news, it's the power of God, because when you gain the knowledge of it, you will gain some faith.

*Now faith is the substance of things hoped for, the evidence of things not see.*          *(Hebrews 11:1)*

The evidence then, is the faith. **And faith stands in the place of the thing until the thing appears.**

When the thing appears, you don't need the faith in it anymore. You have the reality of it; it's in the natural realm. But until it is manifest, faith is the only evidence that you have.

Remember, we are talking about God's kind of faith. It has to do with nothing but the Word of God. It has to do with only the things that God has promised.

Some say, *"Well, what if God doesn't want them to have what they are confessing?"*

## FAITH AND THE PROMISE

This faith I'm talking about has nothing at all to do with anything outside of what God has promised. **Would it be wrong for us to believe God for the things that He gave us,** the things that He promised us?

I believe it hurts the heart of God when His people do not take advantage of the provisions that He has made. Now He has made a way for us. It's through faith. The apostle Paul says the only way that you can enter into the grace of God is through faith. (Ephesians 2:8-9) You can't be saved any way other than through faith.

> *For by grace are ye saved through faith: and that not of yourselves: it is the gift of God:*
> *Not of words, lest any man should boast.*
>
> *(Ephesians 2:8-9)*

There are some things that God will not do. You cannot enter into some things unless you enter in through faith.

Salvation is one of them. You can't be born again without believing the Word of God.

Faith is the substance of things hoped for. Somebody said, *"If God has given us all these things, then where are these things? Why don't I have them?"*

# FAITH IS THE SUBSTANCE OF THEM

*Through faith we understand that the worlds were framed by the word of God, so that things which are seen were not made of things which do appear.* (Hebrews 11:3)

When we move down two verses from Hebrews 11:1, we learn the worlds were framed by the Word of God. We could say it this way. *"We understand that it was through faith that the worlds were framed by the Word of God."* That's the way God framed the world. It was through the Word; His Words which He spoke. He spoke words which brought creation into existence. There was nothing created without words. All things were made by words.

*In the beginning was the Word, and the Word was with God, and the Word was God.*

*The same was in the beginning with God.*

*All things were made by him; and without him was not any thing made that was made.*

(John 1:1-3)

Without Him — Him who? Him, the Word. Without the Word, nothing was made that has been made. In the beginning, all creation was made by the Word. If the Word was with God, the Word was God. **The Word is still God over every situation.** When you use the Word of God and quote it by faith to bring a situation under control, you will sometimes have religious people say, *"You're just trying to act like God."* They will get upset about it. They don't like people acting like God.

**I am not trying to be God. I'm acting as God** would act in this situation.

Just simply say what God said about things, regardless of what the circumstance says. That doesn't mean that you ignore the circumstance. I'm doing something about the circumstance. We will get into that in some of the later chapters, when we can go into more detail about it.

You see, this faith is the evidence of things not seen. God did not see the world when He said that, except through the eye of faith. In the beginning, God created the heaven and the earth. Then we see the recreation, the reforming of this earth when God looked out and saw darkness, and He said, *"Light, be."*

## GOD'S WORD TRANSPORTS FAITH

What God saw was darkness. But **God spoke what He desired.** God spoke His will. God's Word was His will, and it carried power. It was a spiritual force. This is why Hebrews says we understand it is through faith that the world was framed by the Word of God.

He framed the world with His Words. You just can't build without substance. He took words. Faith-filled words were God's substance.

Here, essentially, is what God did. He took His words and filled them with a spiritual force that the Bible calls faith. God filled His words with that faith. And the way God got His words out there where they could do something to the trouble spot was by speaking them out there. He used His words as containers to hold His faith and contain that spiritual force and transport it out there into the vast darkness and say, *"Light, be!"*

That is the way God transported His faith to cause creation. That is the way God creates. You find it all through the Bible, from Genesis to Revelation.

*God never does anything without saying it first.*

That may sound simple, but it is also profound. If you will check up on yourself, you will find that you hardly ever do anything without saying it first. You usually say it several times before you do it. That's the way we are made. We are made in the image and likeness of God. We have the ability to conceive God's Words in our heart. That brings into our spirit being, into our heart a spiritual force called faith. We can take that faith which comes from the Word of God, fill our words with it, and use our words as containers to transport our faith into our situation, into the circumstances of life, **and transform that circumstance.**

This is not magic. This is the power of God. The gospel is the good news. It is the power of God unto deliverance, preservation, healing, and soundness. We are talking about using the faith of God. We are talking about using the power that is in God's Word to bring faith into us — that spiritual force which will cause us to be triumphant over any circumstances of life which disagree with the Word of God.

We are not out to get something that God doesn't want us to have — as some people want to imply. We are out to get what God promised to us by His method. And God's method is by faith.

## Chapter Two

# LIFE AND DEATH IN WORDS

### WORD POWER

In this chapter we are going to be studying words and the power of those words. Most people do not realize the power of words. Before we get through with these study sessions, you will realize that the things you are speaking out of your mouth are setting the cornerstones of your life.

Words deceive us. Words transmit. Think about that. The words that you speak **transmit faith or transmit fear.** So when we are talking about your spoken words, we are talking about things that are powerful.

We will start in Genesis where God looked out over the darkness that was over the earth.

*In the beginning God created the heaven and the earth.*

*And the earth was without form, and void; and darkness was upon the face of the deep. And the Spirit of God moved upon the face of the waters.*

*And God said, Let there be light: and there was light.*                                          *(Genesis 1:1-3)*

Notice the Bible said that in the beginning God created the heaven and the earth. The Spirit of God was hovering over the water. The water was there, the darkness was there and the Spirit of God was there. But you will notice that nothing happened until words were spoken. God said, *"Light"*. Now, that's powerful when God speaks it. When God speaks, it comes into existence.

27

You always have some who say, *"Now, I can understand that, because you see, that was God."*

You have heard people make statements like this — *"sticks and stones may break my bones, but words will never hurt me."* Nothing is further from the truth. Words can **kill you.** If you don't know what you are doing with words, they will destroy you.

*The integrity of the upright shall guide them: but the perverseness of transgressors shall destroy them.* (Proverbs 11:3)

Perverseness is crooked and contrary speech. Proverbs has a lot to say about perverse lips — crooked and contrary speech, or speaking things that are contrary to what we actually believe.

Many people speak perversely. I don't know why we do it, but we do. But you have to break yourself of it.

Often you speak the very opposite of what you mean. You have heard people say, *"Oh, isn't that a big dog!"* when it's a little bitty Chihuahua.

That is what the Bible calls perverse speech. It's crooked or contrary. You are speaking contrary to what you actually mean.

God created man in His own image and in His likeness. **God's Word is His will for man.** When I say man, I mean mankind. Man was created in the image of God. Man's word — your words — should be your will toward God. We really should not speak **anything that we don't desire to come to pass or that is not our will.**

## DEATH AND LIFE
## IN THE POWER OF THE TONGUE

You've heard people say, *"What you don't know won't hurt you."* **What we don't know is what is killing people.** Proverbs says,

*Death and life are in the power of the tongue: and
they that love it shall eat the fruit thereof.*

*(Proverbs 18:21)*

We are talking about how to get our spoken words
in line with the Word of God. God's Word conceived in
the heart, then formed with the tongue and spoken out
of the mouth becomes a spiritual force releasing the
ability of God. These are words that you conceive in the
human spirit. Then you form them with the tongue.
Have you ever noticed that your words or syllables are
separated by the tongue when you speak?

The Word of God conceived in the human spirit
(what the Bible calls the heart), then formed with the
tongue and spoken out of the mouth releases the ability
of God. Let's put it this way — it should do that. This is
how you conceive God's Word.

You also conceive and speak other words. For
instance, if it's the devil you are quoting, you are
releasing the power of the devil. It's just that simple.

Many have failed to understand why there is so
much teaching on confession. They criticize us because
of our confession, and teaching the power of God's
Word in the mouth.

Actually, what we are doing is simple Bible truth.
We are simply **showing you how to operate in the
principle of God's Word.**

## GOD'S PRINCIPLES

God's principles are involved in confession and the
principles of faith. The Bible says faith comes by
hearing, and hearing by the Word of God.

It didn't say that's the only way we can get faith.
We thought that was what He said, but that's really not
what He said at all.

Faith in God's Word comes by hearing the Word of
God. By the same token, you could say that faith in the

29

devil would come by the same method. Faith in the devil could come by hearing the words of the devil.

So you see, we shouldn't take **a truth and try to make the** truth out of it. Paul said,

*So then faith cometh by hearing, and hearing by the Word of God.* (Romans 10:17)

Hearing the Word of God causes faith in God and in His Word to come to you. This is the spiritual force which is released out of your mouth when you begin to speak God's Word. It actually releases God's ability inside of you as an individual. This is one of the reasons why Paul made this statement.

*I can do all things through Christ which strengthened me.* (Philippians 4:13)

He understood that the Word conceived inside of him and spoken out of his mouth actually set the cornerstones of his life.

When I first saw some of these principles, I knew they were true — I knew they were in the Bible. In my teaching, I even made some statements about them. In fact, I even made this statement, *"God's Word that is conceived in the heart, formed with the tongue, and spoken out of the mouth becomes spiritual force, releasing the ability of God within you."*

But I didn't know **why** this was true. And I didn't know how this was true. Now, over a period of years I have found why it's true, and why it works.

## WHY GOD'S WAY WORKS

God's way works. When you find out why it works, that makes a difference.

Why is creative power released inside you when you speak God's Word out of your mouth? This is essentially what God told Joshua back in the old covenant — in the Old Testament.

*This book of the law shall not depart out of thy mouth; but thou shalt meditate therein day and night, that thou mayest observe to do according to all that is written therein: for then thou shalt make thy way prosperous, and then thou shalt have good success.* (Joshua 1:8)

Do you want to make your way prosperous? Do you want to know the key, the secret of being successful in the things of God, or in anything in life? It is to do exactly what God told Joshua to do. Do what God told the children of Isreal to do. **Put the Word of God in your mouth.**

Let me share with you why this principle is so important. The words you speak are more important to you than to anyone else. The reason your words are so important to you is that they affect you more than they affect anyone else.

The individual who is cursing someone, using God's name in vain, is not going to hurt the other person, but he is hurting himself. He is actually going to bring damnation on himself by speaking those curses.

## EARS TO HEAR

Most of you have heard yourself on a tape recorder. When you heard your voice, you said, *"Who is that? That couldn't be me. Oh, no, that's not me."*

But that's how others have been hearing you all the time. That is exactly the way you sound.

God created you with two sets of ears — not just an ear on each side of your head. You have an outer ear and an inner ear. The inner ear is made up of a bone structure inside your head. The inner ear feeds your voice directly into the human spirit — what the Bible calls the heart. This is why the words you speak are more important than the words that anybody else

31

speaks to you or against you. The words you speak affect your whole being.

Medical research has discovered that the part of the brain which controls human speech is connected to every nerve of the body. The words you speak about yourself can even affect your health. For years, people didn't understand it. But now medical science has found that there is some connection between what you say and what happens to you.

Jesus knew that two thousand years ago. He said that a man will have whatever he says, if he will believe and doubt not in his heart; if he will believe what he says will come to pass. (Mark 9:23, Mark 11:23-24)

Now let's pull this together and point out what we are talking about here regarding words. In the beginning God spoke, *"Light, be!"* **when light was not there.** God saw darkness and He said, *"Light."*

This is God's method. This is not man's method. We just followed along after God with His method. When God saw something that didn't agree with His will, He spoke the thing desired. When God saw darkness, He said, *"Light."* If it had been some of us, we would have looked out there and said, *"Oh, it's dark out there. It's getting darker, and I don't believe it will ever get light."*

Then, you see, that would have affected our situation. It would have affected us internally. If we had the power that God had, the faith that God had, such talk would have turned the thing into darkness forever.

God was smarter than that. He told us all through His Word what works. When He spoke light, then that is exactly what appeared.

Have you ever wondered why it is impossible for God to lie? God releases sufficient faith in every word He speaks to cause that which He spoke to come to pass. I'm going to say that again. **God releases sufficient faith in every word He speaks to cause it to come to pass.**

# WHY JESUS HAD GREAT FAITH

Have you ever asked yourself why Jesus had so much faith? Sometimes people say, *"I wonder why Jesus had so much faith."* Jesus said, I say only that which I hear My Father say. Jesus had faith because He only spoke that which He heard His Father speak.

> *And if any man hear my **words, and believe not,** I judge him not: for I came not to judge the world, but to save the world.*
>
> *He that rejecteth me, and receiveth not my **words,** hath one that judgeth him: **the word** that I have spoken, the same shall judge him in the last day.*
>
> *For I have not spoken of myself; but the Father which sent me, He gave me a commandment, **what I should say, and what I should speak.***
>
> *And I know that his commandment is life everlasting: **Whatsoever I speak therefore, even as the Father said unto me, so I speak.***
>
> *(John 12:47-50)*

Jesus spoke the words of His Father. When He did, it caused the faith of his Father to come inside of Him. That's the spiritual force we are studying. *"Faith cometh by hearing, and hearing by the Word of God."* Faith that is in God's Word gets into your spirit when you speak it.

Quite often we have read Romans 10:17 and said, *"Well, that just means that I just need to read the Bible."*

It didn't say that faith comes by reading, it says faith comes by hearing. In order to hear something, it has to be spoken.

It's more powerful when you hear it spoken out of your mouth. Because you are the way you are, you like what you say more than you like what anyone else says.

33

Now, if you don't, there is something wrong with you.

The words you speak affect you more than the words that anyone else speaks. You can get **some faith by hearing me speak** the Word of God, or read the Word of God. But faith will come to you more quickly if you speak it out of your mouth. That's why God told Joshua, *"Keep My Words in your mouth day and night. Keep saying what I said."*

When Satan came against Jesus, tempting Him in the wilderness, Jesus responded by speaking only what His Father said, *"It is written."* (Matthew 4:4,7,10)

Now, if you went around speaking everything God said, then the faith of God would develop inside of you. You would get highly developed in the God kind of faith.

## CROOKED SPEECH MEANS LESS FAITH

This is where we have nullified our faith in days past; we have spoken crooked speech. We have spoken things that we didn't mean. We have said, *"isn't that a big dog?"* when it's just a little dog; *"Oh, isn't it hot outside?"* when it was 20 below zero. By doing that we have developed ourselves to not release faith in the words we speak. But God releases faith in every word.

If you are going to get faith out of God's Word, there must first be faith in God's Word. If you had an empty bucket, you couldn't pour water out of it. If there is no water in the bucket, you can't pour water out of the bucket. Now that is very simple, but it's also profound. If there were no faith in God's Word, you couldn't get any faith out of God's Word. But God's Word is filled with faith.

That faith which is in God's Word will get inside of you, if you will speak it. Remember when you heard your voice on a tape recorder? You said, *"Oh, that couldn't be me."* But it was you.

The reason it didn't sound like you to you, when it sounded like you to everyone else, was because you have been hearing yourself all these years with the **inner ear.**

Your voice is picked up by your inner ear and fed directly into your human spirit. That's the way you hear yourself speak.

The way you hear your voice isn't like you sound to us at all. When you heard yourself on the tape recorder, then you heard your voice just exactly the way we have been hearing it — and you got embarrassed about it. You said, *"Oh, that couldn't be me. I just don't believe that's me."* But it was you.

## WRITE GOD'S WORD ON YOUR HEART

Why would God create us with two sets of ears — some on the outside, and some on the inside? Because there's a part of us on the inside that also needs to hear. It's our spirit. It's what the Bible calls the heart. The writer of Proverbs makes this statement.

> *Let not mercy and truth forsake thee: bind them about thy neck; write them upon the table of thine heart.*  (Proverbs 3:3)

How are you going to write things on the table of your heart? The Psalmist David found out how. He broke into that revelation. He says, *"My tongue is the pen of a ready writer."* (Psalm 45:1)

Now let's connect these things that we are talking about. God told Joshua, *"Don't let the Word depart out of your mouth. Meditate therein day and night. Observe to do all that is written therein. And then you'll make your way prosperous."*

God told the children of Israel, "If you shall harken diligently to the voice of the Lord thy God, and observe to do all His commandments, then all these blessings will come upon you and overtake you." (Deuteronomy 28:1-2) Harken means to hear intelligently and declare.

In other words, they were admonished to speak what God said.

*"Faith cometh by hearing, and hearing by the Word of God."* The spiritual force of faith (which is the substance of things hoped for, the evidence of things not seen) comes to you when you hear the Word of God. And in order to hear the Word of God, the Word of God must be spoken.

The force of Faith will come to you more quickly and be more profound if you speak it out of your own mouth. When you do, your voice is picked up by your inner ear, and fed directly into your spirit, or what the Bible calls the heart. That's the way you write these things on the table of your heart. You do it by speaking them out of your mouth.

I think we have lost this down through the years. The Apostle Paul understood it. The New Testament saints, and even Old Testament saints understood it. But somehow we have missed it. We have underestimated the power in words to affect the human spirit or the human heart. James said it this way,

*If any man among you seem to be religious, and bridleth not his tongue, but deceiveth his own heart, this man's religion is in vain.* (James 1:26)

In other words, what he believes is in vain, if he doesn't bridle his tongue. For his tongue will deceive his heart.

## HEART DECEPTION

Why would the tongue deceive the heart? Because the tongue speaks the words which are picked up by the inner ear and fed directly into the heart. And your heart or spirit assumes that what you speak is what you want. Your tongue can deceive your heart into believing that words spoken are exactly what you want. Your spirit will say, *"Let's see to it that it comes to pass."*

We are going to hit this from so many different angles, and say it so many different ways that you are going to get an understanding of it.

Let's look at Mark 4. One could hardly teach this without getting into this chapter. This is the parable of the sower. Jesus talked about the sower sowing the Word. We are not going to deal so much with the parable, but I want to deal with some of the things Jesus said about it. Jesus said this when He interpreted the parable for them.

*The sower soweth the Word.*          *(Mark 4:14)*

What is the man sowing? Words. Words that are spoken are seed. Now, here specifically, Jesus is talking about the Word of God. That is what God was talking about when He told Joshua, *"Don't let **the Word of God** depart out of your mouth."*

## WORD-INCORRUPTIBLE SEED

Since the Word of God is incorruptible seed, then there is a parallel between it and every other word you speak. This means that every word you speak is a seed. Whether they grow, and what they produce, depends on how you use them and which way you use them.

God's Word is incorruptible seed. I farmed for thirty years, and I didn't have incorruptible seed. But thank God, when you operate a spiritual law, you have incorruptible seed. If I could have gotten hold of incorruptible seed when I was farming, I wouldn't have had to plant as many seeds. God's Word is incorruptible seed. When you put God's Word in your mouth and speak it, that Word becomes incorruptible seed. That seed will always work.

That doesn't mean you will always have the harvest you intended. It simply means the seed will work. **You can do things to stop the harvest,** or cause the seed to fail to produce. But you can't stop the seed from

37

working. It will do its part. This is why James made the statement that if any man seems to be religious and bridleth not his tongue, he will deceive his own heart, and his religion will be in vain. In other words, what he believed is in vain, if he doesn't bridle his tongue. His tongue will deceive his heart. When he gets that deceit in his heart, it will lead him in the direction of his deceitful words, thinking and believing that is the direction he has ordered.

## THE KINGDOM AND THE SEED

Now let me show it to you in the scripture. I know some of you think, *"Where in the world did he get that?"* In Mark 4. Remember, in this parable Jesus has established that the sower sows the Word of God in verse 14. The Word was sown in the heart of man in verse 15.

> *And he said, So is the kingdom of God, as if a man should cast seed into the ground;*
>
> *And should sleep, and rise night and day, and the seed should spring and grow up, he knoweth not how.*
>
> *For the earth bringeth forth fruit of herself; first the blade, then the ear, after that the full corn in the ear.* (Mark 4:26-28)

The Kingdom of God is as if a man cast seed into the ground. Now we are at an intersection here. We could go a lot of different directions with this parable. But I want to say just enough about it that you understand what we are talking about.

**The kingdom of God is within you.** Jesus said that in Luke 17:20-21.

> *Behold the kingdom of God is within you.*
> (Luke 17:20-21)

You need to get this into your spirit and understand that Jesus is saying that the kingdom is within you — there is power in **you.** God's Word is the spiritual force of power that operates in that kingdom. The kingdom dwells within your heart.

This kingdom that dwells in your heart is no less powerful than the kingdom that will be set up in the New Jerusalem. In fact, it is of the same kingdom. But it is a spiritual manifestation of that kingdom. It is capable of bringing into manifestation everything you *IN YOU* have need of in this life. It comes through the human spirit. That's what Jesus is saying here. The kingdom of God is as a man casting seed into the ground. Now, that includes ladies too. When it talks about man it talks about mankind. *KINGDOM OF GOD*

In other words, if an individual casts seed into the ground, who is doing it? The individual is doing it.

*And he should sleep, and rise night and day, and the seed should spring and grow up, he knoweth not how.* (Mark 4:27)

Notice, he goes to bed, and he gets up. Now, it's not hard to get God's Word to work. Just have enough faith to go to bed and get up; just go to bed and get up. That's not hard, is it?

Let me stop something here before it gets started. That verse doesn't mean that you just confess the scriptures, and you won't have to work anymore. Sometimes people get turned on to faith and they want to throw away all their good business judgment and quit their job.

If you can't live by faith on your job, you're going to starve without it. **Faith is not a way to laziness.**

The man plants the seed, and he sleeps and rises night and day. In other words, he goes on about his business. He goes on doing the things he has been doing. The seed springs up and grows up, and he

39

doesn't know how. He said in verse 27, you don't have to know how it works.

Somebody said, *"I don't understand how everything that I need could come out from the kingdom that's inside of me."*

## THE KINGDOM SUPPLY

The kingdom inside of you is the kingdom of God. Jesus is in that kingdom. You know what the apostle Paul says . . .

*My God shall supply all your need according to his riches in glory by Christ Jesus.*

*(Philippians 4:19)*

How? By Christ Jesus. Who is Christ Jesus? The Word of God. He is going to do it by the Word of God. How does the Word of God work? **The Word of God works in the human spirit** the same way food taken into the physical body works in the physical body. You eat food, natural food. It is assimilated in the body and produces a power called strength.

When the Word of God is received into the human spirit, it does basically the same thing. It is assimilated in the human spirit and **produces a force called faith;** a spiritual force called faith which is spiritual power.

That force comes from the Word of God. The Bible says that is the way it works. The apostle Paul tells you how it works.

## IN THE HEART — IN THE MOUTH

In Romans 10:6-8 Paul says,

*But the righteousness which is of faith speaketh on this wise, Say not in thine heart, Who shall ascend into heaven? (that is, to bring Christ down from above:)*

40

*Or, Who shall descend into the deep? (that is, to bring up Christ again from the dead.)*

*But what saith it? The word is nigh thee, even in thy mouth, and in thy heart: that is, the word of faith, which we preach;*                    (Romans 10:6-8)

In verse 6 he tells you what he wouldn't say first, and then he tells you what he should say. In verse 8 he says the righteousness which is of faith says, *"The word is nigh thee, even in thy mouth and in thy heart."*

Notice, it first gets in your mouth, then it gets in your heart. This corresponds with what Proverbs 3:3 says: write these things *"upon the table of your heart."* Then bring in what David said: *"My tongue is the pen of a ready writer."* (Psalm 45:1) Then bring in what Jesus said; *"A good man out of the good treasure of the heart bringeth forth good things."* (Matthew 12:35)

The kingdom of God is as if a man cast seed into the ground. So the Apostle Paul says that the Word has to get into your mouth first, then it gets in your heart.

That's why I mentioned hearing your own voice on a tape recorder. You can understand that, because your voice is picked up by your inner ear and fed into your human spirit, or what the Bible calls the heart. That's the way you plant the seed of God's Word in your heart — by speaking it.  *Kingdom of God, within you*

## PLANTING SEED

Speaking what God says does several things. When you speak the Word out of your own mouth, then you are planting a seed. And not only that, *"faith cometh by hearing, and hearing by the word of God."* (Romans 10:17)

The more you speak the Word, the more you believe it. The more you believe the Word, the more you speak it.

41

*We having the same spirit of faith, according as it is written, I believed, and therefore have I spoken.*                    *(II Corinthians 4:13)*

Paul said, *"I also believe and therefore speak."* He was quoting an Old Testament scripture, Psalm 116:10, *"I believed, therefore have I spoken."* Then he said, *"we also believe and therefore speak."*

In other words, what you believe, you will speak. Well, if you believe the Word, you will speak it. If you speak it, you will believe it, and if you believe it you'll speak it, and if you speak it you will believe it. It is God's cycle for producing faith as well as planting seed for harvest.

This is the way you get the process going. It's in your mouth, and it's in your heart. When it's in your heart in abundance, it gets in your mouth. Out of the abundance of the heart the mouth speaketh. That's the reason you can always locate people and tell where they are spiritually by the words they speak. What's abundantly in their heart always shows up in their mouth. Just hang around them a few minutes, and what's in their heart will get in their mouth.

Sometimes they don't like what's in their mouth. I remember a man who was working for me on the farm several years ago. One day he came out with some big curse words. Then he slapped his hand over his mouth and said, *"Oh, no. I don't talk that way."* What he meant was that he didn't intend to talk that way around me. But what was in his heart got in his mouth.

Whatever is in your heart will always tell off on you. If you are in doubt and fear and unbelief, you will always talk about it. If you are in faith, you will talk faith.

Jesus said the kingdom of God is as if a man cast seed into the ground. You need to understand this; God is not sowing seed for you. It's not going to manifest for you just because it's in the Bible and you happened to read it.

When you get it in your mouth and speak it out of your mouth, it is then picked up and fed into your heart or spirit. And that's what Jesus says is the planting of that seed.

Now everyone knows, if you don't plant seeds, you won't have a harvest. That is, you won't have a good harvest.

## DON'T LEAVE PLANTING TO GOD

I have heard people say this, *"Well, I tell you, I'm just going to leave it up to God. Just whatever God wills, that's what will happen to me."* Now, I'll just bring that down on a natural level and see if that is what you want. If I were to say about my farm, *"Well, now, I'm just leaving my farm up to God; just whatever grows out there this year will be God's will for me,"* what do you think I'm going to harvest? I can tell you what I'll harvest. Cockleburs, Johnson grass, pigweeds, and crab grass. But I won't have anything good to eat, nor anything that I could sell.

Why? Because the earth is under a curse. You must force it to produce good things. You have to plant good seeds. Notice Jesus says the kingdom of God is as if a man casts a seed into the ground and he should sleep and rise night and day. The seed should spring up and grow, he knows not how, **for the earth brings forth fruit of herself.**

The earth is going to produce fruit. Isn't that what Jesus said? Notice that in this chapter He has already established that the seed is sown in the heart of man.

We hear people talk about the heart, and they put their hand over their physical heart. Jesus is not talking about the blood pump. He is talking about your spirit. He is talking about the spirit of man, the core of your

43

being. When something scares you, you have said, *"My heart jumped up into my mouth."* Well, where did you feel something? It was down in the pit of your stomach. That's where your spirit is. When nervous, you said, *"I have butterflies in my stomach."* It's where your spirit is. At those times, you were feeling something in your spirit.

That spirit, the heart, is the production center. That is where the kingdom of God resides. It dwells inside of you. That's where Jesus dwells in the person of the Holy Spirit. And this kingdom within you is capable of producing everything that you plant in it.

You can plant good seeds in it, or you can plant bad seeds in it. You can plant the Word of God, or you can plant the words of the devil.

## UNWANTED SEED

We have misunderstood and have been led astray sometimes, for we have said, *"Well, now, I'll just tell you. God knows what I mean."* We speak some doubt and unbelief statement like, *"Nothing I ever do works out. It always turns out bad for me."*

Somebody said, *"Now I wouldn't say that if I were you."*

*"I'm just saying it like it is."*

That person is also planting a seed.

You have heard people say this, *"I have studied the Bible, and I just can't understand it. I just don't get anything out of it."*

They have probably been saying that for twenty years. What has happened? Their spirit picked up on that. Their inner ear fed it into their spirit, which said, *"Shut off revelation knowledge of the Bible, because they have declared they can't understand it."*

Remember, the part of the brain which controls speech is connected to all of the other nerves of the

44

body. So what do you think it does to your whole system when you say this? *"Well, it's flu season. I'll probably be the first one to catch it."*

You probably will; at least you are planting the seed. You say, *"Well, I always get the flu."* Your voice is picked up and sent into your spirit, saying to shut down the immune system, for he is taking the flu.

God designed us that way. But He told us how to operate this mechanism. Jesus said the kingdom of God is as if a man cast the seed into the ground. Now do you realize what Jesus is saying here?

## HEART IS GARDEN

The heart is the garden spot. It is the soil which God has provided for you to produce whatever you need in this life. In Eden, Adam had a garden, which God gave to him. It was called the Garden of Eden. It supplied everything that Adam needed. He sold it out to Satan, and Satan became the god of this world. But Jesus came and restored this thing and got it back from the devil. And now the born again human spirit which God has put inside of you **is a garden which will produce everything you need in this life.**

Your spirit will lead you to anything you need. It has the wisdom to lead you to it. For your spirit is in contact with God's Spirit. God's Spirit knows all about God. The Apostle Paul said this in I Corinthians 2.

> *For what man knoweth the things of a man, save the spirit of man which is in him? even so the things of God knoweth no man, but the Spirit of God.*
>
> *Now we have received, not the spirit of the world, but the spirit which is of God; that we might know the things that are freely given to us of God.*
>
> *(I Corinthians 2:11-12)*

45

He is saying that I don't know all about me, but my spirit does. The human spirit, or what the Bible calls the heart, knows all about me.

No man knows all about me, but my spirit does. Nobody knows all about God, but the Holy Spirit does. Now, if you can get those two spirits together, you will tap the source of all knowledge.

To do that, your spirit would search the avenues of God's wisdom. It would find a way to get you in a position to cause what you are saying from the Word of God to come to pass in your life. It will lead you to it. It will come to you in the night. It may come to you while you are driving down the road.

But if you go around saying, *"I tell you, I never do know what to do. I always make a mess out of things,"* then your human spirit will lead you to make a mess out of everything, then end up blaming it on God. *"Well, it must not have been God's will for me to succeed."*

No, you just sowed the wrong seed in your garden.

The kingdom of God is as if a man cast seed into the ground. You have to put the seed in there. It is incorruptible seed. The Word of God is the seed. The word that you speak out of your mouth will produce. It will bring forth the manifestation of the thing you desired.

## NO HARVEST WITHOUT SEED

The kingdom of God is as if you cast the seed into the ground and it grows. The earth bringeth forth fruit. The earth is the heart. Jesus has already established that fact. It is going to produce the fruit. All you have to do is be smart enough to speak it. Plant the seed and go to bed and get up. Go to bed and get up, and go on about your daily affairs. It means not to worry and fret or be overly concerned. It doesn't mean to quit your job.

So many today have not understood the power of their words. That's why I make the statement that words are the most **powerful things in the universe.**

*In the beginning was the Word, and the Word was with God, and the Word was God.*

*All things were made by Him (the Word); and without him was not any thing made that was made.* (John 1:1, 3)

Without the Word of God there was nothing made that was made. I am convinced that, just as it was then, so is it now. There is no authority exercised without words. And God has given us authority over the devil. Hardly anything can be done without words.

Somebody said, *"Well, you could write it down."* But it's still words. Some of you may think I'm a fanatic on words. When we get through with this teaching, you will know more about words and the words that we speak. It will cause you to set a watch over your mouth. David said,

*Set a watch, O Lord, before my mouth; keep the door of my lips.* (Psalm 141:3)

Some people say, *"Well, that just puts me into bondage, having to watch my words."* But you don't know what bondage is, until you just say anything that you want to. That's the greatest bondage you can get into. God has given us instruction. If you go by the Instruction Book, you will find it always works just like God said it would.

We must realize that God knew what He was talking about. If we will just do what He said, we will have what He said we could have. **Don't be a hearer only, but also a DOER of God's Word.**

47

# Chapter Three

# SEED TIME AND HARVEST

**In this chapter we will continue on the subject of the power of words. We are in Mark, chapter four.**

*And he said, So is the kingdom of God, as if a man should cast seed into the ground;*

*And should sleep, and rise night and day, and the seed should spring and grow up, he knoweth not how.*

*For the earth bringeth forth fruit of herself, first the blade, then the ear, after that the full corn in the ear.*

*But when the fruit is brought forth, immediately he puteth in the sickle, because the harvest is come.*
*(Mark 4:26-29)*

In this passage of scripture, Jesus tells us that you are the one planting the seed. Take God's Word and put it in your mouth. You speak it, it becomes a seed, it goes into the heart — the human spirit — and there it begins to grow and produce. The kingdom of God is **as if a man** should cast seed into the ground.

Notice that Jesus said, *"**For the earth** (the heart of man) **bringeth forth fruit of herself. First the blade,** then the ear, after that the full corn in the ear."* Sometimes people give up before the time for a harvest. Many of you have probably done that. You have said some things that stopped the growth process.

Mark 11:23 tells us the principle of the law of faith. Whosoever shall say, shall believe, shall doubt not in his heart, but believe what he says will come to pass, he shall have whatsoever he says.

49

## THE SEED IS A NECESSITY

That is a law of faith. That's the way it works. Sometimes people think, *"It's going to happen just because I say it."* **Notice that saying it is involved in planting it.** But it won't necessarily happen just because you say it. I want you to get this point, because too many people get hold of Mark 11:23 and run off in left field.

**It won't work just because you say it. But saying it is involved in working it.** It's like saying to a farmer about farming, *"You won't **necessarily** have a harvest just because you've planted. But you will never have a harvest if you don't plant."*

Sometimes we get criticized for teaching people to confess the Word of God and say what God said. People say, *"Well, that's just too mechanical."*

But we are talking about planting seeds. When you're talking about power of words, you're talking about the power of seed. There is life in that seed the farmer plants which causes the manifestation of the very thing that he planted. The life is in that seed.

## LAW OF GENESIS

Genesis 1:11-12 contains what I call the law of Genesis. If you get hold of this, it will help you in all the other things we are studying, because it is God's way all through the Bible. **The law of seedtime and harvest is God's method.** I didn't choose it until after God chose it. But this is God's method.

*And God said, Let the earth bring forth grass, the herb yielding seed, and the fruit tree yielding fruit after his kind, whose seed is in itself, upon the earth: and it was so.*

*And the earth brought forth grass, and herb yielding seed after his kind, and the tree yielding*

50

*fruit, whose seed was in itself, after his kind: and God saw that it was good.* *(Genesis 1:11-12)*

Now let's look at what God said to Noah after the flood. God made a promise to us regarding this earth.

*And Noah . . . offered burnt offerings on the altar.*

*And the Lord smelled a sweet savour; and the Lord said in his heart, I will not again curse the ground any more for man's sake . . .*

*While the earth remaineth, **seedtime and harvest,** and cold and heat, and summer and winter, and day and night shall not cease.*

*(Genesis 8:20-22)*

God said, *"This is the method that I have chosen for this planet, and it will be that way as long as this planet is in existence."* That's the way it works. That's God's method.

Seedtime and harvest is God's method. God's law, the law of Genesis, is that **everything produces after its kind. Everything.** The seed is in itself.

The seed of strife is in strife itself. If you want to create more strife, get into strife with someone. It will create more strife. The seed of love is in itself. If you give love, you can reap a harvest of love. The seed is in itself.

This is God's method — the law of seedtime and harvest. Sometimes people say, *"Well, now, I know why you're saying that. You are just using God's Word, you're just trying to use God's Word to bring a manifestation."*

Yes! That's the way it works!

That's what God said, that's what we have just read. Jesus said the kingdom of God works this way. It's as if a man cast seed into the ground.

The seed is the Word of God. That has already been established. It's God's Word. So what are you going to use if you don't use God's Word?

## ACT AS GOD WOULD ACT

I have heard people say this. *"Well, I'll tell you, those people who confess God's Word and say the promise of God over and over are just trying to act like God!"*

Yes, that's exactly what we are trying to do.

**Act as God would act in a similar situation.** What would God say about a bad situation or circumstance if he were to face it. We know how He would act because of what He did in Genesis 1 when He looked out and saw darkness. He said, *"Light."* What did He do? **He spoke the thing desired.** God is more highly developed in this than we are.

Somebody said, *"But that was God."*

That's right, that is God. But God also said,

*Let us make man in our image, after our likeness: and let them have dominion over the fish of the sea, and over the fowl of the air, and over the cattle, and over all the earth, and over every creeping thing that creepeth upon the earth.*

*(Genesis 1:26)*

How is man going to have dominion? I can understand how Adam could run the jack rabbit out of the cabbage, but what is he going to do when the elephant goes to tromping down the cabbage? What is he going to do then?

God said for him to subdue it. He is going to do it the same way God did — with words; with the power of words. To subdue the earth, he had to do it God's way. When he saw something that he didn't like, he had to **speak the thing desired.**

52

Follow this line through all of the teaching of the New Testament, and even in the Old Testament. Jesus said,

> *What things soever ye desire, when ye pray, believe that ye receive them, and ye shall have them.* (Mark 11:24)

In other words, pray the desire; don't pray the thing that you don't desire. Speak the thing desired, even when you pray it.

## SOW IT THE WAY GOD SAID IT

We have been taught down through the years that we have to *"say it like it is."* **That is not a Bible method.** The Bible method and the law of faith is that you say it the way the Word of God says it.

If your wants are in line with the Word of God, then say it the way you want it. Say it the way the Word says it. **When you see lack and problems in your life, speak abundance and peace.** That's the seed you are sowing. Go to the Word of God, find the promise, and plant that seed. You are seeding for a harvest.

The problem has been that people say a few things and plant a few seeds, then go off and leave them. **You don't necessarily have a harvest just because you planted the seed.** You must care for that seed. It takes time for these things to manifest.

It's not going to happen just because you say it. But saying it is involved in making it happen. The farmer is not necessarily going to have a harvest just because he planted. But planting is involved in obtaining a harvest. **There will be no harvest without planting.**

So the law of Genesis says that everything produces after its kind. So the very thing which God has designed to cause us to be victorious in life, to come into the full manifestation of the promises of God, can also work in reverse for us, if we don't follow the instruction book.

## CHECKING THE SEED

God didn't give these things in the Bible to put you in bondage. I have had people say this to me. *"Well now, this confession stuff just gets me in bondage. I just can't say anything anymore, because I have to watch what I'm saying so much."*

You can see it taking effect when you have to watch what you are saying. Some of the things you continually speak are causing your problems.

When people come to me and tell me all about their problems, I ask, *"How long have you been confessing the negative over this situation?"* Some have been doing it for twenty years. Their problem is just one inch below their nose — their mouth. It's what they have been confessing for twenty years."

In Luke 17:5-6 the apostles came to Jesus and said, *"Lord, Increase our faith."* They said, *"Just give us more faith."* It would be good if we could just ask God to give us more faith. Wouldn't that be great? He would then give us a bushel basket full.

But Jesus replied, *"If you had faith as a seed, you would say . . ."* The King James says it a little differently. *"If ye had faith as a grain of mustard seed, ye **might** say."* But the literal Greek, the interlinear Greek New Testament says, *"If you had faith as a seed you **would** say . . ."* That is a stronger statement than the King James translation.

> *And the Lord said, If ye had faith as a grain of mustard seed, ye might say unto this sycamine tree, Be thou plucked up by the root, and be thou planted in the sea; and it should obey you.*
>
> *(Luke 17:6)*

## PROBLEMS OBEY YOU

This did not say it would obey God, and this did not say it would obey the Holy Ghost. **It says it would obey you.**

54

Now these are the words of Jesus. This is not something I made up. Jesus said it.

Notice the apostles said, *"Lord, why don't you just give us more faith? That's what we need, we need more faith."*

Jesus said to them, (allow me to paraphrase it) *"Fellows, you don't need more faith. You need to understand that faith works like a seed. But unless you plant it, it will not do you any good."*

You see, faith does not come by asking. Faith comes by hearing the spoken Word of God.

## PLANTING THE SEED

A seed is no good unless you plant it. If you had two grains of wheat in your hand, you couldn't make biscuits out of them, you couldn't make any gravy out of them; you don't have enough. It's only good for one thing, and that is to plant.

But if you are smart enough to do what God says to do with them, before long you could feed the world with those two grains of wheat. If you plant them, they will grow up, and they will produce, and you will have a harvest of more just like the ones you planted.

So Jesus is saying to the disciplines here, **"If you had faith that you were willing to plant . . ."** The problem was that they did not have faith they were willing to plant. They did not have faith as a seed. It is possible to have faith that is not as a seed.

You could say, *"Oh, yes. I believe the Bible is true. I believe it from cover to cover."*

Well, Philippians 4:19 says, *"My God shall supply all your need according to his riches in glory by Christ Jesus"* Luke 6:38 says, *"Give, and it shall be given unto you; good measure, pressed down, and shaken together, and running over, shall men give into your bosom."*

55

*"Well, yes, I know that's in the Bible. I believe it."*

*"Is it true in your life?"*

*"Well, no, it's not true in my life."*

*"Why isn't it true in your life?"*

*"Well, I guess it's just not God's will."*

**The Word of God is the will of God.** It is God's will, but it won't happen in your life just because it's God's will. You are not going to get healed just because the Bible says, *"By His stripes you were healed."* You are not going to become prosperous just because the Bible says, *"Whatsoever he doeth will prosper."*

The Word must be inside of you. You can't take a Bible down to the hospital and lay it on someone and get them healed, even though it is full of the Word of God. But if you can get that Word inside them, then it will manifest itself.

## FAITH SPEAKS

Jesus said to the apostles, *"If you had faith as a seed* ***you would say*** *to the sycamine tree."* (A black mulberry tree.) Evidently, they were walking down a path and this tree was right in the middle of the path. This tree was an obstacle growing there in their path.

Jesus said, *"Now, if you had faith as a seed, you could say to this inanimate object, this tree, 'Be plucked up by the roots, be planted in the sea,' and it — the tree — would obey you."* Or, *"It would obey your faith-filled words, if you had faith as a seed."*

Jesus tells two great faith secrets here. 1) Faith ***is as a seed; it works like a seed.*** 2) **You plant it by speaking it.**

Somebody said, *"I tell you, you're not going to catch me speaking to trees and mountains, and talking to things."*

Then you are not going to see them removed. Jesus is not talking about uprooting trees anyway. No more than He is talking about blowing Mount Everest into the sea when he said, *"Whosoever shall say unto the mountain."*

He's talking about problem areas in your life; situations you face; circumstances you don't know how to handle. He tells you to say to that situation, *"Be plucked up; be planted in the sea; depart; be gone."* **Tell it what to do and where to go.**

## DOMINION WITH WORDS

This is the way Adam was to have dominion in the beginning. God told Adam to have dominion over the fish of the sea, the fowl of the air, over everything that creepeth on the earth.

Now that's good news in itself, just to know that you have dominion over creeps; over the elephants, over everything.

How was Adam going to subdue the elephant? He would have to do it with his faith. There wasn't much he could do about it physically. He had to do it with his faith and the power of words. He had to operate in it with his faith and the power of words. He had to operate in it like God operated in it.

Jesus told two great faith secrets concerning the power of words. 1) If you had faith as a seed, 2) you would speak what you believe.

Now compare this with what James said.

> *If any man among you seem to be religious, and bridleth not his tongue, but deceiveth his own heart, this man's religion is vain.* (James 1:26)

## THE TONGUE DECEIVES HEART

James said, if any man seems to be religious, what he believes will be in vain, if he isn't careful about what he speaks. Now, many people seem to be religious, but they don't bridle their tongue. They speak all sorts of

57

things. When they start out, they may believe that everything will be all right. But if they believe and speak everything they hear on television, they will end up having faith in the devil. They will have faith in a depression, instead of prosperity. What they believed in the beginning will disappear, because they have brought on something else.

You can pray one thing and say another. **Then your saying will nullify your praying.** So Jesus simply tells you how to use the power of words with the law of faith.

## SPIRITUAL LAW WORKS

Someone made the statement that those who say they can, and those who say they can't are both right regarding any situation, when that is their continual confession. You can understand that if you just say something one time, that's not necessarily a confession.

Learn to operate in the **power of words and the law of faith.** Faith is a law. We can all understand natural law. There is the law of gravity. You know the law of gravity works. There is always someone foolish enough to say that it doesn't apply to him, but if he just jumps off a building, he discovers it is working.

The law of gravity works when it's cold, and it works when it's hot. It works when the wind is blowing and it works when it's not. It works when it's raining and it works when it's dark. Do you know why? Because it's a law. **Laws work.**

**God's Word is spiritual law.** God's Word works, when you work it properly. But sometimes we have made up our own rules and said, *"Well, I said that but I really didn't mean that. I just said that, but God knew what I meant."*

That's like going to the phone and saying, *"I'm going to dial my father on the phone."* I dial three or four numbers right, but miss one digit in the number.

58

Then I say, *"Oh, well, you know the phone company knows what I meant."*

I am not going to talk to my father. I didn't follow the phone company's instructions.

## UNCONTROLLED POWER WILL DESTROY

We have to realize something; we have to go by God's rules. God has some rules and regulations concerning laws. And when we operate in spiritual law we must operate with God's rules.

## CONTROLLED AND UNCONTROLLED POWER

We have learned how to conform to and enforce laws of electricity. There is a law that governs electricity, and as long as you don't violate that law you can use electricity. It will heat your house, it will cook for you, it will wash your clothes, it will do all of the things that need to be done. We have said, *"My, isn't it wonderful that we have electricity?"* But yet that same force which can do so much good for you, if it's untamed, will kill you in an instant.

I saw this happen one night. A man had a wreck. A power pole fell and the power line was hanging about three feet above the ground. The ambulance crew started down the bank to get the man, and everyone was standing around there within three feet of that power line. I guess they thought it was insulated, or that the power was off. But it wasn't. When they put the man on the stretcher and started back up under that wire, one of the men got too close to it. That electricity — 17,000 volts — arced to his body and killed him instantly.

It was the same power that cooked his food, warmed his house, and did all the things that made his life easier. When he violated the law, it killed him.

As Proverbs says, death and life are in the power of the tongue. The old adage, *"sticks and stones may break your bones, but words will never hurt you"* is simply not true. Words can destroy you, if you don't know how to operate in the way God told us to operate in spiritual law.

## BINDING OR LOOSING

**The spirit world can be controlled by the Word of God.** Jesus said this to Peter in Matthew 16:19.

*And I will give unto thee the keys of the kingdom of heaven: and whatsoever thou shalt bind on earth shall be bound in heaven: and whatsoever thou shalt loose on earth shall be loosed in heaven.*

*(Matthew 16:19)*

You bind with words. With words you bind things or you loose things. Sometimes you think you are just being honest, and you loose the devil against your finances by saying things like, *"Well, we just never can get ahead." "If I ever get a good job, I lose it."* Those words loose the enemy against you.

The Word says,

*Whatever you do will prosper, and no weapon formed against you will prosper. If you give, it will be given unto you, good measure, pressed down, shaken together and running over shall men give unto you. You have favor with men and God.*     *(Psalm 1:3; Isaiah 54:17; Luke 6:38; Acts 2:47)*

That is what God said about it. But sometimes we say, *"Well, nothing I ever do works. It always blows up in my face."* We have said that because we have never understood the power of words.

Do you realize what that does to you on the inside —
to your spirit? It may not affect anyone else much, but it
will affect you. **Words spoken are powerful when you
release them from your spirit.**

You release the ability of God by speaking God's
Word in you. It's very simple. **God's Word in your
mouth produces a force called "faith" in the human
spirit.** What is abundantly in your heart gets back in
your mouth, and when it gets in your mouth, it gets
abundantly in your heart. It starts a dynamo going, and
it starts to produce a spiritual force called faith.

Hebrews 11:1 says this faith is the substance of
things hoped for. It is the evidence of things not seen.
So faith is the evidence of those things that you hope
for. That faith comes from God's Word. Faith is both
the substance and the evidence of it; the things desired.

What is this substance of what a farmer desires? The
only thing he has to start with in the spring of the year
is seed. He has his seed. The seed is in itself. The ability
to reproduce is in that seed. It will produce the same
kind many times more than was planted.

God's Word — His promises — are just as powerful.

Let me share with you what the Lord spoke to me in
1974 in Dallas, Texas. He said,

*There is not one bit of the power departed from
My Word. There is as much power in My Word
now as there was the day that I spoke it. My
Word is not void of power — but My people are
void of speech. They will not speak what I
have said. But they speak what the world
says. They speak what the enemy says.*

God also said this. And I will never forget it.

*Even as there is creative power in My Word to
be released when you speak it, there is even*

*also evil power present in the words of the enemy to afflict and oppress everyone who speaks them.*

We have understood to some degree that there is creative power in God's Word. But I don't think we have ever stopped to think that as surely as there is power in God's Word, there is evil power present in the words of the enemy to afflict and oppress those who speak them.

## FAITH COMES BY HEARING

We talk about speaking God's Word and releasing a force called "faith" inside of you, which is the substance of things hoped for and the evidence of things not seen. There's also a reciprocal of that. Since there is power in God's Word to release faith, which is the substance of things desired, then **there is a spiritual force in the words of the enemy. That force is called "fear."**

Faith cometh by hearing the Word of God. Just so, faith in the devil comes by hearing the words of the devil. Faith in the devil is called *"fear."*

I want to say that again, and I want to say it just a little differently. Hebrews 11:1 says faith is the substance of things hoped for, the evidence of things not seen. It is the substance of things desired, because what I desire is what I hope for. Right? Faith is the substance of things desired, and that faith comes by hearing God's Word. **I hear the promise of God, and then I desire the promise of God.** I speak the promise of God that releases the spiritual force in me called faith — the substance of the thing desired. It becomes the seed of the thing desired.

# FEAR ALSO COMES BY HEARING

Then fear comes by hearing the words of the devil. So if hearing God's Words produces faith, hearing the devil's words continually produces fear. **Just as faith is the substance of things desired, fear is the substance of things not desired.**

That is why you ought to resist fear like you resist the devil. Now you can understand why Job said, *"The thing which I greatly feared is come upon me."* (Job 3:25) *"The thing that I was afraid of has come unto me."*

When you get out there in the world, or into the ministry, you must come against fear. For Satan uses the fear tactic.

Somebody said, *"How do you overcome fear?"*

Speak the Word of God. Do you remember what Jesus said in reply to the devil's temptation to turn stones into bread?

> *It is written, Man shall not live by bread alone, but by every word that proceedeth out of the mouth of God.* (Matthew 4:4)

If you live by every word of God, then you would die by the words of the devil. Because the Word of God produces life giving faith, the words of the devil produce death. When you are speaking contrary to the Word of God, you are producing fear.

Sometimes people don't realize that they are quoting the devil. **We quote the devil when we speak things that are contrary to the Word of God.** Anything that is exactly opposite of what God has said has to be the words of the devil.

Whether or not you realize it, those are the two sources. Things either come from God or from the devil. When we speak contrary to the Word of God, we are also releasing spiritual forces out of our mouth. Those forces will get in our spirit (heart). That's the way we receive them. Our tongue is as a pen of a ready writer. Remember — God said, *"Write my Word on the table of your heart."*

## DON'T AGREE WITH THE ENEMY

If you speak the words of the enemy, you are writing the words of the enemy on the table of your heart. The reason some people are so filled with fear is that they believe everything they see on television. Jesus Himself said this about the last days.

*Men's hearts failing them for fear, and for looking after those things which are coming on the earth.*        *(Luke 21:26)*

Now I want you to take note of this. Jesus did not say men's hearts will fail them because of the things which are on the earth. He said men's hearts will fail them because of **looking after those things which are coming** on the earth — in other words, worrying and fretting over tomorrow.

Jesus is not talking about heart attacks. It could be, by the law of double reference, but you cannot find in the Word of God where Jesus ever talked about the human physical heart. He is talking about the garden spot. He's talking about *"soil"* that He put in you — where the kingdom abides.

Jesus is saying that kingdom in the heart of man, into which He sows the seed, will fail to function properly because of fear.

You may have faith when you are around lots of other Christians who believe as you do. But when you get out into the world where it's right down to the nitty gritty, you will have to resist fear like you resist the devil. And you do that by quoting what God said, in the face of every situation and every circumstance. I don't care if all hell breaks loose, say what God said about it. It causes faith to come.

64

# WORDS OF LIFE

You live by every Word of God. There is life in every word of God. In fact Jesus said it this way.

*The words that I speak unto you, they are spirit, and they are life.* *(John 6:63)*

In other words, Jesus said there is spirit life in every word of God.

Since that is true, there is spirit death in the words of the devil. Your words affect your spirit. You can speak words of life to your spirit by agreeing with God, or **you can speak words of death to your spirit by agreeing with the devil.**

Proverbs put it very aptly when the writer made this statement.

*The spirit of a man will sustain his infirmity; but a wounded spirit who can bear?*

*(Proverbs 18:14)*

The spirit of man, the human spirit, will sustain his weakness. One translation says **the human spirit will hold off, or hold in the weakness or infirmity.** It will work either way. The human spirit, the heart of man, will hold off, or hold in the weakness, depending upon what you say about it.

That is what the Word of God says about it. I'm just declaring what the Bible says. It will hold it off, or it will hold it in.

Whatever you bind on earth will be bound in heaven. Whatever you loose on earth will be loosed in heaven. The power of binding and loosing is here on the earth. Binding and loosing is done with words. We speak words; either words of faith, or words of fear. Words of faith release God and bring God on the scene and release His ability. Words of fear bring the devil on the scene and release his ability.

Words are important. Just as people learn to use the natural laws, we can learn to operate in these spiritual laws. Your words become as little seeds that are sown. They are going to produce a harvest just as surely as you plant them.

## CHECK SEED BEFORE SOWING

You should be careful about what you plant. Be careful about what you speak, for words are powerful.

Sometimes people even pray the wrong things. Have you ever caught yourself praying what the devil said? That's an embarrassing situation. Once I was praying and I said, *"Lord my prayer is not working out. Things are getting worse."*

The Spirit of God said, *"Who told you that?"*

I thought for a minute and said, *"It must have been the devil, because You sure didn't say it in Your Word, did You."*

He said, *"No. And I would appreciate it if you would stop telling Me what the devil said."*

Sometimes, people will go to prayer and pray the problem. But that is unscriptural.

If you pray the problem in prayer, you will then have more faith in the problem. **You can destroy your faith by your praying, when you pray wrong.**

If you go to God and pray, *"Now, Lord, You know that John lost his job, and we don't have any money coming in, and we're not going to be able to make the car payment, and we are surely going to lose our house by the end of the year, because the note is due at the end of this year, and, Lord, You know that we can't get a job."*

Then you will get up from that kind of prayer having faith that you can't get a job and that your needs will not be met. You will feel so pious about it, and think you have really been religious. What you have done is to open the door to the devil.

Somebody said, *"Well, what do you do?"*

66

## PRAY THE ANSWER

Go to the Word of God and pray the answer. If you say, *"Now, Father, Your Word says whatsoever things I desire, when I pray, believe that I received them and I shall have them. Therefore, in the name of Jesus I pray that John gets a job; that he gets a good job; that he gets a better job. I pray that we will have all of our needs met according to Your riches in glory, thank God. I believe I have received when I prayed, and I thank You for it. I rejoice over it and praise You, Father, that we will get this house paid off and have $10,000 to give to missions."*

You'll get up from that prayer having more faith in the promises of God to meet your need. Not because you asked for faith, but because you quoted the Word of God in your prayer. And faith cometh by hearing the Word of God.

Faith in God comes by hearing the Word of God. You can also turn that around. Faith in the devil comes by hearing the words of the devil. When you understand that, you will be careful about what you hear. For we have all prayed negative prayers.

We need to control the words that come out of our mouth. God created man with the ability to operate on His level of faith. Jesus said, *"all things are possible to him that believeth."* (Mark 9:23) All things are possible with God. So believe it, and speak it, and release your faith in it, and develop yourself in it.

There is more to this. We will get into the developing stages in later chapters.

## WORD IS MAGNIFIED

God has magnified His Word above His Name. There is power in the name of Jesus, but God has magnified His Word above His Name. That is why God's Word is important in our lives.

We must set a watch on our mouth. Determine to only speak things which agree with God's Word. That doesn't mean you go around just quoting the Bible all the time. I'm talking about not speaking anything that is contrary to the Word of God. You don't have to just quote God's Word all the time, but say things which are in agreement with it.

You will see things change in your situation. Begin to confess, *"I have the wisdom of God. I have the direction of God. I hear the voice of the Good Shepherd."*

Then you will hear the voice of the Good Shepherd, and you will have the wisdom of God in every situation and every circumstance of life. It will always come to you because God's Word will work for you to bring the manifestation.

## DON'T TELL GOD WHAT THE DEVIL SAID

The Lord said this to me several years ago and I have never forgotten it and don't intend to. When I told Him, *"Lord, I have prayed and things are not working out, but getting worse."*

He said to me, *"I'd appreciate it if you wouldn't tell me what the devil said."*

Actually, it was my finances I was praying and fussing about. God said, *"If you don't change your confession, it won't get any better."*

I said, *"Well, Lord, what am I going to do?"* I said, *"It is true that I have all these financial problems."*

He said, *"Go to the Word of God and see what I said about it, and just confess what I said about your finances. So I began to do that. Then one day during my confession time I stopped and said to the Lord, "Lord, I'm confessing all these things and it just seems like I am lying."*

He said, *"Son, how can you lie, saying what I said?"* How could anyone lie when they are quoting what God said about their situation?

I made this statement to the Lord: *"Now, Lord, You said in Your Word to resist the devil and he will flee from you. I resisted him, but he didn't flee from* **me.***"*

And, He replied, *"But I said he did!"*

I said, *"Yes, but the devil didn't flee from me."*

He said, *"But I said he did!"*

I responded, *"I know You said that, but he didn't."*

God said, ***"But I said he did!"*** That's all God ever said to me about it. I finally understood what He was saying. God said he did and I said he didn't, and he didn't. So the law of faith was working; I got what I said. See, I was releasing faith on the negative side; faith in the devil. Another time when I was praying I said, *"Lord, I just don't hear Your voice. I know You said we will hear the voice of the Good Shepherd, but I just don't hear Your voice."*

I was talking to Him and telling Him I didn't hear His voice. You know, sometimes we get caught up in wanting to hear an audible voice. But He said to me, *"Go to the Word of God where I said My sheep hear My voice.* **You confess that you do hear the voice of the Good Shepherd; and you know His voice, and the voice of a stranger you will not follow. Confess that the Spirit of Truth that abides in you teaches you all things, and guides you into all truths. Confess you have perfect knowledge of every situation.** *Confess this over and over and make it a daily confession."*

He said, *"If you will do that,* **over a period of time** *you will call that into manifestation until* **you will hear accurately the voice of God,** *and of the Good Shepherd."*

Now, it won't happen overnight. It didn't happen to me overnight. It's a process of renewing your mind.

## TUNE YOUR SPIRIT TO RIGHT FREQUENCY

You hear so many people saying, *"I don't know what God is saying. I don't ever hear from God."*

But some of those same people are quick to tell you what the devil said to them. How is it they hear the devil, but don't hear God? Think about that for a minute.

Some Christians go around saying the devil said this to them, the devil said that to them. But they never hear what God is saying. They were too busy talking to the devil. They were too busy listening to the devil. If you are doing that, you need to **tune in to a different frequency** and confess, *"I don't hear the voice of a stranger, I hear the voice of the Good Shepherd."* Confess that for eight or ten months and see how much you hear the voice of the Good Shepherd. It will then be just as easy to hear the Good Shepherd as it was to hear the devil.

We have been taught wrong. We have assumed some things, and we have been taught some things which are wrong. When you confess these things, **you will find there is enough power in each promise to cause it to manifest itself in your life.** It will manifest itself in every aspect of your life.

## BE A DOER NOT JUST A HEARER

**But you must do it.** It is not a matter of saying, *"Well, it's in the Bible. I guess it will happen to me."*

The kingdom of God is as if a man cast seed into the ground. You must sow the seed; the harvest will come. The harvest has no choice; it must come. If you will sow the seed, you will eventually receive a harvest, for the law of seedtime and harvest is still in effect. It will never cease as long as the earth remaineth. This is God's method. Seed time & Harvest

# Chapter Four

# WORDS TRANSMIT IMAGES

We are still talking about words. We are going to enter into some other things in this chapter that will carry us further in the same direction.

We have talked about the power of words and how powerful words are when released out of your mouth because they carry spiritual forces. Jesus said it this way.

> *The words that I speak unto you, they are spirit, and they are life.* (John 6:63)

I think sometimes we miss what he said here. He said, *"There is spirit life in the words that I speak."*

That's why it is important for us to agree with God, and to say what God says. When we talk about *"confession,"* that is actually what we are talking about: *"agreeing with God."* When we mention confession, most people think we are referring to confession of your sins. No, we are saying, agree with God — it is the confession of God's Word.

Words are important because they carry spiritual forces. **Words transmit fear; words transmit faith.** Words transmit your image to others. God's Word transmits God's image — the devil's word transmits the devil's image.

If I wanted to give someone an image of my car, I would start describing it. Every word I speak would transmit a clearer image of that car to you. Inside of me right now I can see that car. I can see it; I can walk around it. That is a mental image. I can describe it to you in so much detail that you could go to a parking lot and pick it out. You would know it is my car, even though you have never seen it. My words produce an

71

image of that car inside you. I can transmit to you the image I have with words.

Words are powerful transmitters. Words transmit fear images. Words transmit faith images.

Remember, Paul said,

> So then faith cometh by hearing, and hearing by the word of God. (Romans 10:17)

That is **a** truth; it is not **the** truth — the whole truth. I want to point this out to you again. When Paul said that in context, he was talking about **faith in God** and **faith in God's Word.** That is the way faith in God's Word comes — by hearing what God said. But the opposite end of that, what we would call the *"reciprocal"* of that truth is this. If faith in God comes by hearing the Word of God, then faith in the devil comes by hearing the words of the devil. The opposite force from faith is fear. Fear is actually faith in the devil. So that's why I say, don't ever take **a** truth and make **the** truth out of it. For if you dogmatically declare that the only way anyone can ever obtain **any** faith is by hearing the Word of God, then you have missed what Paul was saying, because you can have faith **in me** by hearing what I say.

## SAME SPIRIT OF FAITH

Faith comes by hearing, whether you are hearing me, hearing the weather forecast, or hearing what the devil says to you. Faith comes by hearing. Words spoken transmit a corresponding spirit.

The apostle Paul said, *"We having the same spirit of faith."* (II Corinthians 4:13) You can transmit the spirit of faith with words. That is one reason Jesus said, *"The words that I speak unto you, they are spirit and they are life."* Jesus was transmitting the spirit of the faith and life that was in Him to you through the words He spoke.

72

Then the apostle Paul continued in Romans 8:2.

*The law of the Spirit of life in Christ Jesus hath made me free from the law of sin and death.*

How did that spirit of life which was in Christ Jesus get in him? It was transmitted by God's Word.

That is why Jesus admonished the disciples,

*Take heed what ye hear.* ✳            (Mark 4:24)

This is very important. People ought to take heed to what they hear. **You should not continually sit under teaching that you know is error, because that same spirit will be transmitted.** I don't care how wrong it is and how wrong you know it is. If you continue to subject your spirit to that false teaching, some of that same spirit will seep into you, because it is transmitted by words you hear.

Somebody said, *"Well, you ought to be as smart as an old cow. They eat the hay and spit out the sticks."* That sounds good and there is some truth in that. But we had a horse once who wouldn't eat anything. We called the veterinarian. He opened that horse's mouth, ran his arm down the horse's throat, and pulled out a big stick that was down his throat. That horse couldn't eat anything, and he would have died before long if someone had not found the stick and removed it.

Some people don't know to spit out the sticks. The spirit of error is transmitted through words. If you continually sit under teaching that is wrong, the spirit of error will be transmitted to you. That's another reason Jesus said, *"Take heed what you hear."*

Let me give you some Bible evidence of what we are saying in regard to words creating power. The Lord said this to me when I was preparing to teach. *"Faith is the ability to conceive God's Word."*

I had never thought about it that way. But **faith is ability to conceive.**

It is spiritual conception. The ability is developed by hearing the Word of God. When you first hear it, you don't necessarily receive it.

If you have been raised in certain denominations, you may have been taught that healing went out with the apostles. You may have been taught that the baptism of the Holy Ghost with the evidence of speaking with other tongues is not for you today. Well, if you have been taught that way, then you are going to believe that way. When you heard that it was for you, it took you a while to decide whether or not you were going to receive it. Faith had to come before you would conceive that Word, which is a seed of truth. Once the Word is conceived in your spirit, it will eventually manifest itself in you. I want to show you Bible evidence for that, and show you how it is connected with faith.

## A HEARER OF THE WORD

In Luke, chapter one we find a classic example of a man who heard a word from God, but did not receive it. Zacharias and his wife Elisabeth had been desiring a child. In fact, the Bible says they had been praying that they would have a child. But they had not had a child because his wife Elisabeth was barren. Then an angel appeared to him.

*And when Zacharias saw him, he was troubled, and fear fell upon him.*

*But the angel said unto him, Fear not, Zacharias: for thy prayer is heard; and thy wife Elisabeth shall bear thee a son, and thou shalt call his name John.*

*And thou shalt have joy and gladness: and many shall rejoice at his birth.*

*For he shall be great in the sight of the Lord. . .*

74

*And Zacharias said unto the angel, **Whereby shall I know this?** for I am an old man and my wife well stricken in years.* (Luke 1:12-15, 18)

Allow me to paraphrase that. Zacharias said to the angel, *"How do I know you are telling the truth? Give me a sign."*

He was not willing at that point to receive the Word of God without a sign.

## CONDITIONAL AND UNCONDITIONAL PROMISES

**Some things that God says are conditional. Then some things are unconditional; God declares them, and He will bring them to pass.** Many of the promises in the new covenant are conditional. But there are some promises God made to Israel, and some promises God made to Abraham which are not conditional. God had established them, and God set in motion exact principles that caused those things to come to pass.

When Zacharias answered as he did, the angel replied with this.

*And the angel answering said unto him, I am Gabriel that stand in the presence of God; and am sent to speak unto thee, and shew thee these glad tidings.* (Luke 1:19)

*And, behold, thou shalt be dumb, and not able to speak, until the day that these things shall be performed, because thou believest not my words, which shall be fulfilled in their season.* (Luke 1:20)

In other words, God knew if He didn't get Zacharias' mouth shut up, this wouldn't happen. Evidently this was not a conditional promise. For Gabriel said, *"my words, which shall be fulfilled in their season."* This shall come to pass. No man shall stop it.

God instigated this action of closing his mouth, causing him to not be able to speak for that period of time until what God declared came to pass.

There are many things God desires to do, but unless you get in agreement with God, many of them will never come to pass. Somebody said, *"If it's the will of God, it will just happen. And if it's not the will of God, it wouldn't happen anyway."*

Some things will happen whether you believe them or not. Jesus is coming back. You can believe it or not believe it; He is still coming. Your unbelief is not going to change that. **But there are some things that your unbelief will change.** When it comes to the promises of God and entering into the provisions that God has made, then your unbelief can change that. You can change it for the better, or you can change it for the worse.

Can you see God's method here with Zacharias? God declared a thing, and Zacharias failed to conceive that word. So God rendered him speechless until it came to pass. Many of us would be better off if we couldn't speak. When our words are unbelief.

You will notice after the child's birth Zacharias still couldn't talk. Others were trying to name the child Zacharias after his father, but Elisabeth said, *"No, we are going to call him John."*

They objected, then asked Zacharias what he was going to name the child. He couldn't talk, even after the child was born.

> *And they made signs to his father, how he would have him called.*
>
> *And he asked for a writing table, and wrote, saying, His name is John. And they marvelled all.*
>
> *And his mouth was opened immediately, and his tongue loosed, and he spake, and praised God.*
>
> *(Luke 1:62-64)*

After everything was performed as God said, after they named the child John, immediately Zacharias' tongue was loosed and he could speak.

He got in agreement with God at this point. Sometimes God will do things because He has declared them, and it is something that is not conditional.

You see, God didn't just say, *"Well, just let him go ahead and talk unbelief, but we will just make it happen anyway."* There are some things God cannot do for you, if He can't get you to agree with Him or just be quiet.

## GOD'S WORD CONCEIVED BY MARY

Let me show you the opposite of that in that same chapter. This same angel appeared to Mary and said to her,

> *Hail, thou that are highly favoured, the Lord is with thee: blessed art thou among women.*
>
> *And the angel said unto her, Fear not, Mary: for thou has found favour with God.*
>
> *And, behold, thou shalt conceive in thy womb, and bring forth a son, and shalt call his name JESUS.*
>
> *He shall be great, and shall be called the Son of the Highest: and the Lord God shall give unto him the throne of his father David:*
>
> *and he shall reign over the house of Jacob for ever; and of his kingdom there shall be no end.*
>
> *(Luke 1:28, 30-33)*

Mary didn't get into unbelief, but yet she asked a question. She simply didn't understand how this could happen.

> *Then said Mary unto the angel, How shall this be, seeing I know not a man?*
>
> *And the angel answered and said unto her, The Holy Ghost shall come upon thee, and the power*

*of the Highest shall overshadow thee: therefore
also that holy thing which shall be born of thee
shall be called the Son of God.* *(Luke 1:34-35)*

Notice what Mary said in response, then compare
this with Zacharias' response.

*And Mary said, Behold the handmaid of the
Lord;* **be it unto me according to thy word.** *And
the angel departed from her.* *(Luke 1:38)*

If God is going to give the same treatment to
everyone, why didn't He also strike her dumb? God is
no respecter of persons. **Why would He strike
Zacharias dumb and not strike Mary dumb?** God
brought a message to her through Gabriel just like he
brought a message to Zacharias.

The problem was that Zacharias did not have faith to
conceive it. And God didn't have time to preach faith to
him. So God just stopped the unbelief.

But Mary received the Word of God. Notice what
she did. **She actually conceived God's Word sent by
an angel.** Zacharias didn't exactly do that, did he? Mary
agreed with God, after the angel explained to her that
this would be an act of the Holy Spirit.

The Holy Spirit is the author of the Word of God. So
the Holy Spirit would overshadow her. Here came the
Word of God to Mary, *"You are going to conceive and
bear a child,"* contrary to all natural thinking and
everything they knew. It was impossible. But the Bible
says it is not impossible for God to perform His every
declaration. He releases sufficient faith in His words to
cause it to come to pass. It will cause things to come to
pass, if it is received in faith.

Now, we are talking about a conditional promise.
Sometimes they are unconditional. The rapture is going
to happen, Jesus is coming back. Whether you believe it
or not, it will still happen.

Mary received the Word. Allow me to paraphrase what Mary said.

*"Look. You have found the woman who will believe you. Be it unto me according to your Word."*

Faith is the ability to conceive what God has declared. Mary conceived God's Word in the womb of her spirit. That is what it means to have faith in the heart: having the ability to conceive in the womb of the human spirit what God declares.

Once that is done, it will manifest itself in the physical realm. In Mary's case, it manifested itself in her physical body.

I was meditating on this one day. I said, *"Lord, I would like to know how this happened. Mary asked the question, but I would like to know more in detail how it happened."* He said it was through an act of the God kind of faith. *"I sent My Word to her. **She heard the Word, she conceived the Word, she received it into her spirit, and then she spoke it.**"*

You will notice in Luke 1:38 Mary said, *"Be it unto me according to thy word."* In today's language, Mary said, *"It is done unto me just like You said."*

Now compare that with what Zacharias said. He said, *"How do I know you are telling the truth? Give me a sign."*

Mary didn't need a sign. She left there and went to Elisabeth's house. She said,

*He that is mighty hath done to me great things; and holy is his name.* (Luke 1:49)

How did she know? **She had no physical evidence whatsoever.** All she had was the Word of God. She conceived it. Her faith gave her the ability to conceive God's Word in her spirit.

## SPIRIT LIFE OR DEATH

**There is spirit life in God's Word.** There is a faith force, a spiritual power that is capable of bringing to pass what God has promised. But it has to be received. It has to be conceived in the human spirit, or what the Bible calls the heart. It is designed by God to operate on the Word of God. You will die a spiritual death if you do not have the Word of God. The Spirit of life comes from the Word of God. God breathed Spirit life into Adam. And without that Spirit life, the human spirit will die a spiritual death.

That doesn't mean the human spirit ceases to exist. That means it just simply is not alive to God. Adam died spiritually when he sinned. That didn't mean that his spirit ceased to exist.

We wrongly equate death with ceasing to exist. But the spirit always exists. Adam was simply spiritually dead.

There is Spirit life in the Word. Mary **received it. She spoke it when she conceived it in her spirit.** Then it manifested itself in her physical body.

## WORD BECAME FLESH

This is the key to understanding the virgin birth. God's Word is full of faith and Spirit power. God spoke it. God transmitted the image to Mary. She received the image inside of her. She **spoke** it and faith came. Faith cometh by hearing. She immediately began to say what God said: *"Be it unto me according to thy word."* When she did, the angel left. He said, *"This is going to work fine. I might as well go on, because she's in agreement with it."*

The embryo that was in Mary's womb was nothing more than the Word of God.

That is why people become confused mentally about the virgin birth. They say it could not have happened.

80

## • Custom Design

Medium size designed to fit your new
personal size Bible.
Other sizes available to fit most popular
Bible product.

## • Convenient Pocket

Outside pocket carries notes and study materials.

## • Choice of Colors

Soft and durable vinyl comes in three tasteful
styles and colors: Rich Burgundy, Royal Blue and
Natural Brown.

## • Craftsmanship

Sturdy nylon zipper and heavy-duty stitching
exhibit superior quality craftsmanship for years of
dependable service.

## • Affordable

Enjoy the distinction and practicality of a Zondervan Bible cover at an affordable price.

**Cherish and protect your new Zondervan Bible
for a lifetime of Bible reading.**

ZONDERVAN
BIBLE PUBLISHERS

ZZI19254
Printed in USA

# Cherish

your new Zondervan Bible
by protecting it with a
Zondervan Bible cover.

*Quality craftsmanship and unique features
provide you years of lasting use*

They look at it biologically. It was both biological and spiritual. She conceived the Word of God.

Somebody said, *"Well, I don't see how that could happen."* Peter gives us some insight into this when he said,

> *Being born again, not of corruptible seed, but of incorruptible, by the word of God, which liveth and abideth for ever.*　　　　　*(I Peter 1:23)*

The Word of God is a living, incorruptible seed which permanently dwells and abides.

In Genesis, chapter three God prophesied Satan's defeat.

> *And I will put enmity between thee and the woman, and between thy seed **and her seed; it shall bruise thy head.**　　(Genesis 3:15)*

We know and medical science knows the woman does not have a seed. The seed is carried by the male. The sperm is considered the seed. But God said the seed of the woman. And God knew what He was talking about. What seed is He talking about when He said the seed of the woman? The seed of the incorruptible Word of God. It is that incorruptible seed talked about in I Peter 1:23.

Mary conceived the Word in her spirit. It manifested itself in her physical body. It was the incorruptible seed.

> ***And the Word was made flesh,*** *and dwelt among us, (and we beheld his glory, the glory as of the only begotten of the Father,) full of grace and truth.*　　　　　*(John 1:14)*

One translation says **the Word took upon itself flesh.** Took upon itself flesh. That proves what was conceived in Mary's womb was **the Word of God.** It was the seed the woman received from God.

It was conceived in Mary's heart (spirit), and it manifested itself in her physical body.

The Lord said something else to me about this type of conception. He said, *"Any believer who will receive My Word concerning any promise in the New Testament (any promise that is for today), conceive it in their heart the way that Mary conceived it, **it will manifest itself.** If it is a healing scripture they are speaking and quoting, it will manifest in their physical bodies."*

Notice it didn't happen overnight to Mary. It was a process. There was a time span involved. If you already have cancer and you are just starting to confess the Word of God to build your faith for healing, you could die before faith comes.

Now, I'm going to say some things that haven't been said. But they need to be said. This is a process. **Confessing God's Word is a process. It's a way of life. It takes time to build faith.**

Some start too late — when it's a life or death situation. If doctors can help you, don't be condemned over that. God wants you alive and well. For most people are not developed to that level of faith. Some have died trying to develop their faith. If medical care can help you, get some medicine. Get well. Get in the Word and stop the next attack before it gets there.

Here is the point I want to make. Confessing the Word of God is a process of building it into your spirit. You do it continually. And then over a period of time it will manifest itself.

## FINANCIAL IMAGE

The Lord went on to say this to me regarding finances. Now get hold of this and learn to conceive God's Word concerning finances. Learn what God said about your finances.

He said to me, *"Any believer can conceive My Word concerning finances by being obedient to the promise; give, and it shall be given unto you. When you give, then start confessing,"*

*It is given unto me, good measure, pressed down, shaken together and running over, will men give unto my bosom. I have favor with God and men, and I sow bountifully. I reap bountifully. My God makes all grace abound toward me, that I, having all sufficiency of all things, do abound to all good works.*

*(Luke 6:38; II Corinthians 9:6, 8)*

What are you doing? You are transmitting that image which God has of you into your spirit. You are receiving the spirit of life for that promise. That promise has no life in printed form. It will not manifest itself while sitting on your bookshelf. It gets inside of you as you speak it. **That spirit life comes from the Word, gets into you,** and causes that promise to be manifest in real life situations. It will cause the good deals to come your way. It will cause things to happen to you that never would have happened if you hadn't received that image inside of you.

## HOLY SPIRIT IMAGE

He said to me, *"Any believer who will conceive My Word concerning the baptism of the Holy Spirit and speaking with other tongues, conceive it in their spirit and act upon it, it will manifest itself through the prayer language, and their spirit being."*

The Holy Spirit will come in, but we must conceive it. That's the way salvation comes. That is the way divine healing comes. That's the way the baptism of the Holy Spirit comes. He said, *"**that is the way all the promises of God are manifest. They have to be conceived in the spirit.**"*

Everything that you receive from God is going to come first into the human spirit, where it is conceived.

## WOMB OF SPIRIT

Brother Cho says it this way, and I like it. It is conceived in the *"womb"* of the spirit. The spirit, or what the Bible calls the heart, is the conception center or the reception center of everything you receive from God. You must receive God's Word first on any subject. Then that Word will bring spirit life into it.

But it does not happen just because you heard it once, or just because you said three hundred times, *"I have a new car."*

You don't get a new car just because you said it three hundred times. First, you must **believe** what you say will come to pass. That may take weeks or months.

I'm saying some things which haven't been said, but they are very much needed.

**The first stages of confessing God's Word are doing little more than causing faith to come.** There is little or no creative ability when you first start confessing the Word of God. People say, *"Well, I confessed it for three days. I don't understand why it didn't come to pass."*

You hung in there for three whole days then gave up.

**This is a way of life. This is not a fad. This is not a formula,** but is a way of life.

Take that Word which is filled with Spirit power, the power of God, and speak that Word. Then that Spirit life in that Word gets inside of you, because your voice is picked up by your inner ear and fed directly into the human spirit. You get it in your mouth, and it gets into your heart. When it gets into your heart in abundance, it gets in your mouth. When it gets in your mouth, it gets back into you heart even stronger.

The miraculous conception came this same way. Mary was the only one who ever received a child that way, and we are not talking about someone else receiving a child that way. We are talking about the promises of God. God gave that promise to Mary. It was a personal promise to her. It doesn't apply to other women.

But all of these promises in the New Testament will come the same way. They have to be conceived. We must receive them.

## BELIEVING GOD IS A DECISION YOU MUST MAKE

I'm going to say it again. **Faith is the ability to conceive God's Word into the human spirit.**

You don't always want to believe God. You must make a decision to believe God.

You don't just wake up some morning saying, *"I just feel like believing God today."* In fact, most mornings you wake up thinking, *"Dear God, I wish I didn't have to believe that today. I know it says that in Your Word.* ***But it looks so different in the natural.*** *I wish I didn't have to believe what You said."*

But you have to make a decision to believe it. Sometimes it's in the face of apparent defeat, in the face of lack. When things are going wrong we need to button our lips and just believe God. The apostle Paul said it this way.

> *Let no corrupt communication proceed out of your mouth, but that which is good to the use of edifying, that it may minister grace unto the hearers.*
>
> *And grieve not the holy Spirit of God.*
>
> *(Ephesians 4:29-30)*

If you can't speak in agreement with God's word, then don't speak at all. But there are some times we must force our mouth to speak and declare God's Word over the situation.

85

Our words should always be filled with faith, and they should minister grace to the hearer. Have you ever stopped and asked yourself who is the number one hearer of what I say? If you look in the mirror, you are looking at the number one hearer. You are the one to hear it first. First you hear it in your thought. Then you speak it.

Remember we talked about you hearing your voice on the tape recorder. When you heard it, you were embarrassed, because it didn't sound at all like you thought you sounded. The reason was that you have heard yourself mostly with the inner ear. If you plug up your ears and speak, your voice sounds louder to you. Why? **Because your inner ear is picking up the sound. Your voice is picked up by the inner ear and is fed directly into the human spirit.** This is the way you get God's Word into your heart. This is why faith will come more quickly when you speak God's Word. For your spirit will receive the words you speak more quickly than it will receive words that I speak. I can read the Word of God to you, but it will not get faith in you nearly so fast as if you speak and declare the Word of God yourself.

Your voice speaking the Word of God has a force that enters into your human spirit, and you receive that force. That is why Proverbs says,

> *Let not mercy and truth forsake thee: bind them about thy neck; **write them upon the table of thine heart.*** *(Proberbs 3:3)*

You write these things on the table of your heart by speaking them. The Psalmist David says,

> *My tongue is the pen of a ready writer.*
> *(Psalm 45:1)*

That is how you write God's Word on your heart. That is how faith comes. Faith comes by hearing the

Word of God. To hear it, someone must speak it. And you speaking the Word of God is the quickest way for you to receive faith. **Faith will come more quickly if you quote it yourself.**

## CONFESSION - THRUST

Confession is to your faith as thrust is to an airplane. If you don't have thrust, that airplane will not get off the ground. It is heavier than air. You must have something pulling it through the air. You must have thrust, for there is a law of lift which supercedes the law of gravity. You don't stop the law of gravity from working when you get in the airplane. You supercede the law of gravity with a higher law, which is a combined law of thrust and lift.

## UNSEEN LAW

What if I had gotten in the airplane and I looked out on the wing and said, *"I don't see any lift on this wing today. There isn't any there. I don't see a thing. I can't fly today; there isn't any lift. Maybe it is not God's will for me to fly today."*

Now see, that's a good example of being able to see and use things you cannot see. Actually, that lift is not there. But the design is there that will create lift, if you combine the thrust with it. But starting out without any lift, how do I know, when I get to seventy knots, that there will be enough combined law of lift and thrust to get that airplane off the ground? If it doesn't, I will be in the salt bayou in less than a minute, for it's right at the end of the runway.

But we all have faith in the unseen. How did I gain faith in the unseen? With words. They told me this wing is designed aerodynamically so that when air passes over this wing, it creates a low pressure area on the top of it, because the air travels farther over the top than it does under the bottom. So it has to go faster. And when it does, it creates a low pressure area. And the air underneath is trying to push up to this low pressure area. This creates what they call lift.

## THINGS THAT ARE NOT
## BRING TO NAUGHT THINGS THAT ARE

Through words they transmitted faith to me; enough that I would have faith to get in that thing and say, *"This thing will fly."* Somebody said, *"How is it going to fly? It weighs over two tons."*

I may not understand all I know about lift, but I have faith in the law. I have at least come to agree it will work if I make it work by adding thrust.

Faith is a law also. You must have faith in the law of faith, and then make the law work by applying confession. **For confession is to your faith as thrust is to that airplane.** Without the thrust there will be no lift. Without confession of God's Word, speaking and meditating God's Word, you won't develop much faith.

Then on the other hand, you can get an airplane in the air flying like a bird. You can pull back on your throttles, and reduce the thrust and it will still fly. You are sitting up there doing 250 mph. You can pull it back to half throttle. You are producing half as much thrust, but it's still flying. But now you are only doing about 150 mph.

You may think, *"Well, I'm saving gas. Let's pull this thing back to a quarter."* So you pull the throttle back to one-fourth power. You are saving more gas, but now your speed is down to about 90 mph. You can still hold the same altitude. But to do so, you must increase the angle of attack — that is, hold a nose-high attitude. And you decide, *"Well, that's doing so good, I'm just going to shut the engine off."*

You are coming down!

And that's what happens to your faith without confession. **Your faith will never rise any higher than your confession.**

Let me say this to you. I'm going to say it three or four ways, so you won't miss it. **Your confession is the ceiling for your faith.**

Your faith will not exceed your confession. The more you develop your confession of the Word of God — the speaking of what God says — the higher you will get developed in your faith. You don't get there overnight.

It takes time. I didn't learn to fly an airplane overnight. You have to develop yourself in faith. You are going to make some mistakes. The people you teach will make some mistakes. But it takes time, and you have to develop yourself in it. It's just like a child who gets up to walk, and he falls. He doesn't say, *"Walking doesn't work. Forget it. I'm going to crawl."*

No, he knows it works. He sees too many people walking.

You must develop yourself. To do that, you have to start where you are.

This thrust to an airplane is what causes the lift. Without the thrust, without the airplane moving through the air, there will be no lift. **Without God's Word in you, there will be no faith.**

Being a faith person today and having faith in God today doesn't mean that ten days, thirty days, six months from now you will have faith. **If you shut off the Word supply** — pull back on the throttles — **you can coast for a while. But you are about to come down.**

In fact, I learned this by saying to the Lord one day, *"I want to know why things are not going as well as they were a year or so ago. It seems as if now it's a struggle to do things that just came easy back there a year ago."*

89

When I asked the Lord the question, I prayed in the Spirit, and I was listening for the Spirit of God.

I heard this coming up in my spirit. *"You've pulled back on your throttles."*

I said, *"I've done what?"*

He said, *"Confession is to your faith as the thrust is to that airplane. And you have been pulling back on your confession."*

Then the question came up in my spirit, *"What were you doing a year ago when things were going much better, and your faith was to a higher peak?"*

I stopped, and I thought about it. A year ago, every day, I was confessing the Word of God from the little booklet, *"God's Creative Power."* I wouldn't dare miss a day. Not that I was in bondage to it, but I wanted to feed by spirit. I did it daily, and meditated in the Word of God. I said, *"Come to think of it, I have been doing it hit and miss the last several months."*

That was my answer. *"You have been pulling back on your confession, and your faith is dwindling. You are losing the thrust."*

The Lord said, *"If you get that thrust (confession) back into it, then that lift will show up again."*

When I did what God said, I got exactly what He said. You know, it's amazing. God knows some things. He wrote the book, you know. He can tell you how to get out of situations. You see, you have to check up on yourself. Have you ever said, *"I can't believe in something I can't see?"* I have said that in the past.

But now when I sit down in my airplane, **I am expecting air that I can't see to flow across a wing (I don't understand) fast enough to cause a law (I can't see) cause an airplane that weighs over two tons to fly like a bird. The unseen law brings to naught what is seen.**

Now, in my natural mind, if I think about that long enough, I would go home and crawl under the bed, instead of flying on that plane.

But you must put faith in all of those things that you don't understand every time you fly. You can't see them, and you don't understand them. You know that you believe in it because you see them fly, and you've heard people talk about riding in them. Someone will talk you into it. They will transmit the image they have of airplanes to you, and you will believe it, even though you don't fully understand it.

Seeing and understanding some things inspires your faith. When you see it work long enough, certainly that will have some effect on your faith. It inspires your faith. Now you can see what we are talking about in the power of words.

That's the long way around, but these things will help you get hold of this principle.

## DEVELOPMENT OF PRINCIPLES

I want to point out to you that we are talking about principles. Confessing God's Word is a principle that must be developed. It is not just a formula. **It is not going to work just because you say it. But saying it is involved in working it.**

It's a process. It takes time. It takes weeks. Sometimes it takes months. It must become a way of life to you.

Quite frankly, the first stages of confessing the Word has very little effect on the problem areas. It will affect them only when you believe it. But speaking it is involved in causing faith to come. And it's not just a mechanical formula. It's a matter of being in obedience to God's Word. You speak abundance, and keep speaking abundance until faith comes.

91

Don't do like some people have done. They said, *"Well, I'm a faith man, I'm just going to confess the Word of God. I'm going to quit my job and live by faith."*

You are going to starve!

No, don't quit your job. Use your faith on your job. Don't just throw all good business sense aside. But take the Word of God and build it into your spirit **until you know, that you know, that you know God's Word is true in you.** When you are that sure, you will have a manifestation of it.

**The more highly developed you get in either fear or faith, the quicker the manifestation will come.** Some are highly developed in fear. Some are highly developed in faith. Develop your faith in the Word of God. Remember these two things.

Fear comes by hearing the words of the devil.

Faith in God comes by hearing God's Word.

## Chapter Five

# THE RIGHTEOUSNESS WHICH IS FAITH PRINCIPLE

In the last chapter we looked at the fact that the power of God's Word conceived in the human spirit produces a spiritual force called faith. It will manifest itself in your life.

We looked at the fact that Mary conceived God's Word in her spirit. It manifested itself in her body.

In this chapter I want to share with you the principle upon which God operates, and **how you can operate in the same principle.** Sometimes people don't realize that they can operate in the same principles as God. They are divine principles. They are spiritual laws. **But we can operate these principles also.**

## PRACTICE BRINGS UNDERSTANDING

To be effective with the teaching of the Word of God and the principles of the Bible, we must learn to practice these things. Many people practice what they are preaching. But when you **preach what you have already practiced,** you will be far more effective. Then you have already practiced it and found what makes it work and what will short it out, causing it not to work.

Remember to practice it. Set it in motion. Get it working in your life. You're not as effective when you have not practiced it for yourself. You have heard someone preach the same sermon as some great man of God. They said the same words. But unless they have practiced it in their life, it just came out of their mouth and fell to the ground. There was no authority behind it. It was what someone else experienced. Preach or share something you have already experienced. It will be more effective.

In Luke chapter one we found that Zacharias lost his speech for more than nine months, until what God said came to pass, because Zacharias doubted what the angel said. God sent the angel to him. But he didn't receive God's Word. Then on the other hand, we found that Mary said, *"Be it unto me according to thy Word."*

## FEELING OR BELIEVING

Now let's notice what Abraham did about believing God. It is recorded several times that Abraham believed God, and it was accounted to him for righteousness. Righteousness means right standing. In other words, he was in right standing with God because he decided to believe God's report.

I'm sure Abraham didn't always feel like believing God. But **he made a decision to believe God.**

> *For the promise, that he should be **heir of the world,** was not to Abraham, or to his seed, through the law, but through the righteousness of faith.* (Romans 4:13)

You will notice the promise was not through the law, but through the righteousness of faith. What was this promise he was talking about? That he should be heir of the world. Did you realize God's promise to Abraham was that **he would be heir of the world? The whole world.**

Somebody said, *"Well, what does that do for me?"*

It will do a lot for you, if you realize the Bible is saying we are heirs of the world!

> *And **if ye be Christ's, then are ye Abraham's seed,** and heirs according to the promise.* (Galatians 3:29)

Somebody said, *"Yes, but by the time the meek inherit the earth, the taxes will be so high they won't want it."*

But I don't believe that. We are heirs of the world. It was to Abraham, not through the law, but through the **righteousness which is of faith.**

I want to take time to share with you some things about this righteousness which is of faith. This promise is *"through the righteousness of faith."*

Now look at Romans 10:6. Notice what the Apostle Paul says about the righteousness which is of faith.

## WHAT RIGHTEOUSNESS WOULDN'T SAY

**First** he is telling you what the righteousness which is of faith **did not say.**

*But the righteousness which is of faith speaketh on this wise, **say not** in thine heart, Who shall ascend into heaven? (that is, to bring Christ down from above:)*

*Or, Who shall descend into the deep? (that is, to bring up Christ again from the dead.)*

*But what saith it?* (Romans 10:6-8)

Sometimes it helps you to find out what something is not before you find out what it is. I believe that is what Paul does here.

He said the righteousness which is of faith would not say, Who is going to reverse the process of death? Who is going to bring Jesus back from heaven, that He may come to us and heal us and do things for us again as He did in the days when He walked the earth? **The righteousness which is of faith would not say it that way.**

I know you are thinking, *"Well, I wouldn't say that either."*

But have you ever said this? *"Lord, come down and touch me!"*

95

Surely you have. That is what we are saying when we say that. We say, *"Jesus, if You just come down here and touch me, I know I would be healed."*

Well, I have news for you. He's not coming. Hebrews 10:12-13 tells us Jesus is seated at the right hand of the Father until His enemies are made His footstool.

You see, Jesus is there in His physical body. He is seated there. And He is not coming back until His enemies are made His footstool.

Somebody said, *"Do you mean He's not going to heal me?"*

He has already healed you. He sent His Word and healed you. This is what the Bible said about it.

*He sent his word, and healed them, and delivered them from their destructions.* *(Psalm 107:20)*

Then the scriptures reveal more insight in the book of John.

*In the beginning was the Word, and the Word was with God, and the Word was God.*

*All things were made by him; without him was not any thing made that was made.*

*And the Word was made flesh (took upon itself flesh), and dwelt among us.* *(John 1:1, 3, 14)*

## WORD PERSONIFIED

The Word was with God in heaven in the beginning. The Word was made flesh; when the Word became flesh He was called Jesus. One translation says the Word took upon itself flesh. The Word walked upon the earth in flesh form. God had sent His Word and healed and delivered them. That includes us also.

It happened this way: Mary conceived the Word of God in her spirit. And then it manifested itself in her physical body. The Word actually, literally took flesh upon itself and dwelt among us. What the Word did in heaven God would prove beyond any doubt that the Word would do the same things in the earth today. He clothed His Word with flesh (Jesus), and sent him here to live among us, and He showed us that the Word could do the same on earth.

**Jesus was the personification of God's Word on this earth.** He came here to heal the sick. He raised the dead; he cast out the demons. The Amplified Bible says He came to destroy, loosen, dissolve, undo the works the devil had done. The Word came to destroy the works of the devil. When we talk about Jesus, we often disassociate Him from the Word and from what John 1:1 says about Him. **Jesus in Word form was the creator of all things.** God used the Word **to create.** God used the Word **to frame the worlds.**

Then to prove to us that the Word is as powerful on earth as it is in heaven, He clothed His Word with flesh, sent Him to the earth, and He did the same works here on earth. Then He told us,

*He that believeth on me, the works that I do shall he do also: and greater works than these shall he do; because I go unto my Father.*

*And whatsoever ye shall ask in my name, that will I do, that the Father may be glorified in the Son.* (John 14:12-13)

So when God says He sent His Word and healed us, that is exactly what He expects His Word to do — heal and deliver from destruction.

Somebody said, *"Do you mean Jesus is not healing anyone on earth today?"*

Yes, Jesus heals today. But Jesus is not coming in His physical form to heal you. He dwells in you in the person of the Holy Spirit. **It is through the Word that**

**you receive healing.** Someone may lay hands on you, but it is the Word that gives you faith to expect healing to come when hands are laid on you. But regarding Jesus coming personally and touching you, He's not coming to do that. He is seated at the right hand of the Father until His enemies are made His footstool.

Somebody said, *"Well, I have heard of people who saw Jesus. He came in, stood by their bed and touched them, and they were healed."*

They had a spiritual vision. That was not Jesus in his physical body. They saw a spiritual vision. That still happens today. But Jesus is seated at the right hand of the Father until His enemies are made His footstool.

## WHAT RIGHTEOUSNESS WOULD SAY

Now allow me to repeat, because we have gone so far around to get to this. This promise to Abraham was not through the law, but through the righteousness which is of faith. That is the way you enter into this promise. This is the way you become heir of the world through the promise God made to Abraham.

**Next,** Paul tells you what the righteousness which is of faith **would say.**

> *What saith it?* ***The word*** *is nigh me,* ***even in thy mouth, and in thy heart:*** *that is, the word of faith, which we preach.*     (Romans 10:8)

Notice that the Word gets in your mouth, **then *"in thy heart."*** The Word is first in your mouth. If it doesn't get in your mouth, then it won't get in your heart. You can **learn about the Word.** You can **hear about the Word.** But until you put the Word of God in your mouth, it has not reached its highest form. For faith cometh by hearing; and to hear the Word, it must be spoken.

The righteousness which is of faith **would not say,** *"Jesus will have to come back and touch me."* It wouldn't say, *"We'll have to reverse the process of death and raise Jesus up from the grave and let him walk in his physical body so He can meet our need."*

The righteousness which is of faith says, *"Jesus is not here physically. But the Word is nigh me."*

It is the same Word that created heaven and earth. Do you realize that God's Word is just as powerful as Jesus was when He walked the face of the earth? There is as much power in His Word under the new covenant as there was in Jesus as He walked the earth. God sent His Word and healed them, whether it was through Jesus or the new covenant Word of promise.

So this is the way you become heir of the world, heir of this promise: **through the righteousness which is of faith.** The righteousness which is of faith speaks. It speaks faith, not fear and doubt. Now let's bring verses eight and nine together.

> *But what saith it?* **The word** *is nigh me, even in thy mouth, and in thy heart: that is, the word of faith, which we preach.*
>
> *That if thou shalt confess with thy mouth the Lord Jesus, and shalt believe in thine heart that God hath raised him from the dead, thou shalt be saved.* (Romans 10:8-9)

## ACTIVATING THE PROMISE BY FAITH

Paul instructs us to confess Jesus as Lord. When a sinner comes to repentance, if he goes by this scripture, he confesses Jesus is the Lord of his life. He confesses because he believes the Word of God. He may say, *"I believe Jesus died for my sins and I confess that He is the Lord of my life."*

When he said that, Jesus wasn't the Lord of his life. The devil was. But because **he made the decision and by faith said it,** all the demons of hell can't stop it from coming to pass. He has come to right standing with God. This is the righteousness which is of faith. He probably didn't feel like he was righteous. He didn't really feel like Jesus was his Lord. But he made the decision to believe it and to proclaim it. This is the way the righteousness which is of faith works. You believe unto righteousness. Notice the next verse.

*For with the heart man believeth unto righteousness; and with the mouth confession is made unto salvation.* (Romans 10:10)

With the heart man believes. It's a function of the inner man, or the heart. He believes with his whole inner being or heart. **Faith works in the heart. It doesn't work in the head.** When the sinner made a confession of faith, he released God's energy force within him. **He spoke it into existence.** All the demons of hell couldn't stop it, because a man took God's Word and decreed it by faith. If he believed it in his heart and said it with his mouth, then it came to pass, regardless of how he felt, for it was by faith, not feelings.

But you could believe in your heart and be saved. If you couldn't, any person who couldn't speak couldn't be saved. *"With the heart man believeth unto righteousness."*

For example, I have heard of people who got up at the altar call and started down the aisle to receive Jesus as their Lord. And before they got there, they were speaking in tongues. They were saved and baptized in the Holy Ghost, and hadn't spoken one word in English. They made the decision in their heart. Their very action said something.

The scripture says with the heart you can believe unto righteousness. *"And with the mouth, confession is made unto salvation."* Then someone may say, *"You must confess it before you are saved."*

But notice this. Salvation is from the Greek word *"sozo."* It is an all-inclusive word. It means deliverance, preservation, healing, and soundness. All of those ideas are included in that word sozo. But sometimes we just take it to mean being saved, or born again. We miss what the apostle Paul was saying here.

Let's put it in perspective. He said with the heart, man can believe and be born again. But if you want deliverance, preservation, healing, and soundness, then you must get your mouth in motion. Begin to speak the promises. For with the mouth confession is made unto deliverance, preservation, healing, and soundness. Here Paul is not referring to being born again. He is referring to possessing the promises of God.

This is why he said this promise of being heir of the world was not to Abraham through the law, but through the righteousness which is of faith. This righteousness which is of faith speaks the Word of God. It says, *"The Word is nigh me. I can possess the promise. The promise is nigh me."*

**You may have a need. But the promise is nigh you.** You take the promise and put it in your mouth and speak it. When it is spoken, it is heard and releases divine energy to the hearer.

Oh, you can believe to be born again. But if you want deliverance from the pressures of life, the situations and the problems of life, if you need supernatural deliverance, then you must get your mouth in motion and speak in agreement with God.

When God says something, it is truth. When you look at the situation that says, *"You aren't going to make it, Mack,"* **the Word of God says whatever you do will prosper.** The Word says *"that ye may prosper in all that ye do."* (Deuteronomy 29:9) *"No weapon formed against you will prosper."* (Isaiah 54:17)

We put God's Word in our mouth and speak it. That is what the righteousness which is of faith does.

> *Therefore it is of faith, that it might be by grace; to the end the promise might be sure to all the seed.* (Romans 4:16)

## GRACE IS GOD'S WILLINGNESS

Somebody said, *"That promise was not to us. It was just to Abraham."*

It said the promise is to all the seed. *"It is of faith, that it might be by grace."* **Grace is God's willingness to use His power and His ability on your behalf, even though you don't deserve it. God is willing,** and His grace is His willingness.

We have always heard that God's grace is unmerited favor. But ask yourself this. If God could have been in favor of you being saved, but was nót willing to get personally involved in it, would it have helped you? What if God had said, *"If the world can save itself, it's all right with Me, but I am not going to get involved in it. I'm not going to send My Son. I'm not going to do anything. **But I am in favor of the world being saved!"***

We would have all died and gone to hell, wouldn't we? But **God did get personally involved in it.** Grace is God's willingness to get involved. Read the Bible with that interpretation of grace, and you will find it's a different Book. Grace is the willingness of God. Jesus said to the apostle Paul, *"Paul, My grace, or my willingness is sufficient for you."* God said, *"I'm willing, Paul, but you have to do something."*

Paul was asking Him to get the devil off of him — the messenger of Satan that was buffeting him. But Jesus kept telling him, *"Paul, My grace is sufficient. I am willing, but you have to act."* He was telling Paul, *"I'm not going to do it. It's up to you."*

Finally, after the third time, Paul understood it. There are some things we have to do. It doesn't happen just because it's in the Bible. The promise must be activated.

> *Therefore it is of faith, that it might be by grace;* **to the end the promise might be sure to all the seed;** *not to that only which is of the law, but to that also which is of the faith of Abraham; who is the father of us all.* (Romans 4:16)

The scriptures tell us that God preached the gospel of faith first to Abraham. (Galatians 3:8) You notice in the Old Testament there is not much taught about faith. There is not much insight into it. But they operated in faith. They knew they were to believe what God said — and it was imputed to them for righteousness. Hebrews 11 tells of all the mighty men and women of faith. But yet, there was not much said about how to receive faith, or how to exercise faith.

God taught the gospel of faith first to Abraham. He taught it to him by example. In Romans 8:17, Paul refers to Genesis chapter 17 where God spoke to Abram.

## PRECEPT

> *(As it is written, I have made thee a father of many nations,) before him whom he believed, even God, who quickeneth the dead,* **and calleth those things which be not as though they were.**
> (Romans 4:17)

This is the way God talks. Paul gives reference to Genesis 17, where God said **I have made you the father of many nations.** Notice that God didn't say He was **going to** do it. Remember, we talked about **now** faith being the substance of things hoped for, the evidence of things not seen. (Hebrews 11:1)

There was Abraham. He did not have the promised child. The first time God spoke this promise to Abraham, he was *"only"* 75 years old. But before it came to pass, he was 100 years old.

Now you can see why it says where there was no hope Abraham believed in hope. **He believed God for 25 years before it came to pass.**

We will come back to that, but I want to share something here about the time of the promise.

God sometimes reveals things to us which won't happen overnight. You may get revelation in your spirit of things God is going to do. Twenty years ago I saw things about the ministry I am in that are finally happening right now. They didn't happen the next year. They are happening twenty years later. I saw it through the eye of faith. God revealed it to me by revelation of faith. But I didn't go out and tell everybody. We make a mistake when we tell everything we know.

## GUARD GOD'S SECRETS

Joseph told God's secret, and it almost got him killed. **It wasn't God's will for Joseph to go through all the suffering he went through to become the ruler in Egypt.**

We have thought that was just God's way of doing it. But it really wasn't God's way. Joseph told God's secret and let it out to the devil. Then the devil tried to kill him to stop it from coming to pass — and almost did it.

His brothers threw him in a well rather than kill him. The Bible said the Word of the Lord tried Joseph. He had God's Word concerning it. The revelation tried him to see whether he was going to believe God's Word, or believe the circumstances. But every place they put

104

Joseph, he ended up being the doer of everything that was done. No matter where they put him, he ended up on top.

The cream will always come to the top. If you put milk in a separater and shake it up, the cream will always come to the top. The same is true of people.

But here was Joseph. He had God's Word. Like Abraham, he just decided to believe it, even though there was trouble for many long years, starting as a young man. It looked like he had missed it. But he had decided to believe God. When he was taken into Egypt, he ended up in prison. But he still believed God. He would not let that dream depart from him.

Sometimes God reveals some things to you that He doesn't want you telling everyone. For one thing, God doesn't want the devil learning about it. God would reveal much more to us about situations and circumstances of the future if we wouldn't let it out to everyone. For if you let it out, the devil will eventually get hold of it.

Did you know the devil doesn't know everything? Sometimes we let out God's secrets. Sometimes we do this even when we are praying. **There are some things you ought not to pray about in English.** You ought to **pray about them in the spirit.** Then they will come to pass before the devil finds out about it.

This will answer many questions about some things God revealed to you, but they didn't happen that way. God revealed it, and you told everyone. Then the devil brought people across your path who told you that it wouldn't work, and that it wasn't God. They talked you out of it.

We must be sensitive to the Spirit concerning these things God revealed.

## BELIEVING IN HOPE

Now let's pick up where we left off in Romans four concerning Abraham's faith. In verse 17 we find that God called things that were not as though they were. And He taught Abraham to do the same. Then in verse 18 He tells what to do when there is no hope.

*Who **against hope believed in hope**, that he might become the father of many nations, according to that which was spoken, So shall thy seed be.* (Romans 4:18)

This says that Abraham, when there was not hope, **decided to believe** in it.

You might say, *"What do you mean, he believed in hope when there was none?"*

He went to the Word of God and found some hope. There was no hope naturally. But there was hope supernaturally.

What are you going to do when there is no hope? It might be about a financial situation. Maybe you are in that situation — no hope naturally concerning a financial situation.

Well, go to the Word of God and get some hope. Check to see what God said about your finances. God believes in miracles. If He can get you to believe in them, you can get one manifested in your life. **But only if you keep His Word in your mouth.** That's the key to it. Confess what God said is true in your finances.

Abraham *"against hope believed in hope, that he might become the father of many nations."* It didn't **look** that way to him. But he decided to believe *"So shall my seed be,"* just as God said they would be.

*And being not weak in faith, he considered not his own body now dead, when he was about an hundred years old, neither yet the deadness of Sarah's womb.* (Romans 4:19)

Notice it says that he would not consider his own body, now dead. He refused to consider this fact. Naturally speaking, one hundred year old men do not father children. But Abraham would not consider the fact that his body was dead. He was not just ignoring it. He was doing something about it.

Sometimes people just ignore a situation. They think it will go away if they ignore it. But **things won't go away just because you ignore them.**

Abraham decided to do something about it. He believed what God said and he started saying the same thing.

Abraham could have said, *"It sure doesn't look like it's going to come to pass. I sure don't feel like it. But I choose to believe God, that I might become the father of many nations."* (Romans 4:21)

## BE "FULLY PERSUADED"

*He staggered not at the promise of God through unbelief; but was **strong in faith,** giving glory to God.*

*And being **fully persuaded** that, what he had promised, he was able also to perform.*

*And therefore it was imputed to him for righteousness.*

*Now it was not written for his sake alone, that it was imputed to him;*

***But for us also, to whom it shall be imputed,*** *if we believe on him that raised up Jesus our Lord from the dead.* (Romans 4:20-24)

God didn't put this in the Bible just so Abraham would know it was imputed to him as righteousness. It is recorded that it might be imputed to us in the same way.

107

Abraham didn't have the Bible we have, to read the account of this. Don't you know, Abraham would have loved it if he could have read what we are reading. **And Job could have been far ahead if he could have read the first chapter of Job and found out the devil did it, and not God.** But we forget sometimes that they didn't have the same information we have.

Abraham staggered not at the promise of God through unbelief. He would not consider his body. That is actually what it means. He wasn't putting faith in his body. He was putting faith in God's Word.

The first thing God did to Abram to build his faith was to change his name.

## GOD'S FAITH PRINCIPLE

It is obvious he is too old to father a child. And his wife is 90. But God called things that were not as though they were. Then in order to get Abram to do the same, God changed his name. God said, *"Your name will no longer be Abram, but Abraham, which means 'Father of Nations,' or 'Father of a Multitude.' And Sarai, her name no longer be Sarai, but Sarah, which means 'Mother of Nations,' or 'Mother of Multitude.'"*

God was not playing make believe. This was **God's way** of getting Abraham to operate in the principle of faith. God uses His own principles and laws. He knew if He could get Abraham to say what He said, it would produce faith. For faith cometh by hearing the Word of God.

But Abraham couldn't read Romans 10:17 to find this truth. God knew there was enough faith in the name to cause it to come to pass. So God just changed Abram's name. Every time Abraham walked up to someone and said, *"My name is Abraham,"* he was saying, **"I am the father of many nations;** or, *"Thus saith the Lord: I am the father of many nations."*

Can you imagine, with all the people who worked for Abraham, how many times his name was called each day? They said, *"Oh Abraham, what do you want to do with this fence? Abraham, what do you want to do with the sheep? Abraham, what do you want to do with the cattle? Abraham, Abraham, Abraham . . . ."*

Abraham didn't hear the word *"Abraham"* at all. He heard **"Father of nations. Father of nations. Father of nations. Father of nations."**

I like to use my imagination. I imagine he was probably on a cane, getting around slowly. And he kept saying, *"I am Father of nations. I am Father of nations."*

Others wanted to laugh, but they didn't dare, because all the people in the county worked for him. They kept saying, *"Oh, Father of nations. Oh, Father of nations."*

Finally he threw away his cane and said, *"Praise God, I believe I am."* And he started walking better and standing straighter because he believed God. Faith cometh by hearing.

## EXAMPLE OF GOD'S METHOD

There are many others who believed God in a similar manner. God told Joshua,

*This book of the law shall not depart **out of thy mouth;** but thou shalt meditate therein day and night, that thou mayest observe to do according to all that is written therein: for **then thou shalt make thy way prosperous, and then thou shalt have good success.*** *(Joshua 1:8)*

We see God changing Abraham's name so he would say what God said. God is giving these as examples of operating this principle of faith. What you speak is what you believe. And what you believe is what you speak

109

over and over again. That's why it is important that you be careful how you speak.

You will notice that Abraham and God **called things that were not as though they were.**

It did not say they were **calling things that were as though they were not.** Be sure you understand this, for there is a great difference between those two statements.

Abraham did not go around saying, *"I'm not old. I'm not old. No, I'm not old. I'm not old."*

If he had said that, he would have been lying. Some don't understand the difference between a lie and a confession. **A confession is based upon the Word of God.** It may seem to the world that it is a lie. But if God said it, how could you lie saying what God said?

I'm glad some people I know didn't live in Abraham's day. They would have done their best to talk him out of believing God's promise. They would have said, *"You just ate too much chili. You didn't really hear from God. You're just an old man; you just had a dream."*

*But God knew how faith worked. So He just fixed it so Abram would have to say, "I am the father of nations."* Every time he said his name, he heard the Word of God. He heard the Word of God. And he heard the Word of God. **And faith came. And faith came. And more faith came.** For faith cometh by hearing God's Word.

Faith came for many years before the manifestation of it came. This is something I really want to stress. You don't become highly developed in faith overnight. **It doesn't happen overnight. It takes time.** It takes a process of learning and applying the principles of God.

People get in trouble when they think they will go to a seminar and come out a three-day wonder. They make you wonder what happened to them. You wonder if their mind went out for lunch and didn't return. They go back into their church and do all kinds of crazy things and call them faith. More on that subject in a later chapter.

Abraham did not say, *"I'm not old. I'm not old."* He did not deny facts. But **he called it the way God called it, and it overcame the facts.**

You will notice it was 25 years from the time God made him that promise until it came to pass. We make a mistake when we think everything is going to happen overnight.

**Growing in faith is a process.** You are today a sum total of the things you have practiced in the days past. Now **you are not going to change that overnight. But you can change it.**

But it will take time to do it. You must learn how to operate the principles.

I mentioned before that I am a pilot. I learned to fly. I've been flying for 30 years.

I could say, *"There's a 747 out at the airport. And I'm a pilot. I guess I can fly it."*

Well, I might stick it up like a dart somewhere. I don't know how to fly a 747. Now, I can fly a small plane. But I can't fly a 747. I don't have any experience with that. That is beyond my capabilities at this point.

Some people try to go beyond the capabilities of their faith level. **You can overload your faith.** You must learn and know the level to which your faith is developed. Operate on that level.

A man could buy a brand new pickup. Then he buys a yacht. He tells them to load that yacht onto his pickup. They lift that one hundred ton yacht and set it down onto the pickup, and it breaks in half. Then he says, *"Pickups don't work."*

Yes, pickups work. He just overloaded it. It wasn't designed to carry that yacht.

**111**

You see what I'm talking about. Some people try to believe God for millions of dollars, when they haven't learned to believe God for a parking place when they go downtown.

You must develop yourself by starting where you are now. Most people want to start on the top story. You don't start up there. Only flakes start up there. Those who do will come crashing down. It will not work that way. **You must develop yourself in faith. You must grow in faith.**

These are things which have been left unsaid, and they need to be said. **You must start on the level you are on now.**

**God knew where Abraham was, and God started him on his level.** God started Abram out by making him say what God said about him. And that is where you must start.

It doesn't matter how religious you are, how super-spiritual you are, or how long you have been in the ministry. You are required to start on your level by saying what God said. That is where everyone starts.

# Chapter Six

# DEVELOPING FAITH
# IN YOUR CONFESSION

We are studying faith and confession. In the last chapter we got down to some practical things. We talked about overloading our faith. We talked about people trying to believe for millions of dollars to do great things when they haven't learned to believe for a parking place. Some are operating on ten dollar faith and trying to believe for millions of dollars. We all must learn to operate on our level of faith.

I think this is how a lot of people have caused trouble in churches. They have gone to a teaching seminar, and they heard me or someone else teach *"You can have what you say."* They got only a part of what was taught in the seminar. They went home thinking they were a three-day wonder.

They do all kinds of foolish things and call it *"faith."* Then the pastor has to sweep up the pieces and try to get them put back together. They overloaded their faith and made a big splash, but couldn't swim. Then the pastor thinks that's the way we taught them. In this chapter we will look at this problem of people going out beyond their level of development.

You must stay within your level of development, and you can grow from there. But **you always have to start where you are.** That may sound elementary, but it's profound. Many will be helped by understanding that fact.

Start where you are. Then you develop your faith by confession of God's Word.

## COUNT THE COST

I remember a certain individual who heard some teaching on faith and confession. He was a professional man, but he was just beginning in his profession. He found a house that he wanted. It was expensive — around a hundred thousand dollars. He started confessing that he was going to buy this house. He started believing for it and confessing the Word of God over it.

He ended up getting the house. The way it happened was almost supernatural, because he did not have the assets to warrant the loan he received. But he pushed the deal through to completion.

That worked so well that he started confessing and believing for an airplane. He bought a twin-engine airplane that same way. Soon he had more than he could maintain. He didn't have the income to support the things he had bought.

I am not saying this to belittle that individual, but as a matter of instruction to keep others from making the same mistakes. Sometimes people throw away all common sense when they get turned on to faith. Don't develop your faith just in the areas of obtaining things. You may get so many things that you get yourself in trouble.

These aspects of faith have been left unsaid. But they need to be said, for they will keep you from falling into the same trap. Develop your faith to support the things you are believing for.

Yes, you can use your faith and obtain things that you cannot afford. So be careful. Don't go out beyond your level of development.

Many have missed it by not developing their faith to bring in the money to take care of what they believed and obtained. Then they turn thumbs down on faith and say, *"Ah, this stuff doesn't work."*

But it worked so well it got them in trouble. They didn't understand how to work it properly. They found how to get things, but didn't have the common sense to sit down and count the cost.

**Always count the cost. Look before you leap,** as an old saying goes — and that is good advice. If this person figured his income, he would have known right away that he didn't have the income to support those things. But he probably thought it was faith.

## FAITH OR PRESUMPTION

**You must draw a line somewhere between faith and presumption.** You must have common sense with faith. **Don't throw away all common sense and all good business practices when you get turned on to faith.**

A man came to me in a seminar where I was speaking. He said, *"Several of us came over here because we heard you're a farmer, and you're a faith man. We want to know if you use fertilizer on your farm."*

I replied, *"Yes. Do you put gas in your car?"*

Well, no question is stupid if you don't know the answer. Will Rogers once said, **everybody is ignorant — just about different things.** And I'm not making fun of the individual, I'm just pointing out to you the way people think. They want to please God, but sometimes they have more zeal than knowledge. You don't throw away all good business sense and all common sense and all knowledge just because you get turned on to faith. Use your faith in good business practices.

Hebrews 11:1 tells us,

*Now faith is the substance of things hoped for, the evidence of things not seen.*

## NO SUBSTITUTES

When you substitute faith for good business practices, you are headed for trouble. On the other hand, **don't substitute good business practice for faith.** Don't ever settle for good business practice alone. Every day, good people go bankrupt operating in good business sense, but with no faith. They talk negative. They quote the ten o'clock news. They are filled with negative things.

**You must mix faith with what you do. Exercise your faith in what you are doing.** (Psalm 1:3)

A man came to me after calling me regularly for some time. He said, *"Now, Mr. Capps, I'm doing what the Word said. I'm confessing God's Word over my finances. Why isn't it working?"*

Well, the very fact that he had to ask me, *"Why isn't it working?"* proved that he didn't believe. He was not in faith. He is looking at circumstances. Faith would just hold fast to its confession and know that it is working.

The man said, *"I have done everything the Word says to do."*

I said, ***"Well, just keep doing it."***

The ballgame isn't over. Just keep doing it. It doesn't happen overnight. It takes time to change some things. You didn't get that way overnight, and you can't change it overnight.

He called back again in about a month. He again said, *"Well, it still isn't working."*

## YOUR FAITH —
## PLUS TIME — CHANGES THINGS

I finally told him, *"The problem is one inch below your nose. Your mouth. God says it is working; you say it is not."*

116

He called about a year later and said, *"Glory to God! It's working. The Word works."*

It was working all the time, but it just takes time.

Many fail to realize it takes time for things to develop. It takes time to turn things around. If you have been negative for fifteen years, you are not going to change it in four days.

First, you must set things in motion, even in the spiritual realm. 750 years before God sent Jesus into this earth, God spoke it through the prophet Isaiah. God started saying it 750 years before it came to pass. But sometimes we want it to happen overnight.

God's Word has given us insight into the power of words. God's Word is filled with faith power.

**But don't overload your faith. Don't go out beyond your level of development.** Stay within your level of development.

## LACK OF KNOWLEDGE

When I first heard the message of faith and confession, I said, *"I didn't know that was in the Bible."*

I had never heard anyone preach on it. I didn't know Jesus said you could have what you say. I thought, *"If that were true, they would have taught that in my church."*

But they didn't know anything about it in my church. When I heard about it, I got into the Word of God and checked it out. It was there. Jesus actually said it.

*And Jesus answering saith unto them, Have faith in God.*

*For verily I say unto you, That whosoever shall say unto this mountain, Be thou removed, and be thou cast into the sea; and shall not doubt in his heart, but shall believe that those things which he*

117

*saith shall come to pass; he shall have whatsoever he saith.*

*Therefore I say unto you, What things soever ye desire, when ye pray, believe that ye receive them, and ye shall have them.*                   *(Mark 11:22-24)*

## SAYING AND BELIEVING BRINGS RESULTS

Notice this says, *"whosoever shall say."* You can ask people, *"Who will this work for?"* and most will say, *"It will work for 'whosoever'."*

**But it only works for whosoever dares to say.** And that narrows it down some. But that isn't all of that statement. It continues, *"Whosoever shall say . . . and shall not doubt in his heart, but shall believe"* **what he is saying.**

Believe just what he said to the mountain?

No. **Believe everything he says.** He must believe everything he says will come to pass.

That's where I had missed it for a long time. I had heard different people preach on it. But I was reading it one day, and those words just jumped out at me. *"**Those things** which he saith shall come to pass."* **Those things which he saith.**

I realized it was more than just what you say about the circumstance or the mountain of problems. **You must develop yourself to believe that what you are saying day by day shall come to pass.**

**The only way that can be done is by speaking what you desire. Don't speak the things you don't desire. Don't confess things you don't desire.**

For instance, what if Jesus appeared in your church? What if He came walking down the aisle touching everyone and telling them, *"After I touch you, every word you say will come to pass just like you say it."*

Would that change your conversation?

In most churches, if Jesus were to do that, half the congregation would jump up and say, *"Wow! That tickles me to death!"* You'd be two weeks burying the dead.

We have developed ourselves to say negative things. Most of our common sayings are negative. Our everyday speech has been influenced by the enemy to keep us from releasing faith in our every word.

Jesus said whosoever shall **say, believe, doubt not** in his heart, but **believe what he says** will come to pass, **he shall have whatsoever he says.**

## KEEP YOUR WORDS
## HONEST AND BELIEVABLE

It will take you a period of time before you can believe that everything you say will come to pass. You don't get there overnight, because you have talked foolishness and perverse speech for so many years.

You have said, *"I'll tell you, every time I eat that, it makes me sick." "That tickled me to death." "Laugh — I thought I'd die." "I'm just dying to go." "Going to die if I don't." "I am dead in my tracks."* You'd better not be releasing faith in those words.

Why do we have all of these negative things in our conversation? The devil has put it there. It's the devil's way of perverting your words and bringing them to a point where they will work against you, instead of working for you.

We must learn to release faith in everything we say. Keep it simple and honest. Jesus said it this way.

*But let your communication be, Yea, yea; Nay, nay: for whatsoever is more than these cometh of evil.*                                        *(Matthew 5:37)*

*Let your Yes be simply Yes, and your No be simply No; anything more than that comes from the evil one.*                          *(Matthew 5:37 Amp.)*

The apostle Paul said almost the same thing in II Corinthians 1:17-20. So we must clean up our conversation and our speech, if we are going to believe what we say shall come to pass.

The more highly developed you get in your faith, the quicker the manifestation will come. I have had people say, *"I have confessed the Word of God. I have confessed abundance and no lack. I have given, and I am confessing it is given unto me good measure, pressed down, and shaken together. I have to confess it for weeks and sometimes months before it ever comes to pass. But just let me say one negative thing, and it happens overnight."*

I can tell you why. **You are more highly developed on the negative side than you are on the positive side.**

Faith cometh by hearing. (Romans 10:17) So if you are hearing yourself speak the negative, and if you have been doing that for years, then you are more highly developed in those negative things coming to pass.

## SET A WATCH OVER YOUR MOUTH

When you switch over and begin to confess on the positive side and begin to agree with God, it must be conceived in your spirit. It takes weeks and months to cause that to become a reality in your life. Then there are some things you will have to shut off from your vocabulary because they work against you. They cause you to not have faith in what you say. It weakens your words so there is no positive faith at work for you.

Job gave us great insight when he said:

*. . . the thing which I greatly feared is come upon me, and that which I was afraid of is come unto me.*        *(Job 3:25)*

Job wasn't just in fear. He was **highly developed** in that fear. *"The thing which I greatly feared."* You must resist fear like you would resist the devil. Learn to operate in the principles of the Word of God.

Don't expect to become highly developed in faith and confession overnight. But develop yourself by practice. You can be developed in it to the point where you can speak words of faith which will change the course of your life. Remember, just saying something once doesn't mean that thing will manifest. But you can grow in faith until you become highly developed in it.

## FULLY PERSUADED

You can be fully persuaded. The Bible said Abraham was *"fully persuaded that, what he (God) had promised, he was able also to perform."* (Romans 4:21) How did Abraham get fully persuaded? He certainly didn't get that way by saying what the devil said, or what the world said, or what it seemed to be.

The secret to becoming fully persuaded regarding what God said is to keep God's Word in your mouth. And that is essentially what God had Abraham doing. It is what God told Joshua to do in Joshua 1:8. And in Deuteronomy 28 we find a classic example of God teaching Israel how to obtain faith in His promises.

*And it shall come to pass, if thou shalt **hearken diligently unto the voice of the Lord thy God,** to observe and to do all his commandments which I command thee this day, that the Lord thy God will set thee on high above all nations of the earth:*

*And all these blessings shall come on thee, and **overtake thee,** if thou shalt **hearken unto the voice of the Lord thy God.***

*Blessed shalt thou be in the city, and blessed shalt thou be in the field.*

*Blessed shall be the fruit of thy body, and the fruit of thy ground, and the fruit of thy cattle, the increase of thy kine, and the flocks of thy sheep.*

*Blessed shall be thy basket and thy store.*

*Blessed shalt thou be when thou comest in, and blessed shalt thou be when thou goest out.*

*(Deuteronomy 28:1-6)*

## OBEDIENT TO DECLARE

Notice these promises are conditional. Notice again verse one. *"It shall come to pass **if thou shalt hearken diligently unto the voice of the Lord thy God, to observe and to do all his commandments."***

The voice of the Lord thy God which we have today is the Word of God spoken. In reading this, if you are not careful, you will miss it because of the King James language.

As I was studying this, the Lord said, *"You look up that Hebrew word that is translated 'hearken'."*

I thought I knew what it meant, but looked it up. Here is what I found.

*"Hearken"* first means to **hear intelligently.** It also means to hear intelligently, be obedient, and declare.

After looking up that word, the Lord said, *"Look up the word 'diligently'."*

I was sure I knew what it meant to be diligent about something. But to my surprise, I found that the Hebrew word translated *"diligently"* means wholly, completely, far, fast, louder and louder. Those are the ways it is used.

So allow me to paraphrase the way the Hebrew said it.

*It shall come to pass, if thou shall hear intelligently, be obedient to, declare wholly, completely, far, fast, louder and louder what God has said, to observe and to do all His commandments, then all these blessings will come upon you and overtake you.* (Deuteronomy 28:1)

Isn't that amazing! What God is saying here is almost exactly what He told Joshua.

God says, *"Just declare what I have said. Hear it intelligently, begin to declare it wholly, completely, far, fast, louder and louder."*

He is just telling them to get the Word of God in their mouth.

Then God says, *"When you do all that, all these blessings will* **come upon you and overtake you.***"*

Well, that doesn't happen overnight. Obedience is first, and then the blessings.

Next, God tells of all the cursings. We know the curses came only after the people were disobedient. Remember, we are talking about faith and confession. This faith force works only in the heart. And God told Israel how to develop heart faith for the blessings. The secret was to continue to declare God's promises until they possessed their declaration.

II Peter, chapter one gives us much insight into possessing new convenant promises.

*Simon Peter, a servant and an apostle of Jesus Christ, to them that have obtained like precious faith with us through the righteousness of God and our Saviour Jesus Christ.* (II Peter 1:1)

Notice that Peter is talking to those who have *"obtained like precious faith with us."* He is speaking of other born again believers — which includes us today.

*Grace and peace be multiplied unto you through the knowledge of God, and of Jesus our Lord.*
(II Peter 1:2)

## GOD'S WILLINGNESS MULTIPLIED

Remember, grace is God's willingness to use His power and His ability on your behalf. This grace is multiplied to you through the knowledge of God. When you gain the knowledge of God, of what God will do, it **multiplies His grace — His willingness —** to you. God is willing already, but you can't believe any further than you have knowledge. So **when you gain the knowledge of God it multiplies God's willingness to use His power and His ability on your behalf.**

*According as his divine power hath given unto us all things that pertain unto life and godliness, through the knowledge of him that hath called us to glory and virtue.* (II Peter 1:3)

## KNOWLEDGE OF HIM

How has God given us all things that pertain unto life and godliness? **Through the knowledge of him.** You can't believe for something if you have no knowledge of it. When you get knowledge of a promise, you will gain a certain amount of faith regarding that promise. If you will speak that promise, your faith will grow concerning that particular promise.

Peter says, *"According as his **divine power hath given. . ."** This is how God gives it to us — through His divine power of God. **The Good News, the Word of God is His power.** Paul said, *"The gospel of Christ. . .is the power of God."* (Romans 1:16) So He is sending the divine promise through His divine Word. In other words, He has given us all things through the promises of God. Notice *"**He hath given.**"* He is not going to do it, **He has already done it.**

*Whereby are given unto us exceeding great and precious promises: that by these ye might be partakers of the divine nature.* (II Peter 1:4)

# GOD'S DIVINE ENERGY

The word *"whereby"* means by way of these, or by way of these precious promises.

Sometimes people say, *"You must think you are God, going around saying what God said."*

No, but I am one of the *"partakers of the divine nature."* The divine power of God has already been given to us. **God's power is in His Word.** He is *"upholding all things by the word of His power."* (Hebrews 1:3) He created all things with His Word. His divine power is in His Word. And through His divine power, **He has already given.** This divine power is His divine Word. Verse four verifies it when it says, *"Whereby (or by this means) are given unto us exceeding great and precious promises."* The seed to produce the promise is in the promise itself.

The divine power gave us the promises — which is the Word of God. The word *"power"* here is the Greek dunamis. This is the source of our words *"dynamite"* and *"dynamo."* The idea present here is that God has given us a dynamo that will produce spiritual power, causing us to possess the promise which He gave us. Through God's dunamis power, this dynamo or self-energizing, self-reproducing power, we possess the promises.

Now remember,

> . . .*Faith is the substance of things hoped for, the evidence of things not seen.* (Hebrews 11:1)

Faith is **the** substance. You must have the spiritual energy to bring the thing hoped for into manifestation. The energy itself comes from the Word of God. Through these promises of God, He hath given us **all things that pertain to life and godliness.** (II Peter 1:3) But it won't come until you have the knowledge of it. **Once you have the knowledge of it, you must decide whether or not you are going to act on it.**

125

Paul tells us how it works.

*The righteousness which is of faith speaketh on this wise,*

*The Word is nigh thee.* (Romans 10:6, 8)

## PROMISE IN MOUTH
## MULTIPLIES ENERGY IN HEART

Let's say it this way. The promise is nigh you, even in your mouth. And then it gets in your heart. That's the way it gets into your heart. You speak the word of promise out of your mouth. And as you speak it out, it is picked up by your inner ear and fed into your human spirit. Once it is in your spirit (heart), it gets back in your mouth. For what's in your heart gets into your mouth. And when it gets into your mouth, it gets back into your heart stronger than before. When it is stronger in your heart, it gets stronger in your mouth. When it's in your mouth, it gets stronger in your heart. It's in your mouth and in your heart. It's in your heart and in your mouth.

Every time it goes through that process, it gets stronger. God's Word is self-energizing, a self-reproducing dynamo of power that generates faith which will move mountains in your life.

The key is keeping it in your mouth. You can't go to Mark 11:23 and say, *"Because Jesus said you can have what you say, then everything I say will come to pass."* For there is more to the Bible than Mark 11:23. Other things go with that scripture. Mark 11:25 goes with it; *"And when you stand praying, forgive."* If you don't forgive, it will shut your faith down.

## SPIRITUAL HEART ATTACKS

Some people are operating in strife, and wondering why their faith won't work. Well, **their heart condemns them. They have had a spiritual heart**

126

**attack.** They can't operate in faith from their heart because their heart condemns them. It condemns them because they are not obedient to the whole Word of God.

> *For if our heart condemn us, God is greater than our heart, and knoweth all things.*
>
> *Beloved, if our heart condemn us not,* **then have we confidence toward God.**
>
> *And whatsoever we ask, we receive of him, because we keep his commandments, and do those things that are pleasing in his sight.*
>
> *(I John 3:20-22)*

Some would like to live by only certain scriptures and forget the rest of the Bible. But we must live by every Word of God. Some people do crazy things and call it faith. You wouldn't think people would be that foolish.

Once a woman came to a certain minister and said, *"You must agree with me — you* ***just have to agree with me*** *that this man will marry me."*

The minister said, *"Wait a minute. Tell me more about this first."*

She said, *"But you have to agree with me. The Bible said if two agree, it shall be done."*

The minister said, *"Does this man want to marry you?"*

She said, *"Do I have to tell you?"*

The minister replied, *"Yes. How am I going to agree, if I don't know some more about it?"*

She said, *"Well, to tell the truth, he's already married — but you have to agree with me that he will be my husband."*

Now you wonder about people like that. When they get up in the morning, how do they find the floor? Her heart was condemning her. What she wanted agreement on was against God's Word. That is against the

Word of God. How in the world could you release faith for God to do something like that, to break up a home so he could marry another woman.

## GOD'S WORD IS HIS WILL

You have to say these things, because there are some people who don't know any better.

**The things that God has given come through the promise of God.** You don't just take Mark 11:23, or a part of that verse which says you can have what you say, and start saying, *"I have nine million oil wells."*

The principle will work, if you could believe that, and doubt not in your heart, and believe that what you are saying would come to pass. But you can't believe that when you haven't learned to believe what you say in small things. If you use your faith on things like that just to be Mister Big, then your heart will condemn you, and it won't work anyway.

Some people believe you should not prosper, and you should not use the Word of God to obtain what He promised. They are always concerned that you are going to get something God didn't want you to have.

But there is a law built into faith. There is something which will keep it in balance. Jesus shared it with us in John 15.

> *If ye abide in me, and my words abide in you, ye shall ask what ye will, and it shall be done unto you.* (John 15:7)

Someone said, *"That couldn't be true, because it left God's will out of it. Why — you couldn't just ask what **you** will. What if it was not **God's** will?"*

Well, sometimes we miss the first part of that verse. *"If ye abide in me, and my words abide in you."*

What is the will of God? The will of God is the word of God. God's Word is always His perfect will.

128

# A BALANCE BUILT INTO THE LAW OF FAITH

If **the Word** is abiding in you, **then the will of God abides in you.** The problem is that many people keep casting out the Word. They cast out the Word, and just do their own thing. An example is the woman who wanted to believe for a married man to marry her. Just because that was what she desired, she wanted to use her faith to violate God's will. Faith wouldn't work on something that is evil. God wouldn't be a partner to evil. There were no scriptural grounds for that kind of agreement.

The built-in balance in the law of faith is this: if your heart condemns you, then your faith won't work.

God didn't say that you are going to get your prayers answered and everything will be lovely just because you did the good part. We must be careful that we don't get the idea that we are **earning** God's answer to our prayer by doing the things that please God.

But by doing the whole Word, you are obtaining a good conscience toward God. Paul said, **holding the mystery of the faith in a pure conscience.** (I Timothy 3:9) How could anyone have a clear conscience about using faith and agreement to steal another woman's husband? Could you have a pure conscience if you were believing and confessing that your needs would be met by someone losing their billfold so you could find it and keep their money? Now that's dumb. Such actions will just shut down your faith. Your heart would condemn you. You will have a spiritual heart attack. By that I mean your own heart will attack your confession by releasing doubt.

So there is no foundation for this idea that people will get through faith a lot of things that God doesn't want them to have. There is a built-in control.

But yet, **God's will is involved here** in verse 7. If the Word abides in you, **then you have the will of God in you.** Always find the will of God before you start confessing and believing for anything. **Base your confession on scriptural promises.** When your confession is the Word of God or a promise of God, then you have God's will in your mouth.

You miss it when you start confessing things without that scriptural basis. It makes a difference when your basis of confession is the Word of God. It's not just mechanical as some would suggest. It's a spiritual operation. This is the way God designed it. Your words plus God's Word works for you. When you work it, it works. If you don't do your part, it won't produce anything God promised.

Remember Peter said God has given us *"all things that pertain unto life and godliness."* And He gives it through the exceeding great and precious promises. Luke 6:38 is one of those promises. II Corinthians 9:10 is a precious promise concerning finances.

## GOD MULTIPLIES THE SEED SOWN

But there are always some people who will say, *"Yes, but I know why you are giving and teaching people to give. You are doing it just so you can get."*

The promise says, if you give, it shall be given unto you. And God furnishes seed for the sower, bread for your food, and multiplies your seed sown. The law of seedtime and harvest is God's law all through the Bible. And as long as this earth remains, that is the way it will work.

If you need finances, you give finances. If you need time, go give time to God, or to other people. It will multiply and come back to you. Everything produces after its kind.

Some still say, *"I know **why** you are giving. You are giving to get."*

Now that's like walking up to a farmer and saying, *"Oh, I know why you are planting those soybeans. You just want more soybeans."*

That's God's law. You don't criticize the farmer because he plants. That's the law of seedtime and harvest. So don't criticize those who are obedient to God's law of giving and receiving.

I understand that **you could have wrong motives.** We do need to guard against wrong motives. But don't throw the baby out with the bath water, so to speak. You don't throw out the whole thing just because some people operate with wrong motives.

They aren't going very far before they fall on their face, because their heart will condemn them. There is that built-in control.

## THE MYSTERY OF FAITH

So there is no validity to the fear that some will take this faith message, and go use it to bankrupt God. Give God credit for being smarter than that.

**The mystery of faith is in a pure conscience. The instant you walk away from a pure conscience, then your faith will begin to fade away. Condemnation will eventually devour your faith.**

You must have a pure conscience before God. Jesus said, *"When you stand praying, forgive."* (Mark 11:25) That is just as much a part of this faith message as verse 23. You must forgive people. You must walk in love. You must obey the principles of the Bible.

There is more to it than just saying a few scriptures. **This is living the Bible, and being a doer of the Word of God.** Jesus said you live by every Word of God.

When God says the way to reap a harvest is to plant, then **how could it be wrong for us to plant and expect to reap a harvest?**

It is unscriptural to give and not expect to receive. You can choose to give that way. You can give and say, *"Well now, Lord, I don't expect anything in return. I'm just trying to be humble."*

Now, be honest. You aren't being humble. You are trying to impress God. You are trying to convince Him that you are so humble that He should bless you much more. You might as well admit it. That's what we have all tried to do in the past. Don't try to con God.

Be honest with God, and just obey His Word, and say, *"Now, Lord, You said if I give, it shall be given unto me, good measure, pressed down, shaken together, and running over. And because of Your Word I believe and confess I receive all You promised.*

## LAW OF GIVING AND RECEIVING

When you give, you set a law in motion. Every time you give to God's work for Jesus' sake and the gospel's, it will come back multiplied. But the problem is that sometimes people don't understand that, and they don't believe in it. It comes all right, but when it comes, they miss it because they weren't looking for it.

I believe the return will always come. Let's say it this way. **Opportunity will always come.** It may be in a business deal. It may be in something that you didn't expect at all. But you can miss out on it if you are not looking for it, if you are not believing for it. You should have your faith out there seeking it out. But some have just pitched their offering in the bucket and said, *"Well, I guess it's gone. But I'll get rewarded when I get to heaven. It will be wonderful then. I'll get all of these riches I'm storing up in heaven."*

What in the world would you do with it then? We sing that song, *"Won't it be wonderful when we all get to heaven?"* Yes, it will be wonderful then. But **what about the here and now?** What are you going to do about the bill that needs to be paid?

We are looking at some practical things. Not everything is spiritual. Don't take a spiritual attitude about everything the Bible says. Don't try to say when Paul is talking about money that he is referring to spiritual things. Paul talked about finances in II Corinthians 8 and 9. For two whole chapters, he talked about money and finances. It's time we begin to believe God for some things, and use our faith for some things in the financial realm.

Don't let people talk you out of what God promised. The things God has given you by promise are not wrong for you. Believe for them; put your confession of faith out there for those promises. But when you do, go by the Bible method. You must speak some things in faith.

*Let us hold fast the profession of our faith without wavering; (for he is faithful that promised.)* (Hebrews 10:23)

## CONFESSION THRUST

The word *"profession"* here is actually the same word that is translated *"confession."* So we need to hold fast to the confession of our faith.

I want to reiterate some things because of their importance. **Your faith will rise no higher than your confession of God's Word.** When you realize that, you can understand the importance of confessing what God has said, instead of saying what the devil said about the situation you face in life. If you could not loose faith you would not need to hold fast to your confession of that faith. **Confession is to faith as thrust is to an**

133

**airplane.** Unless there is thrust, you won't have any lift on the wings of an airplane. When the thrust is gone, the lift is gone and you will come down.

Just so is the confession of your faith. You must confess God's Word to continue in faith. This is not because God is trying to make it hard on you. But God knows that faith — which is the substance of things — cometh by hearing, and hearing, and hearing the Word of God.

## HEARING IT BEST

You will hear it best when you speak it yourself. Many don't realize that faith will come more quickly when you hear yourself speaking, quoting and saying what God said. Hearing someone else speak the Word all day long won't affect you as much as if **you speak it two or three times.** Your voice is picked up by the inner ear and fed directly into the human spirit.

You hear people talk about blind faith. Faith is not blind. Faith always sees. Faith always sees through the storm. Instead of getting centered up on what is at the present, faith always sees the end results. That's the way Jesus operated in this faith.

## THINGS CAN BE CHANGED

The apostle Paul put it this way in Second Corinthians 4:18. The things that are seen are temporal, but the things that are not seen are eternal. So God's method is simply to take eternal forces — which is faith — and change the things that are seen — the temporal things. The word *"temporal"* means that it is subject to change. That means, if you can see it, feel it, touch it, or taste it, then you can take your faith and the Word of God, and change it. For all evil is temporary. There is no permanent evil.

## FAITH AS SEED

Faith in the heart is a spiritual force inside of the human spirit which comes from the Word of God. Faith in the heart gives the human spirit the ability to conceive what God has promised. Then after the conception of the promise, eventually there will be a manifestation.

Jesus said in Mark 10:15, unless you receive the kingdom of God as a little child, you will not enter therein. I am convinced we have misunderstood what He said. We have assumed He meant you must have faith as a little child. However, as you study this more carefully, you will realize Jesus was saying when the kingdom of God is first received in you, it is the least of all the seeds. But it grows up and becomes greater than all herbs. In other words, it will be greater than everything else in your life. Jesus gave a perfect illustration of how it works in you when He said, if you don't receive the kingdom as you would receive a little child, then you won't enter into it.

That's the way it works. It starts small. You never receive a child full grown, and your faith will not start out full grown. Faith in the heart is the ability in the human spirit to conceive. Then it's like a child growing inside its mother. This is what happens concerning the kingdom of God. The kingdom grows inside of you. So you receive it as a mother would receive a child. The Word of God is the seed or the embryo. It grows and develops in the *"womb of the spirit."* That's also the way your faith develops. You don't receive faith fully developed.

## MEASURING FAITH

It is true that God has dealt to every man the measure of faith. But He gave that faith in His Word. So the only way you can measure your faith is to measure the amount of Word that is in you. You don't start out with all of God's faith. You start with a small amount. It grows, and you add to it, and you hold fast to it. It grows within you. When Jesus said, except you receive the kingdom as a little child, He was referring to you receiving it into your human spirit as a seed. It is small — less than all the other things when you receive it. But it grows and it grows, then it becomes the greatest of all. The kingdom grows as your faith grows. God is a God of faith. He shares that faith with us through His Word. **Faith pleases God.**

**Faith in action is God's personality in manifestation.**

> *. . .without faith it is impossible to please him, for he that cometh to God must believe that he is and that he is a rewarder of them that diligently seek him.* (Hebrews 11:6)

It takes faith to please God, because God is not pleased unless we are operating in His laws. The law of faith is God's law. The apostle Paul spoke of this in Romans 3:27.

> *Where is boasting then? It is excluded. By what law? of works? Nay: but by the law of faith.* (Romans 3:27)

Paul calls faith a law. Actually, we could say it this way: **faith is the law of the new covenant.** Works were the law of the old covenant, but faith is the law of the new covenant. Remember I said faith in action is God's personality in manifestation. Hebrews 11:1 says it this way.

## FAITH — GOD'S SUBSTANCE

> *Now faith is the substance of things hoped for, the evidence of things not seen.* (Hebrews 11:1)

Faith is the **substance** of things hoped for, the evidence of things not seen. Substance means the raw material, or the thing that would cause the manifestation. Now let's go to Hebrews 1.

*God, who at sundry times and in divers manners spake in time past unto the fathers by the prophets,*

*Hath in these last days spoken unto us by his Son, whom he hath appointed heir of all things, by whom also he made the worlds;*

*Who being the brightness of his glory, and the express image of his person, and upholding all things by the word of his power, when he had by himself purged our sins, sat down on the right hand of the Majesty on high.* (Hebrews 1:1-3)

Notice the phrase in verse two, *"by whom also he made the worlds;"* it refers to the Word of God. He says, *"His Son. . .by whom also He made the worlds."* And Jesus was the Word of God on the earth. John says the Word became flesh and dwelt among us. So He is referring to Jesus as the Son and the Word here in this scripture. He says, *"Who being the brightness of His glory,"* God's glory, *"and the express image of His person."* The phrase *"express image"* really means the exact expression of God's person. The Word of God, or Jesus, was the exact expression of God's substance.

## EXPRESSED IMAGE

Do you want to know what God is like? Jesus said, *"If you have seen Me, you have seen my Father."* In John 5:19 He said, *"The Son can do nothing of himself, but what he seeth the Father do: for what things soever he doeth, these also doeth the Son likewise."* So Jesus was doing just what He saw His Father do. *"I have many things to say and to judge of you: but he that sent me is true; and I speak to the world those things which I have heard of him."* (John 8:26)

If you want to know why Jesus was so highly developed in His faith, it was because He always spoke that which he heard from His Father. That's how He defeated the devil, and that's how we can defeat the devil.

There is more power in the Word of God than most people have ever realized. Notice the word *"person"* in Hebrews 1:3 where it says, *". . .being the express image of his person."* In other words, Jesus, or the Word, is the brightness of God's glory, and the express image of God's person. **The word *"person"* is translated from the very same Greek word that is translated *"substance"*** in Hebrews 11:1.

You could actually say, *"faith is the **person** of things hoped for."* Jesus was the Word in person form, or the Word personified. We could read Hebrews 1:3 this way; *"Who being the brightness of his glory, and the expressed image of God's **substance.**"* What God was, His Word was.

*In the beginning was the Word, and the Word was with God, and the Word was God.* (John 1:1)

## GOD'S PERSONALITY

Words are expressions of thoughts and desires. God's Word is the express image of His substance, or His person. When you have a promise of God, this is God's expressed image of His faith. It is his own personality. He has expessed it. In that promise is supernatural power. We call it the divine energy of God to cause the manifestation of that promise.

That divine energy, or faith in action is God's personality in manifestation through you. God is a faith God. When we act in faith, it's the divine energy of God causing us to act that way. So it is actually God's personality in manifestation. This is what it means to be partakers of God's divine nature.

> *According as his divine power hath given unto us all things that pertain unto life and godliness, through the knowledge of him that hath called us to glory and virtue:*
>
> *Whereby are given unto us exceeding great and precious promises: that by these ye might be partakers of the divine nature, having escaped the corruption that is in the world through lust.*
>
> *(II Peter 1:3-4)*

Peter stated it very plainly — God gave it through His power, and by receiving the promises, you are partakers of His divine nature.

# Chapter Seven

# FAITH'S
# CORRESPONDING ACTION

*What doth it profit, my brethren, though a man say he hath faith, and have not works? Can faith save him?*

*If a brother or sister be naked, and destitute of daily food,*

*And one of you say unto them, depart in peace, be ye warmed and filled; notwithstanding ye give them not those things which are needful to the body; what doth it profit?*

*Even so faith, if it hath not works, is dead, being alone.* (James 2:14-17)

Faith requires action. But don't fall into the trap of half-truths concerning faith's action. What James said in verse 17 is a true statement. But be careful that you don't take **a** truth and try to make it **the** truth. For instance, this is a truth concerning the context of this scripture. But if you take this out of context and carry it over into a totally different setting, it may not be true concerning that situation. There is some truth concerning almost any situation. But if you carry this too far into a situation different from the one stated in verses 14-16, then you get in trouble.

In the above passage, the word *"works"* is sometimes spoken of as *"corresponding actions"* — in other words, acting out your faith. Certainly you should have some action to your faith as far as you are developed. The problem comes when people try to act beyond their faith. They take action far beyond the manifestation they have received.

141

When your bank statement comes back with red ink, that is bad news. But don't sit there and say, *"My goodness! Every time you come back, you have red ink all over you. I guess we will never get out of debt."*

## CALL FOR PROMISE DESIRED

Don't call things that are. There is no need to call what is already there. But do what Abraham did. He **called things that were not.** Call it the way the Word says it.

*"My needs are met. I have abundance and no lack because I have given, and it is given to me good measure, shaken together, and running over."*

But that does not mean for you to act as you would act if you had thousands of dollars in your bank account. Some have done that and said, *"I'm confessing abundance. I believe God has met my needs, so I will write checks for all these bills and God will put the money in the bank before the checks get to the bank."*

That is not faith. That is foolishness. Some do that and call the checks *"faith checks."* They are not faith checks. **They are *"hot checks,"*** and you can go to jail for that. How in the world could God bless something that was illegal? He couldn't, and He won't. Stay with Bible principles.

## CORRESPONDING ACTION

One might say, *"Yes, but James said faith without works, or faith without corresponding action is dead. So if I don't act as though it were already true, then my faith is dead."*

**Acting as though you have faith when you have none is double dead.** By that I mean their foolish action will not only hurt them, but others also.

142

Many people miss the whole point in this, and act foolishly. Don't do foolish things. Stay with the context of the Bible. You wouldn't have full corresponding action toward anything until you had the full manifestation of it. You can have some corresponding action. But scripturally, you cannot have full corresponding action until you actually have full manifestation of what you ask or believe.

Some people write checks knowing they don't have enough money in the bank, and say, *"God will have to put the money in the bank before my checks get there."*

No. They may be in jail before God puts the money in the bank. God is not making money. He is not a counterfeiter. It is their responsibility, not God's, to put the money in the bank.

Now, it would be scriptural to write out the checks for the bills, then put them in the desk drawer. But don't mail them **until** you have the money in the bank. That would be as far as you could go with your corresponding action until you had more manifestation.

You must use some common sense in these things. Faith is not foolish. But people do foolish things for lack of knowledge.

There is a similar problem with overloaded faith for physical healing. **Many people die needlessly** because they said, *"If I believe I'm healed, I'll throw away all my medicine."* **Their faith was not developed to that level.** Medicine won't heal you; neither will medicine keep you from being healed. But it will hold down the symptoms until you can believe God for something better.

Many try to operate on a higher level of faith than they are developed to. They try to believe God to cure cancer when they haven't developed their faith to get rid of a headache. Many die needlessly when medical science could have treated them and kept them alive to

**143**

live a full life. It is not a good testimony when someone says they believed God and died. No. They **tried to believe God** beyond where they were developed, and died.

There is some common sense to be used with the application of faith and confession. When you are not developed to the level of faith needed, do whatever is necessary to get the situation under control — especially when it is a life or death situation. Then get in the Word and develop your faith in God's provisions.

Hebrews 11:6 says, *"Without faith it is impossible to please him (God)."* When people get turned on to faith, they want to please God. They hear sermons on faith and corresponding actions, and they certainly don't want to displease God. So they say, *"If I really believe that God has supplied my need, then I should have full corresponding action."* So they go write checks, knowing there is not sufficient money in the bank to cover the checks. They believe God will put the money in the bank for them.

But that is not corresponding action. That is foolishness. They don't mean to be foolish. They really want to please God. But because they have not understood corresponding action, they missed it.

There is a balance in every scripture. The key to balance is keeping the truth of the scripture in context of all that is being said about that particular situation.

Here, James is not talking about a need that you have prayed about. He is not talking about a note on your house, or the rent payment when he says, *"faith without corresponding action is dead."*

He is talking about an individual who came and said, *"I don't even have any food. Can you help me?"* James said faith without action to meet that man's need would be dead faith. In other words, you wouldn't have helped that man at all if you said, *"Go, brother, and be warmed* and be fed. *I have faith that you will be fed. I have faith that your need will be supplied. God bless you, my brother.*"

James said faith without **some action** to give that fellow some clothing, or to help him in his need, is dead. That man didn't want faith, he wanted food. He needed some corresponding action to fill that need. He didn't need someone to say, *"I believe,"* he needed someone to say, *"I will help by giving."* James goes further by saying,

> *Yea, a man may say, Thou hast faith, and I have works: shew me thy faith without thy works, and I will shew thee my faith by my works.*
>
> *(James 2:18)*

Remember, he is still talking about this individual who would come and say, *"I have need of clothing, and I have need of food."* Somebody would say, *"I'm going to show you what great faith I have. I will believe God for you, brother, and God will supply your need."*

James says, *"If you're going to show me your faith, by not doing anything but believing, I'll show you my faith by what I do for him. I'll give him some money, and give him some clothes. Then I will believe God to supply **my** need."*

The kind of faith that will say, *"Oh, brother, I believe that your need will be supplied. I believe it will all work out."*

That kind of faith without some action is dead, as far as that man is concerned. That man will go off cold and hungry, and your faith hasn't helped him unless there is some action.

In other words, James said, If you could show me your faith without works, what I'm going to do is show you my faith by my works. Then James admonishes us to be doers, not just hearers.

*But be ye doers of the word, and not hearers only, deceiving your own selves.*

*For if any be a hearer of the word, and not a doer, he is like unto a man beholding his natural face in a glass:*

*For he beholdeth himself, and goeth his way, and straightway forgetteth what manner of man he was.* (James 1:22-24)

This is what a man would do, if he is only a hearer of the Word. He hears what the Word said about him. He hears what the Word said about supplying his needs, and by hearing that, he sees what manner of man God says he is. **The mirror he is referring to is the Word of God,** for the Word of God accurately reflects to us what God says we are.

A hearer of the Word is like a man who looked into the Word and said, *"Thank God, I'm redeemed from the curse of the law. I'm also delivered from the authority of darkness, and I have world overcoming faith residing on the inside of me. Greater is He that is in me than he that is in the world."*

Then he forgets it all when things go wrong, if he is a hearer only.

He saw he had authority. He saw that faith could remove mountains. But when he goes out to face the everyday circumstances of life, he quickly forgets what he saw and he has no corresponding action toward what the Word said he was. He falls back into the negative stream and just says what the world says. *"Well, I knew it, nothing ever works out for me. The devil always throws a monkey wrench in the deal. Nothing works out for me. But that's the way the cookie crumbles."* He is defeated.

But if he is a doer of the Word, when he faces the hard situations in life and it looks like the devil has the upper hand, **he begins to quote the Word of God** and

146

say what God said about it. He says, *"**I proclaim that I am delivered from the authority of darkness.** In the name of Jesus, **I'm an overcomer.** I overcome evil with good. Thank God, **no weapon formed against me will prosper. Whatever I do will prosper.**"*

That would be corresponding action toward that situation. If he does that, he is a doer of the Word of God; he didn't forget what God said about him.

> *Thou believest that there is one God; thou doest well: the devils also believe, and tremble.*
>
> *But wilt thou know, O vain man, that faith without works is dead?*
>
> *Was not Abraham our father justified by works, when he had offered Isaac his son upon the alter?*
>
> *(James 2:19-21)*

Abraham wasn't justified because he said, *"I believe you, God."* It was because Abraham acted on what God said. He had corresponding action.

> *Likewise also was not Rahab the harlot justified by works, when she had received the messengers, and had sent them out another way?*
>
> *For as the body without the spirit is dead, so faith without works is dead also.*    *(James 2:25-26)*

James said you must have correponding action. Faith without corresponding action is dead. Rahab was a harlot, not a righteous person. But she believed that if she would be of help to the spies who came, they would spare her. She could have been negative and said, *"If I protect them, when they come back, I may be one of those killed in the war."* But you can see her faith in her actions.

She befriended the spies and helped them to escape. Even as an unrighteous person, she had faith that she and her household would be saved alive.

147

*"For as the body without the spirit is dead, so faith without works is dead also."* But remember; keep this all in context. It's when people misunderstand corresponding action that they do crazy things, like writing faith checks.

Then some say, *"The answer (or the money I need) will come by Thursday evening at four o'clock."*

Because they have confessed that it's going to happen Thursday evening at four o'clock, they go ahead and send the check on Tuesday. Don't set times for the manifestation. Don't try to put God in a box.

Now, there are some things that confession will not change. Whether you believe it or whether you don't believe it, Jesus is coming back. Your confession is not going to change that. Then it takes time to bring about some things. When you begin to set times, you usually get in trouble.

It is all right to set your faith to that point, or have that as a goal. But if you are saying that it is going to happen on a certain day, when that day passes, then your faith usually goes with it. You do set these things in motion by confession and by faith. Let me show you the balance to this. Let's go to Mark, the fourth chapter. This whole chapter is important to what we are talking about. But we will begin with verse 26. It has already been established by Jesus that the soil is the heart of man, and the seed is the Word of God.

*And he (Jesus) said, So is the kingdom of God, as if a man should cast seed into the ground;*

*And should sleep, and rise night and day, and the seed should spring and grow up, he knoweth not how.*

*For the earth bringeth forth fruit of herself; first the blade, then the ear, after that the full corn in the ear.* (Mark 4:26-28)

148

This is a revelation of how the kingdom works within you. The kingdom of God is **as if a man cast seed into the ground.** Notice, you are the one who sows the seed in this kingdom inside you.

Now remember, the soil is the heart — the human spirit. He said the kingdom works this way — **you** sow the seed into the ground. The confession of God's Word sows the seed. It is important to mix faith with the Word of God. Thousands of God's people missed the promised land, died in the wilderness, and never obtained what God intended for them to attain. It was the will of God for them to enter in. It was their land. God had already given it to them. Then when referring to them, the Bible says:

> *For unto us was the gospel preached,* ***as well as unto them: but the*** *word preached did not profit them, not being mixed with faith in them that heard it.*        *(Hebrews 4:2)*

The children of Israel heard what God said, but they wouldn't mix any faith with what they heard.

Many hear what God says, but sometimes it's hard to get people to mix faith with what God says, or to get them to speak in agreement with Him. They say, *"but I can see it's not that way."*

I know it's not that way, but God said it, so you say it. The divine energy force of God is in that Word, and it will get inside of you. It is the power source. It is the faith of God that causes you to be able to attain to that promise.

## CONFESSION OR LIE

But some get the idea that you are lying if you quote the promises of God. There is a difference between confessing and lying. Confession is saying what God says in His Word. **Confession is agreeing with God.** To lie would be to try to convince someone that you

149

have something you really don't have, and that you have it now. If people hear you confessing *"My needs are met according to God's riches in glory,"* they are just hearing you quote what God said. They might get the idea that you don't have a need, but you weren't trying to convince them that it was already true. You were agreeing with what God said, in order to get that divine energy to flow into you. **The power to attain to the promise is in the Word itself.**

## SEED IS IN ITSELF

The law of Genesis says *"the seed is in itself." "Everything produces after its kind."* God promises you that He will supply your need, and heal your body, and whatever — the seed is in the promise itself. If you put the Word in your mouth and speak it, you sow the seed in the kingdom. That's a kingdom prinicple. Jesus gives us some insight into this in Luke 17.

*And the apostles said unto the Lord, Increase our faith.*

*And the Lord said, If ye had faith as a grain of mustard seed, ye might say unto this sycamine tree, Be thou plucked up by the root, and be thou planted in the sea; and it should obey you.*

*(Luke 17:5-6)*

If you had faith as a seed, you would say. You would speak to the sycamine tree — to the problem area or the situation in your life. He was talking about a black mulberry tree, probably growing in the path. Jesus didn't say it would obey God, He said it would obey you.

You could only get that kind of faith from God's Word. He said it would obey you because the power of binding and loosing is on earth, not in heaven. It must come through you. You must mix faith with God's Word. He said if you had faith as a seed, **you would**

**say.** The King James translation says you *"might"* say, but the Greek says that you *"would"* say and it would obey you. It — the inanimate object — would obey you.

## HARVEST REQUIRES A PLANTING

Jesus tells us how to plant the seed of faith. He tells us two great faith secrets. (1) **Faith works like a seed,** and (2) **the way to plant it is to say it.**

People who want to say something today and have the harvest tomorrow don't understand the law of seedtime and harvest. Any farmer knows that if you are to have a harvest, you must plant seeds months before the harvest.

## PROJECT YOUR NEEDS
## AND PLAN YOUR CONFESSION

You must plan for a harvest. The problem with many people who try to operate in faith is that they don't ever plan for anything. They will quote the scripture where Jesus says to take no thought for tomorrow, and they say, *"Well, Jesus said not to take any thought, so I don't ever make any plans."*

They missed the whole point. He said to take **no anxious thought;** don't be anxious about things. Certainly, you should make some plans. Project when you will have a certain need, and begin weeks, or months, or maybe even years before the need arises, and begin confessing the promises of God concerning that thing. Start out just like a farmer does when he prepares the soil, then plants and fertilizes, and he has corresponding action toward that crop for weeks and months before he ever has a manifestation of harvest. It's a process. It doesn't happen overnight.

Don't go tell people that they are just going to say it, and then receive it in the morning. For it's not going to happen that way. Sometimes, when you get highly developed in your faith, some things will come into manifestation quickly, and will almost shock you. But that is not the first stage of it. That's when you are highly developed in faith and confession. Then sometimes you will get some gifts of the Spirit in manifestation in the things you are saying. But just the normal way of faith and confession is to start sowing weeks and months before the time the harvest is needed.

Sometimes you deal with someone who has a note due at the end of the year, and they will start trying to believe God on December twenty-fifth. They start confessing the Word. But they waited too late. They should have started at the first of the year to confess the promises of God to become manifest in their life.

In Mark 4 Jesus tells us the stages of the manifestation. You plant the seed. Jesus said you plant the seed by saying. God said in Hebrews 4:2 that the Word did not profit them, for they would not mix any faith with it. They had the promise. They knew what God said about the land. You must mix faith with God's Word. Your tongue is the mixer.

Jesus said faith works like a seed. If you don't have faith as a seed, it will not work for you. You must have faith as a seed. Jesus said it again in Matthew 17:20.

*If ye have faith as a grain of mustard seed, ye shall say unto this mountain, Remove hence to yonder place; and it shall remove; and nothing shall be impossible unto you.* (Matthew 17:20)

Jesus said if you have faith as a grain of mustard seed, **you shall say. . .** Sometimes we get so involved with the mustard seed that we often miss the whole point. Jesus is not talking about the size of the seed, He is talking about faith as a seed. The life is in that seed. The seed is in itself, and the way you plant it is by saying it, speaking it, proclaiming it.

Again let's look at Mark 4.

> *And he (Jesus) said, So is the kingdom of God, as if a man should cast seed into the ground;*
>
> *And should sleep, and rise night and day, and the seed should spring and grow up, he knoweth not how.* (Mark 4:26-27)

People say, *"I don't understand how my saying it would cause it to come to pass."*

Well, these people are very scriptural. The Bible said they wouldn't understand it. It is possible to understand it, but you don't have to understand it to get it to work. **If you just have faith enough to believe what God said and do it, it will work for you.**

It does help when you understand how it works. But you don't have to know how it works to get it to work for you. If you just have the common sense to plant the seed and go to bed and get up, the seed will grow up.

Jesus isn't talking about quitting your job. He is talking about doing the things you would normally do. A farmer plants the seed, then he goes on about his daily business. When it comes up, he doesn't know how, but he knows it works. He doesn't understand how that seed germinates. The life of the seed is in itself. **If you have planted the promise of God, the life is in that promise.** You sowed it in the soil of your heart, and it will germinate after a while. But it's a process.

Once the blade appears, you need to have corresponding action toward that blade. But you would not have full corresponding action toward that plant when it is just a blade. If you said, *"Look at the corn coming up (the blades). I'm sure going to have a harvest. I'm confessing a bountiful harvest. Since I'm confessing it and I believe it, and I've already received it in my spirit, I ought to have full corresponding action toward those stalks of corn. We're going to harvest corn today."*

No, **you are going to destroy your crop if you try to harvest the blade.** There are many people doing just that — destroying their crop trying to harvest too soon. They are trying to have full corresponding action toward the blade.

People have taken what James said out of context — *"faith without corresponding action is dead"* — and they have tried to have full corresponding actions when they did not have full manifestation.

They are trying to harvest the blade. **This is where so many get in trouble; they don't use any common sense with their faith.** You must have common sense, or what we call horse sense. Sometimes intelligent people who are highly educated don't have any common sense. When they get turned on to faith, they just seem to throw away all good common sense. They say they are going to *"live by faith,"* but they go do crazy things. They set out to take full corresponding action, because James said faith without works is dead. They say, *"if I believe that my eyes are restored, I'll stomp my glasses. That will be my corresponding action. That will prove I have faith."*

**It may prove you can't see to drive to work in the morning.**

You should have corresponding action. You should speak in line with your faith and make the confessions. That would be watering and fertilizing that plant. When you have signs of it working, you would continue to water and fertilize it. No farmer would just quit watering his crop and say, *"There it is. I have corn. No need to water it. No need to fertilize it. I'm having corresponding action. I'm just going to act as if it already has the full corn in the ear."*

If you do, you may never have a harvest.

## Chapter Eight

# THE LAW OF CORRESPONDING ACTION

## FAITH REQUIRES ACTION

There must be **some** corresponding action to faith. But in every individual case, whether healing, financial situations, or believing for someone else, there are different actions.

**The most common mistake people make is to have full corresponding action before they have full manifestation of what they confessed.** When they do, they get into trouble. When they carry it over into the area of finances, they end up writing hot checks.

You could go this far in this particular situation, if you believed God to supply your need to pay the rent — you could go ahead and write the check and put it in the desk drawer. But don't mail it until you get the money in the bank. That would be as far as you could go toward that particular situation and be legal about it. God will not bless foolishness nor something that is illegal.

Mark establishes the fact that the soil, the ground, is the heart of a man. Jesus says, *"The sower sows the Word"* (Mark 4:14). We know that the seed which is being used is specifically the word of God. It could be other seeds. You could sow all kinds of seeds in this soil — and many people do. But He is telling us to use it this way; to sow the Word of God in it. That's why the confession of God's Word is so important. **Those words are seeds that you are sowing.**

## AGREEMENT FACTOR

The words you are speaking, even when you are not confessing the Word of God, should be in agreement with the Word of God. For they are seeds, whether or not you intend to plant them. **God's law of seedtime and harvest works.** It works all the time. You don't just turn it on and turn it off, and say, *"I'm saying all of these things, but I'm not really planting seed, I'm just saying this."* If you keep saying it, you are planting seed, whether or not you intend to.

James said,

> *If any man among you seem to be religious, and bridleth not his tongue, but deceiveth his own heart, this man's religion is vain.* *(James 1:26)*

He deceives his own heart. He is deceiving the soil of his heart into believing those things spoken are what he wants, and he has planted it. You could say, *"I want a harvest of wheat,"* but if you plant corn, you have deceived the soil. The soil will produce corn. It will not produce wheat, because **the seed determines the harvest, not the soil.**

Let's look again at what Jesus said in Mark chapter four, which puts some balance into corresponding action.

> *And he said, So is the kingdom of God, as if a man should cast seed into the ground;*
>
> *And should sleep, and rise night and day, and the seed should spring and grow up, he knoweth not how.*
>
> *For the earth bringeth forth fruit of herself; first the blade, then the ear, after that the full corn in the ear.* *(Mark 4:26-28)*

## STUDY CONTEXT BEFORE ACTION

Jesus is telling you how the kingdom works. Faith has corresponding action, but we need to define it. When James said, *"faith without works is dead,"* he was speaking concerning an individual who needed clothing and food. James said, *"If you say to him, 'I have faith to believe that God will supply your need,' then your faith is dead,"* as far as that man is concerned.

Corresponding action to that man would have been to give him some food and some clothes.

Someone says, *"I have faith to believe that God is going to supply all of my need."*

But are you a giver? Do you give out of your need? That is corresponding action concerning your need. The Word says, *"give and it shall be given unto you."*

Someone said, *"Yes, but you don't understand; I don't have enough to give."*

If you don't give, you don't have corresponding action toward what you say you believe. **You must give out of your need.** You certainly couldn't give as much as you could if you had abundance. But corresponding action toward that promise would be to give. **Little is much, when you give it in faith.**

Here is an example of this and the corresponding action behind faith. When Jesus was feeding the multitude, the disciples said, *"How can we feed these people? We have only five loaves and two fish."*

Jesus said, *"Bring what you have to me."*

Jesus took it and blessed it and began to break it. Then He gave it to the disciples. Notice that after everybody had eaten, there were twelve baskets full left. Evidently they had twelve baskets that they were using to distribute this food. Jesus broke it, laid it in those baskets, and told them, *"Now go and feed the multitude."*

There were five thousand men there, and with the women and children, perhaps twenty thousand people. They had to have some corresponding action to start out with such little to feed that multitude. They acted on the words of Jesus.

## DON'T ACT ON OTHERS' FAITH

This is where most of your corresponding action is going to be — **acting on the Word of God and the Words of Jesus.** Sometimes people do things because someone else did it. *"They say, Brother so and so gave his car away, and he got a new Cadillac. So I'm going to give mine away, because I have an old wreck, and I'd like to have a new car."*

But God told Brother so and so to give his car away to help someone in need. **He was acting on God's Word; God's Word specifically to him.** He didn't act just to get himself a new car, but because someone else had a need. Sometimes we have done things just because someone else did it and got blessed. We were trying to act on their faith, and trying to get the same manifestation as if we had faith.

## DEAD FAITH IS NO FAITH

**Faith without works is dead, but acting as though you have faith when you're not developed in it is double dead.**

If you give away your car on someone else's faith, you may walk for eight or ten months. You may not get the same manifestation they did, because you didn't do it on your faith. You didn't do it to meet someone else's need. You did it to get yourself a new car — not that there is anything wrong with you having a new car. But you didn't act on God's Word to you. You acted on God's Word to someone else.

158

It makes a difference when you act on the Word of God. Your corresponding action should be because of the Word.

In Mark 4, the seed is the Word, and a man sows it. Jesus said the man would sleep and rise night and day. It will spring and grow up, and he doesn't know how. You just have to believe that it works, and work the principle.

Now let's look at Mark, the eleventh chapter.

> *For verily I say unto you, That whosoever shall say unto this mountain, Be thou removed, and be thou cast into the sea; and shall not doubt in his heart, but shall believe that those things which he saith shall come to pass; he shall have whatsoever he saith.* (Mark 11:23)

## WHEN YOU SAY YOU SOW

In order to better understand this scripture, let's substitute the word *"sow"* for *"say"*. **"Whosoever shall sow to this mountain,** *be thou removed, and be thou cast into the sea; and shall not doubt in his heart, but* **shall believe that those things which he soweth shall come to pass; he shall have whatsoever he soweth."**

Sometimes it helps to say things differently. We are not changing the Word of God, we are just putting it in a little different perspective and looking at it from a different angle.

You can understand if a farmer sows, he is going to have whatsoever he soweth. Nobody would misunderstand that, because it is simple. But people will argue with you that he won't have whatsoever he saith. **The saying is the sowing.** Whether or not you believe it, whether or not you agree with it, whether or not you like the way God set this law in motion, it is still the law.

You can argue with it, you can fuss about it, but it's still going to work that way.

Don't misunderstand me. I'm not saying something will happen just because you said it once. Generally speaking, you must say it over a period of time to really plant it. Words are not planted just because you say them once.

When you put a seed in the soil, that soil has conceived that seed. The things you say won't be conceived in your spirit until you say them over and over again. When you really believe it, then it is conceived. **Faith in the heart is the ability to conceive** God's Word. It won't happen until it is conceived, just as a child is conceived in his mother's womb. You say things over and over before you really believe them. Faith cometh by hearing. This is true, whether they are positive or negative things.

## LAW OF RETURN

*Be not deceived; God is not mocked: for whatsoever a man soweth, that shall he also reap.*
*(Galatians 6:7)*

*And he said, So is the kingdom of God, as if a man should cast seed into the ground.* *(Mark 4:26)*

Notice that Jesus and the apostle Paul are saying the same thing in these two verses.

In the natural realm we clearly understand this. We know it to be true. There is no clearer truth. Whatever a man sows on his farm, that is what he will also reap. How much more would it work with the Word of God, when **God's Word is incorruptible seed.**

Sometimes we have looked at this and said, *"Well, that sounds like it's too good to be true."* That is like saying to a farmer, *"Oh, it's just too good to be true that you can have what you sow. It can't be true. You can't have what you sow."* But you will never convince a farmer otherwise, because he has experienced it.

That's the way it works! It's a principle. This is God's method. When we by simple faith believe what God says instead of trying to figure it all out, it will work for us.

You may not understand it when you start. Understand as much of it as you can, and just be obedient to do what He says to do. Follow all of these things that Jesus said. *"Whosoever shall say to the mountain, be removed" (Mark 11:23), "Whosoever shall say to the sycamine tree, be plucked up by the root"* (Luke 17:6). None of these things were that way when you started saying them. The tree was still there, the mountain was still there, the problem was still there when you started saying it. But Jesus said they would obey your faith-filled words.

Some people say, *"You can't say it unless it has already manifested."*

Well, why in the world would you want to say it then? Everybody would know it then. There wouldn't be any need to use your faith. That's like a farmer saying, *"Well, I'll tell you, as soon as I get a good crop, I'm going to plant."*

I have news for you. Until you plant, there will be no harvest.

## DECEPTION IS BLINDING

You don't realize how the devil has deceived and clouded the minds of people until you begin to teach the principles of God's Word. I'm talking about religious people. I'm talking about Christians. I'm talking about Spirit filled people. Sometimes they just get angry at you because you believe the Word of God. Their minds have been blinded to some truths because they have been closed minded about some things.

161

Someone said, *"Why, you are just trying to live in a fantasy world. How can you confess all of those things? You must think you're divine."*

No, I am just a partaker of the divine nature. I am capable of operating in the principles of God's divine law.

What we say is what we sow. **But it won't happen just because you say it once.** It won't happen just because you say it a hundred times. **But saying it is involved in working the principle.** It takes saying it over and over to cause faith to come. It is conceived when you believe and doubt not in your heart.

Some people even say things about their finances that they don't really believe when they first say it. A businessman might say, *"I'll tell you, we're going broke. Sure as the world, we're going bankrupt."*

He didn't really believe that when he first started saying it, but if he continues to say it, he will believe it. **His voice has a greater effect on his spirit than it has on anyone else.**

Not only businessmen say this, but ministers talk that way. *"This thing is never going to work. We might as well forget it."* That affects their spirit.

## CHRISTIAN SENSE

When you begin to operate in faith and confession, some people say, *"That's just mind over matter. Why, you're getting into mind science."*

No. This is not mind science. This is Christian sense. It's the Bible way. It's God's method.

You will get criticized. They criticized Jesus, and people haven't changed. Religious people haven't changed that much. They will criticize you for operating in the principles of God. God's people are destroyed for lack of knowledge of God's principles.

Remember, we are talking about corresponding action, acting on your faith. Jesus said the man will cast the seed into the ground, and he will go right on with his daily business affairs. He goes to bed, and he gets up. He doesn't stay up all night. This proves that he is not worrying about it all night and walking the floor. And the seed should spring and grow up, he knoweth not how.

## DON'T LET YOUR
## MOUTH DECEIVE YOUR HEART

Many people don't know how they got into the mess they are in. I see a lot of people, and I can talk to them for fifteen minutes and know in my spirit why they are in the situation they are in. I also sometimes know in my spirit that I can't share it with them, because they wouldn't accept it. They wouldn't believe that's the problem.

Most of the time, the problem is one inch below their nose — **their mouth,** the things they are saying. **Their mouth deceives their heart.** They sowed the thing they didn't want. **They prayed the thing they didn't want, and fear came.** Fear replaced faith, and fear caused the manifestation of the thing they didn't desire, the same as faith causes the manifestation of the things desired.

Fear is a destructive force. It is really faith in the devil. Paul said fear did not come from God.

*For God hath not given us the spirit of fear; but of power, and of love, and of a sound mind.*
*(II Timothy 1:7)*

The things we say are the things we sow. The things we say are the things we shall reap. Mark 11:23 establishes that principle. Then the apostle Paul says it a different way in Galatians, chapter six.

163

*Be not deceived; God is not mocked: for*
*whatsoever a man soweth, that shall he also reap.*
*(Galatians 6:7)*

This scripture is a backup for Mark 11:23. It establishes the same truth. Allow me to paraphrase this verse, and we will see it from a different perspective.

*Be not deceived; God cannot be out-talked;*
*whatsoever a man plants, that shall he also keep.*

Whatever you plant is what you are going to keep; and that is what will produce. That is what establishes the end results.

Let's look again at the foundation scripture for the balance in corresponding actions.

*For the earth bringeth forth fruit of herself; first*
*the blade, then the ear, after that the full corn in*
*the ear.*

*But when the fruit is brought forth, immediately*
*he putteth in the sickle, because the harvest is*
*come.* *(Mark 4:28-29)*

The earth brings forth fruit of herself — the human spirit or heart brings forth fruit of itself. The things you say are going into the soil of your heart. The spirit or heart will have action that corresponds with words you have spoken. You contact God with your spirit. Even while you are asleep, the things you have said continue to cause your spirit to act in agreement with your words.

The farmer goes to bed, and he gets up, and the ground (soil) brings forth the fruit. It works the same way with you. The kingdom within you has been sown with the seed of what you have been speaking. You sow the seed by saying, *"My God supplies all my need according to His riches in glory by Christ Jesus; I have abundance and no lack; because I have given, it is given unto me good measure, pressed down, shaken together and running over."* You say and sow those seeds concerning finances. While you are asleep, this principle is working. Your spirit never sleeps, and you have sown incorruptible seed.

## CANDLE OF THE LORD

*"The spirit of man is the candle of the Lord.* (Proverbs 20:27) The human spirit is the light bulb that God uses to *"enlighten"* you. While you are asleep, your spirit remains in contact with God. It continually searches the avenues of God's wisdom to find a way to cause this promise (seed) that you have planted to come up in your life.

Some people think that God is just going to drop money down out of heaven on them. But that is not God's method. God may bring some business opportunity your way, or perhaps cause someone to give to you. But don't always look for it to come the same way. Don't just look for checks to come in the mail. Look for the method God chooses to bring these promises into effect in your life.

It might be a business deal. It might be a land investment. It could be almost anything, including things you didn't expect to happen.

God will honor His promises. But it doesn't always happen the way we thought it would. While you are asleep, that soil is working. It is searching the avenues of God's wisdom.

*For what man knoweth the things of a man, save the spirit of man which is in him? even so the things of God knoweth no man, but the Spirit of God.* (I Corinthians 2:11)

This *"spirit of man"* is the human spirit. This is the human spirit which is *"the candle of the Lord, searching all the inward parts of the belly."* The *"belly"* refers to your innermost being, or where the spirit is; where the kingdom of God abides.

## HUMAN SPIRIT —
## GOD'S SPIRIT ENLIGHTENS YOU

*"What man knoweth the things of a man, save the spirit of man which is in him?"* In other words, you don't know all about you; you don't know all about what you need. Your human spirit does. Your spirit knows all about you. God's Spirit knows all about God. When your spirit is in contact with God's Spirit, you have contacted the source of all knowledge. You have access to that knowledge through your spirit.

Based on what you have planted in your spirit, your spirit contacts God's Spirit night and day and says, *"I'm calling for the information on how to have those needs supplied according to Your riches in glory by Christ Jesus."*

Your spirit has conceived your words that you have no lack, and you have abundance. Your human spirit has corresponding action to the words you speak in faith. So that's what your spirit calls for from God, Who is a spirit. That information will be transferred from the Spirit of God to your human spirit by revelation.

Then sometime, maybe hours, or days, or months later, you won't know how, but the blade springs up. You get an idea and you say, *"Where did that come from?"*

It came from what you said (sowed). You planted that promise in the soil of your heart. Even though it was not that way in the natural, your spirit conceived the promise you spoke: *"My needs are met; I have abundance and no lack."*

So the question goes from your spirit to the Spirit of God, calling for that information, *"How do we bring this to pass?"*

## PRODUCTION CENTER

The soil, the heart, the spirit of man, is designed to produce. From what Mark tells us, we know **the soil is the production center.** The soil is the heart of man. It is designed to produce the thing desired.

You plant the seed and go to bed and get up. The answer may come while you are asleep. Or you may be driving down the highway some day, and suddenly an idea comes to you. You'll say, *"I wonder why I didn't think of that before?"*

You had never thought of that before because you had not planted the seed for it before. Your spirit had not called for it from the Spirit of God. God can give you ideas that will supply all your need according to His riches in glory by Christ Jesus. They come by the Spirit of God through your spirit.

Some people criticize this type of teaching because they don't understand it. They don't know the working of the Holy Spirit with the human spirit. They think you are trying to make it come to pass by forcing God while quoting what He said. No, we aren't trying to force God into something. We are just planting the seed that calls for a harvest.

## CHECKUP FROM THE NECK UP

Those who criticize **don't need your criticism, they need your prayers; they need to be taught.** You have to keep a right attitude toward them. As somebody said, *"Once in a while, you need a checkup from the neck up to keep from getting hardening of the attitude."*

People sometimes criticize because they don't understand. And you must guard against wrong attitudes. So pray for them and teach them; don't criticize them.

They are intelligent people. They wouldn't go to a farmer and say, *"Well, you're just trying to force God to do something by planting those seeds."*

## GOD'S TOTAL PROVISION

This is God's law of seedtime and harvest. And as long as this earth remaineth, it will work that way. The soil will always have action that corresponds to the seed sown. You could call this the law of corresponding action. The Garden of Eden was Adam's total supply. Everything that he needed in life came from that garden.

In Matthew 6:9-10, Jesus told His disciples to pray that the kingdom of God would come, and that the will of God be done on earth as it is in heaven. Jesus knew it was not that way, but they were to pray that it would be that way. In essence, this is what Jesus said, *"It will be possible when the kingdom of God has come that the will of God can be done on earth as it is in heaven."*

This prayer was partially fulfilled on the day of Pentecost. The kingdom of God that came on the day of Pentecost and was set up inside those who were born again is the same kingdom that will be set up in the New Jerusalem. **But it is a different manifestation of that kingdom.** It is as capable of supplying your every need as the Garden of Eden was to Adam. Did you know that you have a garden inside of you? This kingdom has been given to you; it is your garden. (Luke 12:32) That garden will produce whatever you need. It will lead you to, or bring to you the wisdom to obtain any promise in God's Word concerning you.

But you must sow word seed in that garden. **God has furnished seed for the sower — His Word of promise.** Jesus said that seed is the Word of God, and the soil is the heart.

## ACTION THAT CORRESPONDS WITH YOUR PRAYING

Your corresponding action toward what you say you believe would be to thank God that your need is met. Whenever you pray, believe at that time that you receive what you prayed.

> *Therefore I say unto you, What things soever ye desire, when ye pray, believe that ye receive them, and ye shall have them.* (Mark 11:24)

The *"them"* that Jesus talks about is the things you prayed. So pray the desire. Do not pray the problem, because you shall receive *"them,"* the things that you prayed. **If you pray problems, you shall receive problems,** because you will have more faith in *"them"* (problems) than you have in the answer. Pray the desire. **The desire is the answer.** The answer to financial crisis is Abundance! Then pray abundance, not crisis and lack. Pray for *"them"* to be manifest.

When you pray, believe. Believe what you pray when you pray. Don't wait until you have the manifestation to believe. Believe when you pray *"Now faith is . . ."* You believe now. Whenever you pray, it's *"now."* Believe *"now"* and you will receive later.

You know you don't have *"them"* yet. You are not trying to say you already have them in manifestation. But in the spirit realm, if you've conceived it by faith, then as far as God is concerned, you have them. But you don't have them in the natural realm. Jesus said you shall (eventually) have *"them."*

**169**

# DECEPTION IS NOT
## CORRESPONDING ACTION

Don't try to make others believe you already have what you prayed for. They don't have to believe it. You must believe. Some think corresponding action is lying about something you don't possess. *"I have a new car. I already have it. You ought to see my new car. It's sitting in my garage."*

If you deceive somebody into believing you have something you really don't have, then **you have lied about it.** If they heard you confessing the Word of God, and assumed that you already had it, **then you didn't lie.** They just heard you calling things that be not as though they were, as Abraham did.

Don't try to convince someone that you already have something that you don't have. That is not corresponding action. That is a lie. The corresponding action would be to praise God for it. *"Thank You, Father, I believe I've received it."* You have received it in the spirit, but not in the natural.

Then, part of the corresponding action would be to not ask for that again. If you believed you received it, don't pray for it again. Praise Him that you've received it. If you pray for it again the same way the next morning, then that is action of unbelief.

Now, don't let this get you in bondage. Learn the difference between the prayer of petition and the prayer of intercession. There is much confusion about this kind of praying.

# SOMETIMES NO ACTION
## IS CORRESPONDING ACTION

Someone said, *"The Bible said to just keep on praying about it with persistent faith."*

They always bring up the unjust judge (Luke 18) and the man who went for bread at midnight (Luke 11). The *"importunity"* of the man who went for bread at

170

midnight means persistence. But when you say persistence of faith, that's different than saying persistence in anything else. Persistence of faith would be faith that asked for bread and stood its ground until the bread was received.

Persistent faith is faith that believes it receives, and holds fast to that belief until the manifestation comes. Persistent faith does not keep asking for the same thing. (If you believe you received, why would you ask again?) That would be corresponding action to unbelief. Part of the corresponding action would be to quit praying about the thing you believe you receive. That would be proper corresponding action of persistent faith.

Now remember, so far, we haven't been talking about the prayer of intercession, but only the prayer of petition. Let me point out the difference between the prayer of petition and the prayer of intercession.

**In the prayer of petition, you ask God to do something for you.** If you petition God scripturally to do something for you and your faith was based on the Word of God, then you only need to ask Him once. Then begin to praise God for it. Have corresponding action toward that by praising Him. That action is in agreement with your faith.

**In the prayer of intercession, it is legal and proper to pray the Word of God and proclaim it over and over regarding any situation,** for that is not vain repetition. Jesus put it this way:

> *But when ye pray, use not vain repetitions, as the heathen do: for they think that they shall be heard for their much speaking.* (Matthew 6:7)

## PRAYER REPETITION IS NOT CORRESPONDING ACTION

Some time in your life, you have probably been taught that the way to get your prayers answered is to just keep praying the same thing over and over and over. Finally, you will wear God down, and He will grant it. There is no scriptural basis for that kind of thinking. A few people **think** they have some scriptural basis for it, **but if they rightly divide the Word, they will find no such basis.** We will briefly look at some of the commonly misquoted and misunderstood scriptures concerning this.

One is the story of the widow and the unjust judge. (Luke 18:1-6) Almost everyone says the widow just kept coming to the unjust judge, but she only came to him once. Then it was her boldness of faith that caused him to do what he did for her.

The other scripture is the man who came for bread at midnight. (Luke 11:5-8) The Bible doesn't say he ever knocked, but you hear it misquoted so often that the man just kept on knocking. But he just simply stood his ground until he received what he asked for. And that is a good illustration of corresponding action to his faith.

If you had faith, then you believed that it was settled when you prayed; you wouldn't ask anymore. But when you get over into the area of intercession, your intercession is by praying the Word of God. That is something you are doing to change things. You are not asking God to do something. If you ask God to do it, you need only ask it once in faith. Then praise God for it until it comes. If you ask in unbelief, it's all right to pray again and say, *"Father, forgive me for unbelief. I'm going to pray in faith this time."*

## PRAYING GOD'S WORD
## IS CORRESPONDING ACTION

With the prayer of intercession and praying the Word of God over your finances, you could repeat that prayer over and over, day after day. Doing so would build your faith. When you are praying the Word, your words are changing things.

Here is an example of such prayer.

*Father, because You gave me authority to use the name of Jesus, in the name of Jesus I call down the principalities, the powers, and the rulers of the darkness that have come against my finances. I render them harmless and ineffective in the name of Jesus. I break their power, and I loose the spirit of the living God to reveal to me the hidden things and the direction of God. I break the powers of Satanic forces released against me.*

When I say that, I am affecting things by my praying. I haven't asked God to do anything. You can see the difference between this prayer and a prayer of petition where you ask God to do something. For example, *"I ask You, Father, to send laborers across Brother so and so's path, and minister the Word of God to him."*

That prayer is something you asked God to do. If you believe it when you ask it, you would only ask it once.

If you are praying something that is affecting things, you can pray it continually, for it is not vain repetition, but it is action of your faith.

## THE BALANCE TO FAITH'S ACTION

Now let's move it over into the natural realm. As we look at these principles in the natural realm, we can understand some spiritual things better. Let's say, for example, you take your car to a mechanic and say, *"Can you overhaul this engine?"*

He replies, *"Yes, you better believe I can overhaul it. I'm one of the best mechanics in this country. I know when I overhaul this engine it will run like a new one.*

*You have left it in the right hands when you leave it with me."*

So he goes to work on the engine. If he is a man of faith, but he misunderstands corresponding action, he may come to work some morning and say, *"If I really believe that this car is going to run like a new one, I ought to have full corresponding action toward what I believe."*

So right in the middle of the overhaul, when he doesn't even have the head or the carburetor on the motor, he says, *"I'm just going to have full corresponding action and act as if it's already finished."* So he calls the man to tell him his car is ready.

## ACTION EQUAL TO MANIFESTATION

No one would be that foolish in the natural, would they? We all know that would be foolishness. But yet, concerning healing, concerning the manifestation of what they prayed for, some act that way. For example, some pray to have restoration of their vision, and they say, *"In order to have full corresponding action, I'll have to stomp my glasses, or throw them away."*

That is just as foolish, unless you have the manifestation of it, or unless God specifically spoke to you to get rid of your glasses. For, if God said it, it will work. Glasses won't heal the eyes, nor keep them from being healed.

Some think, because they have full corresponding action, they will cause the manifestation to come. *"If I stomp my glasses, that will prove I have faith and bring the manifestation."* **It may prove you will have to feel your way to work the next morning.** This is just as foolish as the mechanic saying he will call the man to pick up his car when the engine repair is only half completed. The car owner would think the mechanic

174

was a nut. He would not have full corresponding action when he had only half of the manifestation.

Now, don't feel condemned if you have done these things, not knowing any better. That's why we are spending so much time on this subject.

## DON'T RUSH THE HARVEST

Let me give an example concerning restoration of eyes. I know of a lady who sat under some teaching on faith and healing. She wore glasses, but she was prayed for by the laying on of hands that her eyes would be restored.

The next day she said, *"I believe I received my healing,"* so she didn't put on her glasses. She started having headaches immediately. She said, *"Lord, I don't understand this. I believe I received my healing."*

She prayed about it, and the Lord said to her, *"You don't have the manifestation yet. Hold fast to your faith. Hold fast to your confession. But go ahead and wear your glasses. Every time you put them on, say, 'Thank God, I believe I've received my healing. I believe my eyes are restored'."*

She started using this confession. She had to mix some faith with what she believed. In pulling off her glasses, she was trying to have **full corresponding actions toward what she believed, but she didn't have full manifestation.** She only had the blade.

Remember, Jesus said, *"First the blade, then the ear."* It is conceived, and it is producing, but she doesn't yet have the mature harvest. If she could see clearly, then that would be the full manifestation.

**Some people are not only living by faith, they are driving by faith, because they can't see.** First, that's illegal; and second, it's foolishness when you don't have the manifestation. If you can see, then take your glasses

**175**

off. But if you can't see, put on your glasses and stay legal.

This lady confessed, *"Thank God, I believe I received my healing; I believe I received my healing,"* every time she put her glasses on.

This went on for some time — several months. Later, she started having headaches with her glasses on, and she said, *"Lord, I don't understand it. Now I'm having headaches with my glasses on."*

The Lord said, *"Remove your glasses."*

This was at least ten years ago, and she is still healed, thank God. She still does secretarial work, and she has normal vision without glasses.

This lady could have destroyed the harvest. She could have gotten over into unbelief by saying, *"Why, this faith stuff doesn't work."* She could have tried to have full corresponding action toward her faith when she didn't have the full manifestation. As Jesus said, she didn't have the *"full corn in the ear."* She had only the blade. She had conceived the Word, and she released her faith in that prayer. Some people would say of her actions, *"Well, that wasn't corresponding action."*

But she did act as far as she had manifestation. This action is described in the text — Mark, chapter four.

> *. . . first the blade, then the ear, after that the full corn in the ear.*
>
> *But when the fruit is brought forth, immediately he putteth in the sickle, because the harvest is come.*

You shouldn't have full corresponding action toward anything until you have the full manifestation.

Live in faith. Confess your faith, and act as far as your faith is developed.

# Chapter Nine

# THE BALANCE TO CORRESPONDING ACTION

We are sharing some practical teaching in this chapter concerning putting balance to our corresponding action. We are spending so much time on this subject because there have been so many things left unsaid in the past.

Let's go again to the foundation scripture in Mark, chapter four.

> *And he said, So is the kingdom of God, as if a man should cast seed into the ground.*
>
> *And should sleep, and rise night and day, and the seed should spring and grow up, he knoweth not how.*
>
> *For the earth bringeth forth fruit of herself; first the blade, then the ear, after that the full corn in the ear.*
>
> *But when the fruit is brought forth, immediately he putteth in the sickle, because the harvest is come.* (Mark 4:26-29)

Let's zero in on the twenty-ninth verse. *"But **when the fruit is brought forth,** immediately **he putteth in the sickle."*** When you have full manifestation of the mature fruit, then the harvest is ready to be reaped.

Many people get excited about faith. But we don't want to excite faith, we want to teach you how to operate in the principles of faith. Sometimes those who get their faith excited, go out beyond their level of development. That is one thing you do not want to do. You don't want to lead or push people out beyond their level of development.

## EXCITED FAITH

That happened to Peter when he jumped out of the boat to walk on the water. (Matthew 14:22-28) He was not developed to that point. But he saw Jesus walking on the water. I am sure they were saying, *"If Jesus was here, things would be different."* They looked up and saw Jesus walking on the water. Peter in his excitement said, *"Lord, if it be you, bid me come."*

Now, Peter was not ready for water walking, but his faith was excited. Many Christians are not ready for water walking either. They have been to a few faith seminars, but they aren't ready. Peter forced Jesus into calling him out of the boat. He said, *"If it's really you, bid me come."*

What could Jesus say? He couldn't say, *"No, it's not me. Forget it, Peter, you're not developed yet."* Anything He said other than *"come"* was going to be a lie. Even if he didn't answer at all, it would still be a lie, for it was Jesus. All Jesus did was answer his question when He said, *"Come."*

Peter did walk on the water. But he was not developed to the point that he was able to hold fast to that Word of faith; he became too involved with the circumstances. When he did, he began to sink. Faith left him. You can excite people's faith to the point where they will get out there and sink. Many people have gotten excited about faith because of some story someone told. They said *"This is the way it happened to me, and it all worked out good."*

## PRACTICE BEFORE YOU PREACH

That person was operating at his level of development. **It may be disastrous for you** to do that same thing. Therefore, **when you operate in the principles of faith, practice them before you preach them.** Many people are practicing what they preach;

178

but you need to be preaching what you have **already practiced.** Don't just excite people's faith. Get them involved with the principles. You can excite people beyond their ability. That is what happened to Peter. He got excited and tried to operate beyond his level of faith. Jesus didn't intend for that to happen. Peter forced Him into it by the way he said it. Some of you have done the same thing. You said, *"Lord, if it's Your will for me to do this, then let this other thing happen to prove Your will."*

**It was God's will for you to do that, but it wasn't God's will for the other to happen.** You forced God into a bad situation.

## EXCITED FAITH IS
## OFTEN DISAPPOINTED FAITH

As in Peter's case, excited faith will sometimes cause other people to do things just because you did. They want to act on your level of faith instead of their own level. Here is an illustration of what I'm talking about. Several years ago I went into a certain church. I told how God supernaturally supplied the gasoline for my airplane. I was lost out in the northwest part of the country and had flown for five hours and twenty-five minutes. The airplane only held four hours and thirty minutes of fuel. When I landed, I still had seventeen gallons of fuel in the airplane.

A man in the church heard my testimony and got excited. After the service that night, he and his wife got in their car and started home. His wife said, *"We'd better get some gas in the car."*

He said, *"No — God put gas in Brother Capps' airplane, He'll put gas in my car."* He drove five miles out in the country and ran out of gas and called the pastor. The pastor had to go get him some gas.

These are some of the things that people do with excited faith. I have learned when I give that testimony to tell them, *"Now remember, this was an emergency."* God is not going to put gas in your car just because it's empty. If it were an emergency situation, and you were developed to that level of faith, it would happen to you. But God is not in the business of supplying gasoline for everyone. This is an example of excited faith. That man did that because I left something unsaid that should have been said, and he read between the lines what he thought I meant.

## CHECK YOUR LEVEL OF FAITH
## BEFORE YOU LEAP

Let's go into the area of divine healing. When people assume the wrong idea of corresponding action concerning healing, they usually end up in trouble. Some of them die. Many of them are not developed to the point where they can believe God for divine healing without a doctor, or without the aid of medicine. They could be over a period of years by confessing the promises of healing. But they are not developed to that yet. If you push them out there by saying, *"If you really believe God, you'll throw your medicine away; If you really believed God, you would quit going to that doctor,"* many of them will die as a result, and that's foolish.

**It may be that you are developed to that level. But don't try to put everybody on your level of development.** People must operate on their level of faith, not yours. These are some practical things that need to be understood. Don't push people out there beyond their level, and don't belittle them for not being where you are in faith.

It takes time to develop in faith. They may get there in a few years. But some of them may never get there if

180

they throw their medicine away. You certainly don't want them to die just because they're not developed in their faith. So don't push them. All individuals have to know their level of development. They can't start where Brother Hagin, or Brother Copeland, or Brother Oral Roberts are now. They must begin on their own level.

Some people can't believe for divine healing at their stage of development. But they can believe if they go to the doctor, God will give the doctor the wisdom to operate on them and they will recover. If that is their level of faith, that is what they should do. Many people have gotten into trouble because they didn't understand the need of operating on their level of development.

There are people **trying to believe.** But when it means life or death, you'd better know what you believe. If the doctor says you have cancer and you must have an operation right now, or you are going to die in a few months, you are the only one who knows your level of faith. If you have any doubt as to whether you are to that level or not, then you need to have the operation quickly. You may say, *"But I want to believe God for my healing."* That is all right if you know your faith is developed to that level.

## IS IT FEAR OR FAITH?

There are some who haven't learned to believe God for relief from a headache, and they want to believe God for total healing of cancer. For many, it's not their faith that makes them want to believe God — it's their fear of the knife. **You will bury most of those people.** Many would have lived if they would have had the operation.

I don't want to discourage anyone's faith, but I caution you to **know where you are before you make a decision, when it means life or death to you or your children.**

The major point is this: **don't push anyone beyond their level of development.** These people can be taught, and if they will practice their faith and develop their faith, then eventually they will be able to receive their healing and not need their medicine.

But if you push them beyond their level of development, some of them will die. Now, that is not watering down the faith message. But these are some of the things that have not been taught in most faith seminars. Yes, James said, ". . . *faith without works is dead.*" That means faith without corresponding action is dead. But he is talking about a man who needed food and clothing. Just to say to that man, "*Go and be warmed and be fed*" is not enough. If you don't give him something, your faith is dead.

Let's look at this from a different angle. Those who are sick need healing. James says the prayer of faith will save the sick and the Lord will raise them up. (James 5:15)

Here is one Bible method of restoration or healing. **If we are to follow what James taught on works or corresponding action, then we must give the sick what they need.** First of all, they need to be anointed with oil and have the prayer of faith prayed over them. Even if you prayed the prayer of faith and the healing power of God flows into their body, the symptoms may linger in that body for several days before they have the total manifestation of their healing. The medicine they are taking does not heal, but keeps the disease from getting out of control, and eliminates the symptoms. Even though there is a divine healing process started in their body when you prayed, the symptoms must be dealt with until they have a total manifestation of their healing.

**Some can handle the symptoms and stay in faith, but some can't.** Now remember, James said, to give the man what he needed was faith with corresponding action. It may be true that the person is healed, but if you take away their medicine, the symptoms will usually cause them to doubt that you prayed the prayer of faith **and doubt that anything happened** when you prayed.

Someone may say, *"But if they are healed, they don't need the medicine."* They really don't need the medicine to heal their body, but they may need it to keep the symptoms down so they don't get into fear. **To some, the medicine is needed until they have the full manifestation of healing.** Others who are operating on a higher level of faith have learned to ignore the symptoms and stay in faith.

We have missed this point that the works or corresponding action that James said would make faith perfect was **giving the individual what he needed, not taking what he needed away from him.** Some may only need prayer to be healed, because they are more highly developed. **Some may always need medicine** because they have not been taught divine healing. Some were even taught it was of the devil. Then there are some who need prayer and the medicine to keep them out of fear until the doctor tells them they are well.

Medicine does not heal. It only aids healing. So if it doesn't heal, neither would it keep you from being healed.

It takes time to develop yourself in faith. Each individual has to determine their own level of faith. Don't ever tell anyone to throw their medicine away. If God tells them to throw it away, if they have the *'full corn in the ear,'* or full manifestation, then it's time to throw it away. Some people think they will be healed just because they are not taking any medicine. No one ever got healed because they didn't take medicine. But they say, *"That proves I have faith."* **It may prove that you will die young, if that's the reason you are not taking it.**

## GOD'S WORD HEALS

You can develop yourself for divine healing, because healing is a fact in the Bible. Psalms 107:20 says, *"He sent his word, and healed them, and delivered them from their destructions."* It is His Word that healed us. Some say, *"Why do you confess God's Word every day?"* Well, I explain it this way. It's like a farmer who needs thirty thousand dollars to pay a note. He says, *"I can make a hundred dollars an acre off of wheat."* So he plants wheat, but he only plants one acre and says, *"I've planted my wheat — I'm going to get thirty thousand dollars."*

But he isn't. He is going to make one hundred dollars. He didn't plant enough wheat.

## CONFESSION OF FAITH, NOT FEAR

Some people are trying to operate on the ultimate level of faith when they are still down on a lesser level. Their planting was too small. The farmer couldn't receive the **manifestion of his total need met when he didn't plant enough seed to produce it.**

Jesus said the kingdom of God is as if a man cast seed into the ground. Casting your seed is a process. The more you sow, the greater the harvest. Confession of the Word is a process of eliminating the negative in your life and sowing the promises of God. It doesn't happen overnight. Some have died confessing the Word of God. Someone said, *"I don't understand why they died. They were confessing the Word."*

Yes, but they were not developed in it. Some were confessing it out of fear. I know one such person who had cancer for two or three years and wouldn't go to a doctor because of fear. The cancer had spread by the time they heard any teaching on faith and confession. She started confessing that she was healed. But she was not developed in it. She wouldn't go to the doctor until it was too late. When she died, someone said, *"I don't understand it; she was saying all the right things."* Yes, she was, but it was too late for confession alone.

## TIMING IS IMPORTANT TO CONFESSION

Confession is a process. You need to start confessing your needs met well in advance — especially in finances when you can project your need, and you know when you need it. But with sickness and disease you won't know in advance. Some people make the mistake of starting to confess that they are healed after they get sick. The Word will heal you and it will also keep you from being sick.

You should confess the promise of God concerning healing, health, and life daily. Confess that every disease germ and every virus that touches your body dies instantly. Say, *"I am healed, well, delivered from the curse of the law."* Say it while you are well. **Use your faith on the front end.** If those who are confessing they are healed **after** they are sick had done it **before**, they probably never would have gotten sick.

What is that old saying? **An ounce of prevention is worth a pound of cure.** Use your faith on the front end and refuse to allow sickness and disease in your body.

## DOCTORS AND MEDICINE

Somebody said, *"What about doctors? Is it wrong to go to a doctor?"*

I will tell you the way I feel about doctors and medicine. If I need a doctor, I'll go to a doctor. If I need medicine, I'll take it. I don't sit around saying I don't want to miss God's best. If I get sick, I've already missed God's best. Confess the Word daily. Build your faith and develop yourself in God's Word. If you get sick, don't feel condemned over that. We have all missed it. But there is no need to die just because you missed it.

Concerning healing, some people are trying to have full corresponding actions when they have the *"blade"* and they do not have the *"full corn in the ear."* You will notice Jesus stated in Mark 4:29, when the fruit is mature or ripe, then he putteth in the sickle. It's harvest time when you have the full manifestation of the healing you prayed for or confessed. That is when you should have full corresponding actions toward that crop; when it is already mature; when you have the full corn in the ear.

You wouldn't want to take medicine if you had no symptoms and the doctor says you are well and the x-ray says the cancer is gone. It would be foolish to be taking medicine then, because you have full manifestation of healing. Your harvest is fully mature.

Several years ago a man said, *"I wouldn't ask you to pray for me."*

I said, *"Why not?"*

He said, *"Well, I'm taking medicine."*

I answered, *"What is the medicine supposed to do?"*

He said, *"The doctor said the medicine would help me."*

I said, *"The Bible says prayer will help you; the prayer of faith will save the sick and the Lord would raise them up. (James 5:15) It seems to me, if we do both, you may get well twice as fast."*

This is one of the things the devil has used. He uses these thoughts to put condemnation on those who are sick. The devil would like for you to go one way or the other, but not both. For he has a better chance if you are limited to one or the other. He will say, *"If you are going to believe God, you can't take medicine,"* or, *"If*

*you take medicine, you can't believe God."* But God
wants you well, even if it takes both methods — or ten
more!

**Too many people are like Peter. They get out of
the boat before they have water-walking faith.** They
may make it for a while, but soon they begin to sink,
because they haven't learned to keep their eyes off
circumstances. When fear comes, that's proof enough
that they are not walking in faith. When they call and
ask, *"Why isn't it working?"* they are not fully
persuaded.

## DON'T GO WHOLE HOG WHEN HALF READY

There was a man in a certain city who got born
again and turned on to faith. He thought this was the
greatest thing he had ever heard. He learned that he
was redeemed from the curse, from sickness and
disease, and that God was his healer (Galatians 3:13,
Exodus 15:26, Psalms 103:3). He had been raised in a
church that didn't believe these things. He just grabbed
it, and began to run with it, so to speak. He wasn't
developed in it, but he had mental assent to these Bible
truths. He had diabetes and five other things wrong
with him. Any one of them was enough to kill him.

He just went whole hog. **He threw all his medicine
away and almost died.** I counseled with him, and some
other brethren counseled with him. I said, *"The insulin
will keep the symptoms down. Is it easier to believe you
are healed when you feel well, or when you are hurting
and about to die? All the medicine does is to keep the
symptoms down and make you able to function. It's not
going to heal you. No one ever got healed by taking
insulin. Then on the other hand, it won't keep you from
getting healed. So, every time you take the insulin, say,
'Thank God, I believe I received my healing.' Mix your
faith with the Word of God."*

So he took our advice. He confessed his healing and confessed the Word over his body daily. Among other things, he had cancer in both lungs, an enlarged heart, high blood pressure. The doctor said he had the highest blood pressure he had ever seen any man have and live.

After ninety days I saw the doctors report. The doctor said, *"You must quit taking insulin — you don't need it any more. Your heart is perfectly normal, your blood pressure is normal. There is no sign or spot in one lung, and just a very small spot in the other, and it's much smaller than it was."*

The man got almost a totally clear bill of health in ninety days. I am convinced that he would have died, if he had not gotten back on his medicine. He was a young Christian with more zeal than knowledge.

This is why you read in the newspaper sometimes where a child died because the parents would not get them medical help. They believed the child was healed. But the child died. Someone may have told them to stop the child's medicine because they prayed for healing. Many tragic things have happened needlessly.

You won't get healed just because you stay away from doctors or medicine. You could die because you stayed away. Ultimately, all healing comes from God. Doctors have just learned how to aid the body process in healing and hold down the symptoms. Some of these things need to be said because so many try to go beyond their faith and get in serious trouble.

## LEPERS' CORRESPONDING ACTION

Let me give you another example in the Bible. In the seventeenth chapter of Luke, you find the story where ten lepers came to Jesus. They were standing afar off. They were required by law to stay about 100 yards away from the crowd.

*And they lifted up their voices, and said, Jesus,
Master, have mercy on us.*

*And when he saw them, he said unto them, Go
show yourselves unto the priests. And it came to
pass, that, as they went, they were cleansed.*

*(Luke 17:13-14)*

When Jesus saw them He said, *"Go show yourself to
the priest."* Now, what kind of an answer was that? The
only reason you would go show yourself to the priest
was if you had been cleansed. That was the law. If you
had been cleansed, and if you no longer have leprosy,
you would go show yourself to the priest and he would
pronounce you clean.

They were standing there and **Jesus did not pray
for them.** He just said, *"**Go show yourself to the
priest.**"* The Bible says **as they went they were
cleansed.** The going was the corresponding action.
They were acting as far as they could with what Jesus
said. And **as they went** they were cleansed. This was as
far as they could go with their corresponding action at
that point, and Jesus required it. They didn't have the
manifestation at that time. They could have said, *"But
Jesus, we're not well yet."* But they acted on the words
of Jesus. It makes a difference when you act on the
words of Jesus.

What would have happened if they hadn't gone?
Only one of them came back. Jesus said, *"Were there
not ten cleansed? But where are the nine?"*

As far as Jesus was concerned, ten of them were
cleansed, because He spoke the Word over all of them,
*"Go show yourself to the priest."*

It is possible that nine of them lost their healing.

*And Jesus answering said, Were there not ten
cleansed? but where are the nine?*

*There are not found that returned to give glory to
God, save this stranger.*

189

*And He said unto him, Arise, go thy way; thy*
*faith hath made thee whole.*        (Luke 17:17-19)

It was his faith. His faith was released in his corresponding action. He went when Jesus said, *"Go."* **It is possible that the other nine did not receive their total manifestation,** even though it doesn't say that in the Bible. Let's look at it from both aspects. They could have gone a way down the road, and began to look at themselves and say, *"We're not going down there and show ourselves to the priest. There is nothing changed. Look! We're just as bad as we ever were."*

**As far as Jesus was concerned, they were healed.** There wasn't anything else for Him to do. He had spoken the Word. There must be some corresponding action to the things we believe. By the time the lepers walked to the priest, they would all have had complete manifestation of their healing. But I question if the other nine kept their healing, because Jesus asked the question, *"Were there not ten cleansed? But where are the nine?"*

## A FARMER'S CORRESPONDING ACTION

When I was farming, I had a crop of wheat. We had planted wheat, and it didn't come up to a good stand. I told the men who worked for me, *"While I'm gone, if it gets dry enough, plow it up, because there just isn't enough to make a good yield."*

My wife said, *"Let's just pray over that wheat and confess the Word of God over it, and believe that it will produce."*

I said, *"Now, you know I'm a faith man all right, but you have to have something to confess over, and it doesn't look like there is enough out there to even use our faith."*

We went to a meeting, and when we came back, it had rained and the field didn't get plowed up. We looked at it, and it began to look a little better. My wife talked me into it, so we went out there and talked to the wheat. We spoke faith-filled words over it. We read Malachi 3:11, Psalm 1:3, Deuteronomy 28:1-15 to the wheat.

We took the Word of God and mixed our faith with it. We confessed the promises of God over it.

When we cut the wheat that fall, we cut fifty bushels of wheat to the acre off that field. That's a good crop. Some of the other fields cut as much as seventy bushels to the acre.

Our corresponding action was not that we went out there and started saying, *"We believe we have a good crop, so let's combine the wheat,"* when we only had the blade. We confessed God's Word over it. We fertilized it and patiently waited for the crop to grow to maturity before we brought the combine into the field.

**Don't throw away good business practices just because you operate in faith. You use common sense with your faith.**

When it comes to the area of healing, there are people who will say, *"If you're confessing that you are healed, then why would you be taking medicine?"* They say, *"You are taking medicine for sickness that you don't have."*

You are sick and you are calling for healing. Just saying you're not sick is not going to make you well. But calling things that are not is a Bible principle. You don't want to go around calling yourself sick. That would be establishing the existing problems. That would be calling things that are already manifest. That doesn't mean that you are denying you are sick. **You just don't give place to the sickness. You don't deny that the sickness exists. You deny its right to exist in your body.**

Confess the Word of God over your body. This is corresponding action toward your healing. You are calling for a manifestation of healing. Until it is

191

manifest, you don't have the *"full corn in the ear."* So you **would not have full corresponding action,** such as throwing away your medicine or stomping your glasses.

Use your faith as far as you can to the point you are developed. Then there will come a day when you will be like the man I referred to who confessed his healing while he was taking his medicine until he had the full manifestation.

Let me give you another example. A piece of property was available to us right next to my office. The man had it up for sale. I made an offer on it, and he turned it down. I thought it was a decent offer. The real estate lady said, *"I believe you will eventually get it. I'll keep an eye on it."*

When I made the offer on it, I went out and walked around the piece of property. I talked to it. I spoke to it, just like Jesus said in Luke six.

> *Whosoever cometh to me and heareth my sayings, and doeth them, I will show you to whom he is like:*
>
> *He is like a man which built an house, and digged deep, and laid the foundation on a rock: and when the flood arose, the stream beat vehemently upon that house, and could not shake it: for it was founded upon a rock.* (Luke 6:47-48)

In other words, He prophesied that if you do His sayings, then when the storms of life come they won't shake you.

I did just what Jesus said, I talked to it. He said, talk to the sycamine tree; speak to the mountain. (Luke 17:6, Mark 11:23) So I walked around that piece of property and talked to it. This is a principle of the kingdom — calling things that be not as though they were. I said, *"ground, I'm talking to you. I call you into the ministry. Jesus said you would obey me, so I say that you are mine, in Jesus Name. I call into you this ministry."*

I just walked around and talked over it; I claimed it with the promise of God.

I said, *"You come to me in Jesus Name."*

As I walked over the property, not only did I talk to it, but I also prayed. *"Father, I claim this piece of property, and I ask you to cause it to come to me. I have spoken to it; I have done everything I know to do concerning it. I have made the man a good offer and it is a fair offer."*

I never did pray about it anymore. I confessed, and thanked God that I received the property. Every time I went past it, I would say, *"You are mine. Come to me, in Jesus' Name."*

One morning several months later we went to work and there was a big sign on that piece of property that said, *"Future Home of the Production Credit Association."* I went in the office and asked my wife, *"Did you see that sign out there on our piece of property?"*

She said, *"Yes, I saw it."*

My head gave me trouble over that sign. Just as Peter had trouble when he got out of the boat and began to see the wind and the waves, I thought about it. In fact, I talked to my wife about it. I said, *"Maybe I ought to go talk to those people about that piece of property."*

I was thinking it may get away. My mind kept bugging me about it. Finally, one morning I realized what was happening. I was walking through the house. That sign kept bugging me, so I just hollered out loud, ***"I know what I'll do. NOTHING!"***

In that particular case, my corresponding action was to do nothing. It would have been foolish to go down to the courthouse and say, *"I want to file a claim on this piece of property."*

They would say, *"Where is the deed?"* You can't record the deed until you have possession of it.

*"Well, it's not manifest yet."*

They would have run me out of there and said, *"you are a nut."* That is trying to have full corresponding action before the manifestation comes. As far as I could go toward that situation was to do nothing, because I had done all I could do. I had made the man an offer. I had talked to the property. I had done everything the Word said to do about it. I had prayed about it, and now it was time to rest in what I had said and what I had done. As David said,

> *Commit thy way unto the Lord; trust also in him;*
> *and he shall bring it to pass.*     (Psalm 37:5)

As far as I could go with corresponding action was to just say, *"I am not going to do anything about it."*

A few weeks went by and they had the plans drawn up to build a building on this property. I was down at White River, where we have a fishing camp, taking dominion over the fish.

I received a phone call from my wife. She said, *"That real estate lady wants to talk to you right away."*

So I called her, and she said, *"Are you still interested in that piece of property?"*

I said, *"Yes, I sure am."*

She said, *"Would you give what you offered for it?"*

I replied, *"I guess I would."*

She said, *"You know, it's funny, they have decided that they want to build over here on the other street."*

I said, *"I don't doubt it."*

Now the full manifestation had come. She said, *"In a few days I will have the papers all drawn up and you can come and pick up the deed."*

You see, **inaction was my corresponding action in that situation.** Sometimes corresponding action will mean that you just don't do anything. **But not always.** Now, if you take this out of the context, someone may say, *"I owe those bills, but Brother Capps said* *corresponding action is to do nothing, so I am not going to look for a job, nor try to get a loan to pay these bills."*

That's taking it out of context, and getting it all messed up, doing crazy things. You shouldn't have to say these things, but you do, or somebody out there will misunderstand it. When you have done all you can do, all the Word of God said to do, all you know to do naturally about the situation, that is the time to rest in what you have already done.

Let's look at another example found in Mark, chapter five.

> *And, behold, there cometh one of the rulers of the synagogue, Jairus by name; and when he saw him, he fell at his feet,*
>
> *And besought him greatly, saying, My little daughter lieth at the point of death: I pray thee, come and lay thy hands on her, that she may be healed; and she shall live.*
>
> *And Jesus went with him; and much people followed him, and thronged him.* (Mark 5:22-24)

Notice, Jesus went with him. They were on their way to heal his little daughter. A woman with an issue of blood came along. She received her healing and testified, telling them all the truth. It probably took them an hour or so for all that to happen. A runner came to them and said, *"Your little daughter is already dead."*

## QUIET CORRESPONDING ACTION

Jairus had done all that he could do. He released his faith that if Jesus laid his hands on his daughter, she would be healed. He had done all he knew to do. **When Jesus heard the bad news He said, *"Fear not, only believe."***

Believe what? Believe what he had established with his own faith.

That is not the time, especially in Jairus' situation, to start making faith confessions. If he had, he would have gotten into fear and unbelief. He probably would have said, *"If you hadn't stopped and healed this lady, you would have gotten there in time to heal my daughter."*

Jesus had said, **"Don't do anything but believe."** He had gone as far as he could go. **His corresponding action was to just be quiet.** Psalm 37:7 says, **"Rest in the Lord, and wait patiently for him."** There is a time to rest in the Lord. Sometimes, corresponding action is to **just rest in what you have already said.** Rest in what you have done in faith. When you don't know anything else to do, rest in the Lord.

Paul said in Ephesians 6:13, *"And having done all, to stand."* Stand! If there is nothing else you can do in faith **rest.** Corresponding action is to say, *"I know what I will do — rest in the Lord, because I have done all that I know to do."*

Then you just rest. But be sure that you have done all you know to do. It is not the fact that you didn't do anything. If you aren't careful, people get the idea that doing nothing is what made it happen. No, it wasn't the inactivity that made it happen. But the inactivity **sometimes** is the corresponding action needed.

In the case of the ten lepers, the corresponding action needed was to go. As they went they were cleansed. Sometimes corresponding action means **doing something in faith.** But not something foolish. Not something crazy. Then on the other hand, sometimes it means to just do nothing at all, but just rest in what you have already done.

Sometimes when people are in a problem and their faith is low, **they start trying to make faith confessions, and they make them out of fear.** You can say all the right things, and say them in fear instead of faith. **You can confess the Word of God in fear.** It can be done. Some people are doing it. That is why we hear of someone who said all the right things, but they died. They may have been doing it in fear.

It has to be in faith. That is why you can't judge things just because of what happens. It looked like they were operating perfectly in faith. You don't know if they were. You don't know what they were really believing. Sometimes they were saying those things because they really believed the opposite was coming. Sometimes they were too late saying them.

Corresponding action is necessary in every situation. Sometimes it's something that you do by faith, and sometimes it's something you don't do.

**Faith in action is God's personality in manifestation.** God has already released His faith in what He said. He believes every word will come to pass, and He acts as though it were true. This corresponding action principle has two sides to it — God's side, and our side. We must do our part. God has done His part.

.. 

## Chapter Ten

# HOPE — A PARTNER TO FAITH

*Now faith is the substance of things **hoped** for, the evidence of things not seen.*          *(Hebrews 11:1)*

Faith is the substance of things, but **hope** is a necessity. Sometimes people say, *"you don't get anything by hoping."* And that's true to a certain extent, for there is no substance to hope.

But hope is a very important partner to faith. Hope is the goal-setter. *"Faith is the **substance of things hoped for.**"* The substance of *"things"* — what *"things?"* The things you **hoped for.** What do we hope for? We hope for the things that God has given us.

That's why the Bible says in Hebrews 11:6, *"But without faith it is impossible to please him."* God is not pleased when we don't enter into the provisions that He made for us. Some things we will never enter into, except through faith. God's willingness is multiplied to us through the knowledge of God. We must know what God has given, or we can't have faith in that promise.

*According as his divine power hath given unto us all things that pertain unto life and godliness. . ."*

*(II Peter 1:3)*

## HOPE IS NECESSARY

Hope is a very important partner of faith. You are reading this book because you hope to receive some insight into faith and confession. But hope alone will not give you that insight. Yet, if it wasn't for hope, you wouldn't have opened the book.

When the sick come into a prayer line they hope to be healed. If they didn't have hope, they wouldn't come for prayer. Since faith is the substance of **things hoped for,** then **there has to be some hope,** or there wouldn't be anything for faith to give substance to.

This will explain to you why some have died, even though they were saying all the right things. Some say, *"I just don't understand why they died."* They gave up hope and there was nothing for faith to give substance to.

## GOD'S WORD GAVE HOPE TO ABRAHAM

I like what Abraham did when there was no hope.

*(As it is written, I have made thee a father of many nations,) before him whom he believed, even God, who quickeneth the dead, and calleth those things which be not as though they were.*

*Who against hope believed in hope, that he might become the father of many nations, according to that which was spoken, So shall thy seed be.*

*(Romans 4:17-18)*

When there was no hope, Abraham believed in hope. There are people today who have no hope **medically.** Doctors have done all they can do. When the doctor says there is no hope, do what Abraham did: go to the Word of God and get some supernatural hope. That's what Abraham did; he decided to side in with God. That's what we are doing when we make a decision to confess the Word of God. We are coming over to God's point of view by saying what God declared about us.

Some might say, *"There is no hope, so you might as well give up."* You can **always** go to the Word of God and get some hope. I don't care if it's physical, financial or spiritual. When it **seems** to be hopeless, go to the Word of God. God's Word is filled with hope.

# DON'T WAIT ON HOPE, POSSESS IT

Hope is a goal-setter. You must have a goal. If you didn't set any goals, if you don't know where you were going, then how would you know when you got there? How long would it take you to get there? You don't know where you are going and you don't know how to get there, unless you have a goal set.

Faith is the substance of things **hoped for. There has to be some direction of faith.** I have seen people who said, *"Well, I'm just waiting on God. I'm just believing God."*

Some of those people are still waiting, and they haven't done anything. They are not waiting on God — God has been waiting on them. You have to make some decisions based on God's Word.

When there was no hope, Abraham decided to believe in hope. **He made a decision** to believe God's Word. That is where his hope came from — the Word of God. Don't try to use faith where hope should be, and don't try to use hope where faith should be. **Hope has no substance.** Faith is the substance of the thing hoped for. So there must be faith and there must be hope. They are partners. Faith is the divine energy of God. It comes from the Word of God and it comes by hearing God's Word. It is the substance of things desired.

In the last chapter we talked about sowing the seed of God's Word. Our words being seeds, we speak the Word of God — the promise of God — into our heart, and then it springs forth and grows up. First the blade, then the ear, then the full corn in the ear. In Mark 4:28 it was established by Jesus that the heart was the production center. Jesus called it the soil.

## REVELATION COMES BY THE SPIRIT

The heart is the production center; Paul adds some light to this subject in First Corinthians, chapter two.

*But as it is written, Eye hath not seen, nor ear heard, neither have entered into the heart of man, the things which God hath prepared for them that love him.*

*But God hath revealed them unto us by his Spirit: for the Spirit searcheth all things, yea, the deep things of God.*                    (I Corinthians 2:9-10)

*"Eye hath not seen, ear hath not heard."* How many times have you heard people quote this scripture and add, *"You never know what God is going to do."* But **you will if you read verse** 10. ***"But God has revealed them to us by His Spirit."***

He is telling us these things won't enter into the heart of man through the natural five senses realm. You cannot get revelation knowledge into your spirit through the five physical senses. But **God reveals them** to us by His Spirit.

God's Spirit bears witness with our spirit and reveals the revelation knowledge of the Word of God. God will do everything He said He will do. God will do everything He promised to do. He will do everything you believe Him to do. But these things have not entered into the heart of man through the **natural eye** or the **natural ear.** But it did enter into the heart of man by revelation, for God has revealed it to us **by His Spirit.** Therefore, God did reveal it, but it didn't come through the five senses.

God has an avenue through which He reveals things. Sometimes it bypasses the carnal mind. God reveals by the Holy Spirit. He is our teacher and guide.

## THE HUMAN SPIRIT SEARCHES

In First Corinthians 2:10, both uses of the word *"Spirit"* are capitalized. The first part of the verse says, *"But God hath revealed them to us by **His Spirit**."* This is referring to the Holy Spirit. But where it says, *"for the '**Spirit**' searcheth all things, yea the deep things of God,"* that is not referring to the Holy Spirit. That refers to the human spirit — your spirit.

> *The spirit of man is the candle of the Lord, searching all the inward parts of the belly.*
>
> *(Proverbs 20:27)*

The human spirit is the light bulb that God uses to enlighten you. God's Spirit beareth witness with your spirit. God's Spirit bears witness with our spirit and enlightens our spirit. *"For **the spirit** searcheth all things, yea the deep things of God."* I believe he is referring to the human spirit. For the Holy Spirit does not need to search the things of God. The Holy Spirit already knows the things of God. It's the human spirit that searches the things of God. When you are asleep, the seeds you have planted in the heart are producing. And you don't really know how. All you did was sow it, and go to bed and get up.

## YOUR SPIRIT KNOWS — GOD'S SPIRIT KNOWS

> *For what man knoweth the things of a man, save the spirit of man which is in him? even so the things of God knoweth no man, but the Spirit of God.*
>
> *(I Corinthians 2:11)*

God's Spirit knows all about God, and your spirit knows all about you. If you get your spirit in contact with God's Spirit, you have tapped the source of all knowledge.

> *Now we have received, not the spirit of the world, but the spirit which is of God; that we might know the things that are freely given to us of God.*
>
> *(I Corinthians 2:12)*

We need to connect this with what the apostle Paul said in verse nine. *"Eye hath not seen, ear hath not heard, neither hath entered into the heart of man,"* through the natural five senses. You didn't see it by the physical eye, you didn't hear it with the natural ear, but God revealed it. It came into the spirit. It came by revelation of the Holy Spirit into your spirit. *"The spirit searches all things, yea the deep things of God."* So after you **sow the seed into your heart,** and sleep at night and are busy during the day, your spirit searches for the wisdom and revelation of God regarding ways and means to bring that seed into production. Then you will wake up some morning with an idea that came from the Spirit of God into your heart, and you didn't know when or how it came.

Verse 12 states that **God gave us the human spirit. We are spirit beings so that He could reveal the things of God to us.**

> *Which things also we speak, not in the words which man's wisdom teacheth, but which the Holy Ghost teacheth; comparing spiritual things with spiritual.*
>
> *But the natural man receiveth not the things of the Spirit of God: for they are foolishness unto him: neither can he know them, because they are spiritually discerned.* (I Corinthians 2:13-14)

## COMPARING SPIRITUAL THINGS

We must compare spiritual things with spiritual. The spirit of man contacts the Spirit of God to find revelation knowledge of these things concerning our everyday life. We don't gain revelation knowledge through the carnal mind. It comes into the spirit.

The natural physical body does not receive the things of the Spirit of God; but the things of the Spirit of God are received into the human spirit, which is the production center.

> *But he that is spiritual judgeth all things, yet he himself is judged of no man.* (I Corinthians 2:15)

Who is **he that is spiritual**? Now notice he said to compare spiritual things with spiritual. He that is spiritual, or the part of you that is spiritual, is the inner man or the spirit. Your spirit judges all things. Your human spirit picks up things about other people that you do not understand with your natural mind. It has not been revealed to you through the eye, or the natural ear, or any of the five senses. You sense some things and you don't know how you know, but you know.

## ENLIGHTENED BY YOUR SPIRIT

You may meet someone, and it seems like your spirit says, *"Get away from them. Don't have anything to do with them,"* and you don't know why. Your spirit will draw up in a knot. Your spirit is searching all things, and it found something, and is warning you. *"He that is spiritual judges all things, but yet he himself is judged of no man."* You cannot judge what is in my spirit; you may only judge my actions.

> *For who hath known the mind of the Lord, that he may instruct him? But we have the mind of Christ.* (I Corinthians 2:16)

We gain the knowledge of the mind of Christ by the Holy Spirit, and through the human spirit.

The spirit of man is truly the light of the Lord. Let's put these two things together. In Mark 4:26, the heart of man is referred to as the soil. It is where you plant the seed of the Word of God so it can produce. It is the

Spirit that reveals things to you and gains the knowledge. **God has given us His Spirit so that we might receive the things of the Spirit of God.** The heart is the reception center. When you speak words, you are sowing seed. When you are speaking the Word of God, you are sowing an incorruptible seed. That seed will not fail. Yet it is possible for your action or inaction to cause a harvest failure. The seed will not fail. What we do with the seed could cause a production failure.

## SLOTHFUL MAN PROPHESIES HIS OWN DOOM

In Proverbs 22:13 we find this statement:

*The slothful man saith, There is a lion without, I shall be slain in the streets.*

The slothful man is one who isn't going to do anything, just sits there and says, *"I'll be eaten."* He doesn't even run. He could at least make an effort to get out of the street. **But he prophesies his own doom.** Those who don't want to act on the Word of God are doing that all the time. *"Well, you know, we're all going under." "Nothing is ever going to work out." "The world's going to blow up in one big atomic blast and we're all going to be doomed."* The slothful prophesies his own doom.

## NATURAL THINGS
## REFLECT SPIRITUAL THINGS

We are capable of conceiving God's Word in our spirit, bringing forth production of what God said in His Word. We are still talking about goal-setting. Hope is a goal-setter. We are talking about how to set goals.

Sometimes when we see these things in the Bible, we tend to take them completely out of their natural setting. When Jesus talked about sowing a seed, He didn't take it away from the soil and say this is a spiritual thing, and it is totally different from sowing a natural seed. **We make a serious mistake when we totally separate the natural from the spiritual.** God's Word is spiritual, but it works like a natural seed. The heart of man is spiritual, but it works like natural soil.

Let me give you an illustration of how the heart is designed to produce. We will bring it down to a natural level of your own house. There is a piece of equipment outside your house that is called a heating and air conditioning unit. It is the heart of that heating and cooling system.

That unit has been designed by an engineer to control the temperature of your house. That's all it was designed to do. It is designed to produce whatever you dial into that little thermostat on the wall, which we will call a goal-setter. The heart of that unit was designed to produce in your house whatever temperature you dial into that thermostat. The numbers on that thermostat represent degrees of temperature. Let's say it's 100 degrees outside, and you want the temperature to be 70 degrees inside. Your job would be to turn that goal-setter to 70 degrees. As long as it is kept on 70 degrees, that unit will work night and day to see that the goal is reached.

You wouldn't have to lay down on the floor and cry and fast and pray that it would get cool in your house. The unit knows how to do it. That is all it was designed to do. You would simply dial the goal-setter and it would send an impulse to the heart of that unit and say, *"Get us some cold air in here it's hot."* With the thermostat on 70 degrees, when it's 100 degrees outside, you have created a problem for the heart of that unit. But it can handle it. That is all it knows to do, but it can do it well.

That unit won't wash your clothes, it won't cook your dinner, it won't keep your house. It wasn't designed to do those things. It was designed for one purpose only: to produce what you have dialed into the goal-setter.

## HEART PRODUCES

Now let's relate this to the heart of man. The heart of the heating-cooling unit is like the heart of a man. You must set the goal for the thing you want produced. Faith is the substance of things hoped for, and hope is the goal-setter. And hope works in the head. What you speak becomes your goal. It is controlled by the head. Your head is the goal-setter. When there is no hope, there is no goal set for the better — although it may set negative goals. Like the thermostat on the wall, your words spoken send an impulse down into your spirit.

By saying, *"In the name of Jesus, by His stripes I am healed; I am redeemed from the curse of the law, and I forbid sickness and disease in this body,"* you set your goal on healing.

What are you doing by that action? Someone may say, *"You are lying, because you are sick."*

No, you are setting your goal. Some people will say that because they don't understand how you can say you are healed by the stripes of Jesus when you hurt. You must decide to plant that goal regardless of present circumstances.

Let's say it is 90 degrees in your house and you come in and turn the thermostat down to 70 degrees. Someone says, *"Hey! You can't do that, that's a lie. It's not 70 degrees in here."*

Well, you know it. That's the reason you set it on 70. You are calling for that temperature. You are calling for those things that are not manifest. That is the way the system is designed. That is the only way it will work. If you set 90 degrees in the thermostat when it is 90 degrees already, there will be no change. The unit will be inactive, producing nothing.

## HEART IS TRUE TO DEMAND PLACED ON IT

Surely no one would be foolish enough in natural things to argue with you when you turned the thermostat to 70 degrees. But they will, when you set your goal on God's promises. Some will argue that you are lying. You have to give some time and meditation to these things to fully understand the design of the heart of man. I know this is a hypothetical situation, and I am using natural things to relate to it. That is the way Jesus taught. It's easy to understand the way that goal-setter on the thermostat works. Faith and confession work that way on your heart. You may not believe it works that way. You may not like it because it works that way, but that is the way it works.

No one would argue with you about turning that thermostat, and nobody would call you a liar. They wouldn't accuse you of trying to live in a world of fantasy because you turned the goal-setter to 70 degrees. For they understand that it will be 70 degrees in the room in a few minutes.

The heart of man is like the heart of that heating-cooling unit. It is designed of God to produce the very thing that you set in it. You put the goal in the goal-setter by speaking it. We talked in another chapter about the tape recorder. When you first heard your voice on a tape recorder, you thought it was someone else. You couldn't believe it was you, because you have been hearing yourself with your inner ear. Your voice is picked up by the inner ear and fed directly into the human spirit. When you heard your voice on the tape recorder you heard it for the first time totally with the outer ear, and you could not believe it was you.

God designed you that way so your voice would feed the impulse of what you desired right down into the garden spot, into the heart, the soil. There it will produce what you are speaking. It is also renewing your mind as you are confessing God's Word.

Suppose someone turns the thermostat to 70 degrees, and then in a little while they turn it to 95. Then, they turn it to 60. It is just going up and down. It will not work properly that way. It will end up blowing a fuse or a circuit somewhere. It is not designed to be flipped from one extreme to the other all at once. It will blow a circuit.

Someone might say, *"Who in the world would be dumb enough to do that?"* Christians do that all the time. They start making faith confessions: *"Glory to God, my needs are met according to His riches in glory by Christ Jesus."* They say that for a little while, then they face the circumstances and say, *"Dear God, it's never going to happen. We will never get these debts paid. I don't know what we are going to do."*

Well, you just changed the thermostat. You have to set it where you want it and leave it there. That unit will work day and night to produce what you have dialed into it. It will never fuss about it, it will never argue with you.

## UNIT DOES NOT MAKE DECISION

Have you ever heard a heating-cooling unit say, *"No, we're not sending cold air. We believe you need hot air, so we're kindling up the fire. We're going to send you some heat."*

If it did that, we would have to say, *"Well, you just never know what that unit is going to do. It has a mind of its own."*

But it doesn't work that way. It is consistent. It always produces the very thing you call for by setting the thermostat.

This is how the heart (spirit) of man is designed.

*The spirit of man is the candle of the Lord, searching all the inward parts of his belly.*

Mark 4:26 tells you the way it works. It is as if a man cast the seed into the ground. That is setting the goal-setter. A seed to a farmer is a goal-setter. If you want to know what goal you have set for your garden, just look and see what seeds you have planted. It will come up just like you planted. You plant the seed and it works. You go to bed and get up. You don't have to hope to God that it will work. It will work because it's designed that way.

## THERMOSTATS HAVE NO SUBSTANCE

Suppose someone who had never seen a thermostat or a heating-cooling unit saw you turn the thermostat to 70 degrees when the room was 90 degrees. It began to get cool when the fan started blowing cool air. He wonders why it was getting so cool. He wants to know what you did.

*"What is that little box on the wall?"*

You say, *"That's a thermostat."*

*"A thermostat. Where can I get one?"*

You can see what he has in mind. He goes down to the hardware store and buys a thermostat. He goes out to his cabin and nails it on the wall. Then he turns it to 70 degrees and sits down and starts to grin.

But it isn't going to work. He gets up and beats on that thing and says, *"Why isn't it working?"*

## THERMOSTAT MAKES DEMAND

It is only a goal-setter. It was never designed to work that way. There is no substance in the thermostat to cool a room. Yet it sends the impulse (goal) to be met. Faith is the substance of things hoped for. Let's say it another way. Faith is substance of everything needed to accomplish the goal hoped for. That cooling unit has electricity connected to it and is available at any time the thermostat makes a demand on it.

That heating-cooling unit won't produce anything by itself. There must be a goal-setter, and you must dial the goal. This is the same way you set goals inside of you. Hope is a goal-setter for you. Always speak your hope. So your goals for your heart are set by speaking those things in faith. Whether that unit feels like it or not, when that thermostat's impulse goes to that unit, it releases the energy that is available, and it immediately starts producing the things you dialed into it.

## YOUR HOPE MAKES DEMAND BY SPEAKING

That is the way the heart of man works. You take the Word of God and you speak it. You set the goal. The divine energy is in God's Word to cause the heart to bring forth the manifestation of it. Even in the summertime, the energy that is bringing forth cool air in a building is the same energy that brings hot air in the wintertime. **The goal-setter is the thing that determines whether it is hot air or cold air. If you are not satisfied with the harvest you're getting, check up on the goal you are setting,** and the seed you are sowing.

That unit won't argue with you. It is not going to argue that you don't need hot air when you send for cold air. It is not designed to decide whether it is right or wrong. It is only designed to produce whatever impulse you send into it.

# SAYING SETS THE THERMOSTAT
# OF YOUR HEART

Jesus says the heart of man is that way. For he will have whatsoever he sayeth. Saying it is the setting of goals. Sometimes we have separated natural things from spiritual things so far that most people believe there is no relationship between them. But Jesus brings them back together when He says, *"If you have faith as a seed you would say. . ."* (Luke 17:6)

Then in Genesis, chapter eight, God says,

*While the earth remaineth, seedtime and harvest, and cold and heat, and summer and winter, and day and night shall not cease.* (Genesis 8:22)

That's the way it works. The Bible keeps referring to sowing. You sow the seeds, you reap a harvest. Whatsoever a man soweth, he shall reap.

The soil in your garden doesn't decide whether what you plant in it is right or wrong. **The soil will produce whatever you plant in it.** Some believe that the human spirit, or the heart of a born again man would not produce anything bad. Ask yourself this question then. Why do some people backslide and go back into sin? Jesus said it this way.

*A good man out of the good treasure of the heart bringeth forth good things: and an evil man out of the evil treasure bringeth forth evil things.* (Matthew 12:35)

I am convinced from what Jesus taught that even a person who is born again can put evil things in his heart. God considers anything that is contrary to His Word to be evil. (Numbers 13:33)

## THE SOIL NEVER ARGUES

I was a farmer for thirty years before I went into the ministry. Never in all the years that I farmed did I plant soybeans and have the ground say to me, *"We aren't going to raise soybeans, we are going to raise cucumbers and bananas."*

Some have gotten the idea that it doesn't matter what they sow, and it doesn't matter what they say, because they say, *"Well, God knows what I meant."*

Would you say, *"I planted radishes, but the soil knew what I meant. I meant to plant tomatoes."*

Certainly not. No one would be that foolish in the natural. You would know you were not going to have any tomatoes, because the soil just doesn't work that way. Just so, the soil of your heart does not decide whether what you plant (say) is right or wrong. Your heart's job is to produce the information needed to cause what you are saying (planting) to come to pass, whether it is right, wrong, or indifferent.

**Mark 11:23 is not a one way street.** But Jesus only told how to operate it on the positive side. He didn't want you to operate the principle on the negative side.

*For verily I say unto you, That whosoever shall say unto this mountain, Be thou removed, and be thou cast into the sea; and shall not doubt in his heart, but shall believe that those things which he saith shall come to pass; he shall have whatsoever he saith.*                                                   *(Mark 11:23)*

## BELIEVE THAT THOSE THINGS YOU SOW WILL COME TO PASS

He tells us to set the goal on removing the mountain, the tremendous problems that are before us. On the other hand, it will work just as fast on the negative side.

Some say, *"This mountain is getting bigger every day. I'll never get over it."*

They are right, because they are working it on the negative side. It will work just as quick, and sometimes quicker on the negative side. Some prophesy that things are getting worse, we will never make it, we will never pay our debts, we will never get this church going.

They are speaking that into the soil. It will cause their spirit to search the avenues of God's wisdom to find a way to bring it to pass.

Remember, the unit won't decide whether you need heat or cold, it just responds to the signal sent from the goal-setter. Hope is a goal-setter or thermostat to your heart (spirit). If you have no hope, there is no impulse sent to the heart, and there will be no production. Even though there is substance in the heart (faith), without **hope** there is no goal to give substance to. Hope causes you to speak the promise.

It is not going to work just because you say it a few times, but it will eventually produce.

Several years ago, when I grasped this truth, I started confessing that I am redeemed from the curse, and in the name of Jesus I forbid sickness to operate in my body — even though I had ulcers. Every so often I would be laid up for two or three days a week, and I couldn't do anything. I drank Maalox by the bottle. I started confessing the Word of God concerning my healing.

Over a period of about three months, it began to get into my spirit. After about three months, the ulcers left my body. They tried to come back a few times. But I would say, *"No, in the name of Jesus I have received my healing."* I am healed. I am well. I am delivered from the curse of sickness.

# CONCEPTION BEFORE MANIFESTATION

I learned how to operate in these principles through trial and error. I made some mistakes, but I continued to confess that I am redeemed from the curse. I confessed I am redeemed from poison ivy. But when I would come in contact with poison ivy it would get on me. Just about every time I went deer hunting, I got poison ivy. Someone said, *"Your confession is not working, is it?"*

I would reply, *"Yes, it's working. Faith is coming; faith is coming."*

I was setting a goal. I kept confessing it, and kept confessing it.

What happened? I got poison ivy again.

What did I do? I put Calamine lotion on it and it dried up. And I kept confessing the Word. I kept speaking it. This happened several times before the manifestation came. It took time to conceive it in my heart by faith.

Remember, faith in the heart is the ability of the heart to conceive God's promise. Once it is conceived, you will eventually have a manifestation.

I continued this for about a year, and then noticed that poison ivy didn't bother me anymore. The corresponding action that I had toward what I believed was that I continued to confess it, even though all natural circumstances and the bumps on my arms and hands said that I was not redeemed from it. I kept saying what God's Word said. I was redeemed from it. (Galatians 3:13, Deuteronomy 28:61)

# GOD'S WORD OVER ALL MATTER

Some people say, *"That's mind over matter."*

But it's not. **It's faith in God and His Word over all matter.** I continued that until it got into my spirit.

216

When it got into my spirit, it manifested itself in my physical body. If I had said, *"I am going to have full corresponding action toward what I'm saying and pull poison ivy off the trees with my bare hands,"* I would have been in trouble. I was just beginning to sow it in my spirit. I couldn't have had full corresponding action toward what I was saying until I had the full manifestation. After a year it didn't affect my body. Now **I can have full corresponding action toward poison ivy.** My skin does not react to it. But it took about a year to conceive God's Word and have it become true in my body. These things are not going to happen overnight. But they will happen, if we are diligent to agree with God and confess what He said about us is true.

## PROCESS OF TIME

Confession of God's Word is a process of renewing the mind. It is causing faith to come. It is being built inside of you. The heart conceives what you are saying and brings the manifestation of it. This is the way it works in your physical body, in your finances, in every situation of life.

**But it takes time. It take a process. This is not a fad. This is a way of life.** This is not something that you try. If you are just going to try it, then it won't work for you. If I had been trying it, then the first time I got poison ivy, I would have said, *"It doesn't work. We can chunk that one; forget it."* But it never occurred to me that it might not work, because Jesus said that it would.

## PRACTICE INCREASES PRODUCTION

Once you find out that these are Bible principles, study them and practice them. Don't back off from them every time things appear to get worse. Just stay with it and confess it until you get developed in it. That doesn't mean that you wouldn't use medicine if it was necessary. Yes, I used Calamine lotion. I took Maalox and everything else I could find to keep the symptoms down until I received the manifestation.

Don't come under condemnation because you take medicine. So many allow the enemy to condemn them just because they take medicine. Don't let anyone force you into operating on their level of faith **if you are not developed to that level.** Use some common sense. Start where you are. Operate on your level. Your faith will grow and your productivity will increase.

## Chapter Eleven

# WHY THE CONFESSION WORKS

Confession is a way to possess the things God has already given by the word of promise. But many fail to grasp this Bible principle. Some run into the ditch on the right side of the road and some run into the ditch on the left side of the road because they have not understood this principle.

When you really understand faith and confession, you can rightly apply it to your life and stay out of the ditch.

There are those who will say, *"This is too mechanical; you are just trying to force God into something."*

No, this is God's principle of faith and confession. Confession is a way to possession. It isn't the only way, but it's one Bible way.

I want you to see what Jesus said about the parable of the sower.

*Hear ye therefore the parable of the sower.*

*When any one heareth the word of the kingdom,* **and understandeth it not,** *then cometh the wicked one, and catcheth away that which was sown in his heart. This is he which received seed by the way side.* (Matthew 13:18-19)

The account of this parable in Mark 4:14-20 is a little different from Matthew's. Let's compare it with Mark 4:15.

*And these are they by the way side, where the word is sown; but when they have heard, Satan cometh immediately, and taketh away the Word that was sown in their hearts.* (Mark 4:15)

219

Mark says when the seed of the Word of God is sown in the heart, Satan comes immediately and takes away the Word. If you read this account and don't read the account in Matthew, you would think that Satan can steal the Word from a person's heart just any time he wants to. But he can't.

Matthew 13:19 says, *"he that heareth the Word of the kingdom **and understandeth it not."*** This is the reason why it's so easy for Satan to steal the Word from some people. **They heard it, but didn't understand it.** If you understand the Word of God that is sown, Satan cannot steal it from you. It can't be taken from you. Jesus established this point with Martha when she was concerned about Mary sitting at the feet of Jesus, hearing the Word.

> *Martha, Martha thou art careful and troubled about many things:*
>
> *But one thing is needful: and Mary hath chosen that good part, **which shall not be taken away from her.*** *(Luke 10:41-42)*

Jesus said the Word that Mary was receiving wouldn't be taken away from her. It wouldn't be taken from her by Satan, for she would understand the Word when Jesus taught it. That's why teaching is so important. That's why we are doing so much teaching on faith and confession. If it is taught accurately, more people will understand and stop Satan from stealing the Word.

There are primarily seven reasons why the confession of God's Word works for you.

## THE SEED MUST BE SOWN

**The FIRST reason the confession of God's Word works is because it is sowing the seed in the kingdom.**

*So is the kingdom of God, as if a man should cast seed into the ground.* (Mark 4:26)

In essence, that scripture says you are sowing seed in the kingdom, which is in the heart.

*And should sleep, and rise night and day, and the seed should spring and grow up, he knoweth not how.* (Mark 4:27)

It is not necessary that you completely understand God's method. This is a principle of God. Just have faith to do it. Be obedient to God's Word and do what He said to do. Hold fast to your confession of faith.

But it helps when you can understand it. Study these things and meditate on them. The more understanding you get of the Word of God, the harder it is for Satan to steal it from you.

There are times when people hear the Word and receive it with gladness. But when affliction and persecution come because of the Word, they are immediately offended. The major problem was **they didn't really understand it.** You have to mix faith with God's Word.

Sowing in the kingdom is the number one reason for success in any area. When you confess God's Word, you are sowing seeds. Mark 4:26 says, *"as if **a man** should cast seed into the ground."* God doesn't sow the seed. The man does it.

The seed is specifically the Word of God. It could be words which are not exactly God's Word, but which are in agreement with God. Then, you could sow the devil's words in your heart, if you spoke what the devil said.

What you confess is important to you. If God said it, it's an established truth. But we have to agree with it. We need to add our faith to it and speak it. Sowing in the kingdom is what God has given us to do.

No one else is going to do it for us. We must speak the Word of God. It becomes a seed that is sown in the heart. **Faith works in the heart. Faith won't work in your head.**

Learn this principle. It is not the saying alone that causes the manifestation in your life. The saying is not an end in itself. However, saying it is involved in causing the manifestation.

## CARNAL MIND NOT SUBJECT TO LAW OF GOD

The head, the carnal mind, is the goal-setter, working through our words. Faith works in the heart. Faith will not work in your head. Some people try to get faith to work out of their head. It will give you a headache! The carnal mind was not designed to operate in the laws of God. Paul gives us insight to this in Romans 8.

> *Because the carnal mind is enmity against God: for it is not subject to the law of God, neither indeed can be.* *(Romans 8:7)*

The law he is referring to is **the law of faith.** Your head will not operate in that law, because it wasn't designed to do so. Your head is a goal-setter. You think with it. What you speak is a product of thought and meditation.

Just because you said something, that doesn't mean it is going to happen. Yet, many things will never happen unless you say it, because it sets the goal.

## IT CAUSES FAITH TO COME

**The SECOND reason why confession of God's Word works for you is that it causes faith to come.**

Setting the goal, the speaking of it, is sowing seeds in the kingdom of God within you.

Some may say, *"If you sow a seed, you only need to sow it once."* But if a farmer wants 300 acres of wheat, he doesn't sow just one acre and say, *"Well, I have the wheat."* He must sow more seed. Sow seeds in the kingdom and **continue to speak** what God said about your situation. It can be in the area of physical healing, finances, or spiritual matters. Speak what God said about you. You speak it, you say it, you confess it. **Speaking it causes faith to come.**

*So then faith cometh by **hearing,** and hearing by the Word of God.*     *(Romans 10:17)*

It did not say that faith cometh by having heard. People sometimes say, *"Well, I've heard that before. I have already said that once."*

**Faith cometh by hearing, and hearing, and hearing, and hearing, and hearing, and hearing.** It's a continual process, and faith cometh. This faith is the substance of things. Remember, hope has no substance, but faith is the substance of things hoped for. Yet, without hope you wouldn't have anything for faith to give substance to.

You set the goal — you plant the seed — by speaking the desired promise. Get in agreement with it. Let your mouth be in agreement with it. That causes faith to come, for faith in God comes by hearing the Word of God. On the other hand, **faith in the devil comes by hearing the words of the devil.** If you are always hearing the words of the devil, then you are probably wondering why you don't have any faith in God. Hearing words of the devil produces fear. Faith is the substance of things hoped for or desired. Then the opposite of faith is fear, which would be the substance of things not desired. You only need to read the book of Job to see this truth. Job said,

*For the thing which I greatly feared is come upon me, and that which I was afraid of is come unto me.* (Job 3:25)

Job didn't just fear; he was highly developed in it. The more highly developed you get in either your faith or your fear, the quicker the manifestation will come. **The words you are speaking will either cause faith to come or cause fear to come. Words transmit faith, and words transmit fear.**

## THIRD REASON — IT RENEWS THE MIND

Did you know that your mind didn't get born again just because you got born again? The apostle Paul said it this way in Romans 12:2.

*And be not conformed to this world; but be ye transformed by the renewing of your mind.*

Paul is writing to the church, the Roman church. He instructed them to do something about their mind. *"Be not conformed to the world, but be ye transformed **by the renewing of your mind.**"*

Confession of God's Word, speaking in agreement with what God says, causes your mind to be renewed to think like God thinks. This in turn will cause you to talk like God talks. Then eventually, talking like God talks will cause you to walk like God walks — in victory over defeat.

If we don't get out minds renewed, we may get into a situation like Peter did when he jumped out of the boat and wasn't ready to walk like Jesus walked.

Peter jumped out of the boat before he was ready. He had learned to talk the talk, but not to walk the walk. Circumstances put him down. Jesus said,

*"Come,"* and there was enough faith in that one word to cause Peter to be able to walk on the water. The problem was that his mind was not renewed. He allowed something that had nothing at all to do with what he was doing to **cause him to begin to sink.**

Think about it for a minute. He had never seen anyone walk on the water, with the exception of Jesus, and that was while the wind was blowing, and they were in a storm. The logical way of thinking about that situation would have been to say, *"I've never seen anyone walk on the water before. I guess the only time you can walk on the water is when the wind is blowing and it is storming."*

Peter stepped out of the boat and walked on the water. But then he began to look at circumstances. He saw the high waves and heard the boisterous wind.

What did that have to do with it? Nothing! Peter allowed circumstances that had nothing to do with walking on the water to cause him to sink.

> *But when he saw the wind boisterous, he was afraid and beginning to sink, he cried, saying, Lord save me.* (Matthew 14:30)

**Fear will put you under the circumstances.** That is why your mind must be renewed in God's knowledge so you won't place circumstances above the Word of God. It is important for you to renew your mind. Do as the apostle Paul said the Colossians had done.

> *. . .ye have put off the old man with his deeds;*
>
> *And have put on the new man, which is **renewed in knowledge** after the image of him that created him.* (Colossians 3:9-10)

225

# KEEP THE ANSWER BEFORE YOU

**The FOURTH reason the confession of God's Word works is that it keeps the answer before you.**

If you are always facing the problem, speaking the problem, praying the problem, then **you will have faith in the problem.** If you are always talking your problems to others, then **you really do have a problem.** If you go to the Lord and say, *"Lord, I have this problem,"* and *"I can't get rid of this problem; it grows bigger every day,"* then **you really do have a problem.**

All you are seeing is the problem. When you wake up in the morning, you see the problem. When you go to bed at night, you are thinking the problem. You eat, sleep and drink the problem. The problem has consumed you — your time, your thoughts, and your prayers. **And faith cometh by hearing.** You will have great faith in the problem, and none in the answer.

But when you begin to renew your mind and begin to keep the answer before you by confessing the Word of God, some will say, *"Oh, you're just ignoring the problem."*

On the contrary, you are doing something about it. When you get accused of ignoring the problem, just quote this scripture.

> *Be careful for nothing; but in every thing by prayer and supplication with thanksgiving let your requests be made known unto God.*
>
> *And the peace of God, which passeth all understanding, shall keep your hearts and minds through Christ Jesus.*
>
> *Finally, brethren, whatsoever things are true, whatsoever things are honest, whatsoever things are just, whatsoever things are pure, whatsoever things are lovely, whatsoever things are of good*

*report; if there be any virtue, and if there be any
praise, think on these things.    (Philippians 4:6-8)*

Paul began with, *"Finally, brethren."* In other
words, this will wrap up the whole thing: whatsoever
things are true, honest, pure, lovely, just, and of good
report, **think on these things.**

Everyone wants to have the peace of God that
passeth all understanding. But not many want to do
what the Bible says to do in order to obtain it. They
want a shortcut. **They want to have the peace of God,
but they also want to confess the problem and pray
the problem.** The more you pray the problem, the more
faith you will have in the problem.

You will never solve a problem by dwelling on the
problem itself. You have to get off the problem and get
over onto the answer. God's Word keeps **the answer**
before you. As you do that, your attitude will change.
You will become a different person. If you see the
problem, if you believe the problem, if you talk the
problem, **you end up being the problem.**

> *Therefore I say unto you, What things soever ye
> desire, when ye pray, believe that ye receive them,
> and ye shall have them.    (Mark 11:24)*

What things? **Those things you prayed.** Even if you
are praying the problem, you are going to have the
things that you prayed. Jesus said,

> *For your Father knoweth what things ye have
> need of, before ye ask him.    (Matthew 6:8)*

So you are not required to pray the problem, or tell
God the problem. He already knows the problem. Isaiah
says,

> *Put me in remembrance: Let us plead together:
> declare thou, that thou mayest be justified.*
> *(Isaiah 43:26)*

227

God said, *"Call to My remembrance what I have said. Remind Me of My Word."* That doesn't mean God is forgetful. You are not doing it for His benefit. It's for your benefit, because faith cometh by hearing. It is not going to make God's faith stronger because He heard it. It's to make your faith stronger because you spoke it and heard it.

If you pray the answer, your faith will grow while you are praying. If you pray the problem, your fears will grow while you are praying.

**Some Christians destroy their faith by their praying.** That is neither the will nor the direction of God. Prayer is not for the destruction of your faith. Prayer is to obtain the answer — whatsoever things you desire. I do not desire the problem, so I don't pray the problem.

I traveled that religious road of praying for twenty years of my Christian life, and I seldom saw a prayer answered. If I did, it was just a faith accident.

Someone stated it this way, and I think it's a good illustration. It's about 35 miles from Dallas to Fort Worth, Texas. If you started out from Dallas to Fort Worth, and drove for three years and didn't get there, wouldn't you know you were on the wrong road? Surely it wouldn't take you three years to figure that out.

Here I was, traveling that religious road of praying **for twenty years.** I never did get where I was going. But when I found in the scriptures that I was supposed to pray the answer instead of the problem, **I got more prayers answered in two weeks than I did in the previous twenty years.**

This will help some of you save twenty years of your life. You **don't** pray the problem. You **pray the answer. Praying the problem is a big problem.**

Notice in Isaiah,

*So shall my word be that goeth forth out of my mouth: it shall not return unto me void, but it shall accomplish that which I please, and it shall prosper in the thing whereto I sent it.*

*(Isaiah 55:11)*

Who is going to return God's Word to Him? He is expecting you to do that. If you return God's Word to Him, it will cause your faith to grow. **It will renew your mind, and it will plant seeds in the kingdom.** God is not trying to make it hard on you. He's trying to make it easy for you.

## CHANGE YOUR HEART

**The FIFTH reason why confession of God's Word works is that it changes your heart.**

Proverbs 4:20-23 gives good advice on this subject.

*My son, attend to my words; incline thine ear unto my sayings.*

*Let them not depart from thine eyes; keep them in the midst of thine heart.*

*For they are life unto those that find them, and health (medicine) to all their flesh.*

*Keep thy heart with all diligence; for out of it are the issues of life.*

You are the one to keep, or guard your heart with all diligence, for out of it are the issues, or forces of life. That is why it's important for us to change our heart. According to Mark 4, our heart can get filled with thorns and stones.

The soil will try as hard to make a stone produce as it will a seed. It does the same thing to a stone as it does to a seed. But the stone will not produce, because there is no life in it. That's why you have to get the stones out of your heart. That's why the parable of the sower said the seed that was sown on stony ground didn't produce. **The soil will give as much time and moisture to a stone as it will to a seed,** but there is no life in the stone. The Word of God is the incorruptible seed, so you must get the stones out and sow the Word. That's what we are doing with this teaching; we are getting some of the stones out so this Word can take root.

## SET THE LAW OF FAITH IN MOTION

**The SIXTH reason why the confession of God's Word works for you is that it sets the law of faith in motion.**

There is a law involved. Paul said this in Romans.

*Where is boasting then? It is excluded. By what law? of works? Nay: but by the law of faith.*

*(Romans 3:27)*

Faith is a law. This is the law that Paul is referring to in Romans 8:7, *"Because the carnal mind is enmity against God."* *"Enmity"* means irreconcilable hostility. You cannot believe with your head what you can believe with your heart. You cannot believe with your head that you can speak to a mountain and it will be removed and be cast into the sea. It won't work in your head. It only works in the heart, in your spirit.

But you can renew your mind and reach a point where your head won't fight you over it. The apostle Paul makes this statement.

*We having the same spirit of faith, according as it is written, I believed, and therefore have I spoken; we also believe, and therefore speak.*

*(II Corinthians 4:13)*

That's the way it works. What you believe, you speak. What you speak, you will believe stonger every time you speak it. This process causes faith to come.

Paul is saying that you are really setting this law in motion — the spirit of faith and the law of faith.

Mark 11:23 and Luke 17:6 fall in line with this same thought.

> *Whosoever shall say unto this mountain, Be thou removed and be thou cast into the sea; and shall not doubt in his heart, but shall believe that those things which he saith shall come to pass; he shall have whatsoever he saith.* *(Mark 11:23)*

> *And the Lord said, if ye had faith as a grain of mustard seed, ye might say unto this sycamine tree, Be thou plucked up by the root, and be thou planted in the sea; and it should obey you.*
> *(Luke 17:6)*

All of these things explain how the law of faith is set in motion. It is not going to happen just because you say it. However, saying it is involved in setting it in motion.

That's why we should speak God's Word, even when outward circumstances say that it isn't true in the natural. Some things are true in the Word of God that should be true in our lives. And as far as God is concerned, it's that way. He doesn't have to do a thing. He has already said all He is going to say about it. It's a matter of us setting the law of faith in motion.

People sometimes say, *"Well, where do I start?"*

**You have to start where you are.** Don't ever try to start up there on someone else's level.

Many get into trouble with the faith and confession message at the very start. They are trying to start out beyond their level of development. That is like trying to build a third story on a vacant lot. You must start where you are. You may want to start by confessing that you will get a parking place when you go to town. Develop your faith and confession in the small things. Don't reach out and try to confess a million dollars when you aren't developed to that level. It will work for you in the small things as well as big things. You will finally get to where you can believe God for bigger things. By experience you learn what makes it work, and also what will short it out.

It is possible to make confessions that sound good, and actually be making them in fear. There are people who confess God's Word out of fear. **It sounds good. They say the right things. But they are doing it in fear.**

Your confession must be done in faith. That's why you have to continue to do it. You will speak some things that you won't believe when you first say them. You know it's true in the Bible. You know the Bible is true, but it's not true in your life. If you speak it, confess it, proclaim it long enough, you will believe it. What you speak, you believe.

## PUT THE ANGELS TO WORK FOR YOU

**The SEVENTH reason why the confession of God's Word works for you is that it puts the angels to work for you.**

Many have never realized this, but the angels are listening to the words you speak. The Bible says in Acts 7:53, *"Who have received the law by the disposition of angels."* They were there when the law was given. The angels were involved in it. But Hebrews, chapter one brings the angels much closer to us than the law.

> *But to which of the angels said he at any time, Sit on my right hand, until I make thine enemies thy footstool?*
>
> *Are they not all ministering spirits, sent forth to minister for them who shall be heirs of salvation?*
>
> *(Hebrews 1:13-14)*

This scripture tells us that the angels are ministering spirits sent here to minister to those who are heirs of salvation. And, thank God, that's us. If you are an heir of salvation, then they are here to minister for you. Supernatural beings, angels, the ministering spirits of God **are here to minister for you.**

In Revelation 22, the apostle John said this:

*And I John saw these things, and heard them. And when I had heard and seen, I fell down to worship before the feet of the angel which showed me these things.*

*Then saith he unto me, See thou do it not: for I am thy fellowservant, and of thy brethren the prophets, and of them which keep the sayings of this book: worship God.* (Revelation 22:8-9)

This angel told John, *"Don't worship me, I am your servant."* We haven't realized this fact about angels. And it's time we did. They are our fellowservants. One translation said, *"a fellow slave of yours am I."* The angel said he is a fellowservant of thy brethren the prophets and **of them which keep the sayings of this book.** If you are keeping the sayings of God's Book, then the angels are your servants.

But you can't tell angels to change the oil in your car. (You shouldn't have to say these things, but you do. Otherwise, someone will take this truth and carry it too far.)

Angels are listening to what you say, because what you say has a tremendous effect on what they do. We have thought God is the only one who tells the angels what to do.

## KINGDOM RULES OVER ALL

God does send messages by angels from time to time. Angels are called messengers. Yet sometimes you

233

are giving them assignments. Psalm 103 gives more insight into this.

> *The Lord hath prepared his throne in the heavens; and **his kingdom ruleth over all.***
>
> *Bless the Lord, ye his angels, that excel in strength, that **do his commandments, hearkening unto the voice of his word.*** (Psalm 103:19-20)*

Notice that the kingdom ruleth over all. Where is the kingdom? It is inside of you. God's throne is in the heavens, but His kingdom (inside of you) ruleth over all.

The angels are doing His commandments. What are the commandments of God? David said the words of God are His statutes and His commandments. Mark 11:23 says that if a man will doubt not in his heart, but shall believe that those things which he saith shall come to pass, he shall have whatsoever he saith. The angels know that is a law. They know what the Word of God says. It seems that the angels are on the earth to minister for us, and to make sure that God's Word comes to pass concerning us. They are listening to what you say, because the words you speak in agreement with God's Word gives them assignments.

If you are saying what God said, then you are assigning angels to go and cause that to come into manifestation. You will notice in Psalm 103:20 that the angels **hearken to the voice** of God's Word. The Bible is the Word of God. But you can hold the Bible up to a microphone and it won't say a word. **It has no voice** by itself. **Angels hearken to the voice** — or we could say they **hearken to the sound of God's Word.** If you give voice to God's Word, then the angels will hearken to what you say, for you have given voice or sound to God's Word.

Luke 6 states,

*Give, and it shall be given unto you; good measure, pressed down, and shaken together, and running over, shall men give into your bosom. For with the same measure that ye mete withal it shall be measured to you again.* (Luke 6:38)

If you sow bountifully, you will reap bountifully. (II Corinthians 9:6) You can lay that scripture on your bank balance and it won't cause it to change. But if you **give voice to** that word of promise and begin to confess it, then the angels that are standing by you daily listening to what you say, will hearken to that assignment. They hearken to the sound you give to God's Word. It becomes an assignment to them. God's Word says a man will have what he says, if he believes and doubts not in his heart. If you are believing and not doubting in your heart what you are saying, then the angels' assignment is to make sure you eventually have what you are saying. It may take weeks, it may take months, it may even take years, but just rest assured that they are working on it. They hearken to the voice of God's Word.

*Let the redeemed of the Lord say so. . .*
(Psalm 107:2)

So begin to say, *"Thank God, I am redeemed from the curse of the law and delivered from the authority of darkness, in the name of Jesus. I am blessed coming in and going out; blessed in the basket and in the store. No weapon formed against me will prosper; but thank God, whatever I do will prosper, because I am like a tree planted by the rivers of water."*

By saying this, you have given voice to God's Word, and the angels have been given that assignment to see that God's Word spoken by you comes to pass.

You influence angels by speaking God's Word after Him.

# Chapter Twelve

# HOW TO PUT YOUR CONFESSIONS TO WORK FOR YOU

Sometimes when you tell people to confess the Word of God, they get all kinds of ideas about what you are talking about. Sometimes they think you mean they should go to their banker and quote scriptures to him, when they can't pay their note.

But that's not what we are talking about. We are talking about confessing the Word of God so you can hear yourself say it in order for you to succeed. It's not up to the banker to hear it; it's not up to the neighbors to hear it; God wants you to hear it.

God said to put Him in remembrance of what He said (Isaiah 43:26). It wasn't that God forgot what He had said; He doesn't want you to forget about it. It keeps the answer before you, and it does the seven things that we discussed in previous chapters.

Let's look at how to discipline yourself to confess God's Word. God is not trying to make it difficult for us. He wasn't trying to make it hard for Joshua when He said,

*This book of the law shall not depart out of thy mouth; but thou shalt meditate therein day and night, that thou mayest observe to do according to all that is written therein: for then thou shalt make thy way prosperous, and then thou shalt have good success. (Joshua 1:8)*

Observe to do all that is written therein. In other words, speak it and meditate on it, and then do it. When **you make your way prosperous,** then you will do wisely. One translation says, **you will deal wisely in all the affairs of life,** once you have made your way prosperous.

## PROSPERITY DESTROYS FOOLS

One of the contentions against the prosperity message is that some contend *"prosperity will destroy you."* But the Bible says that prosperity will destroy a fool (Proverbs 1:32). **If** you go by God's method, and confess the Word of God, **then** when you make your way prosperous you will deal wisely in all the affairs of life. It doesn't sound like it's a curse, as some believe. Prosperity is a blessing and not a curse, if it is gained the Bible way.

When you are confessing the Word of God, what you are saying is setting goals, and planting the seed in the soil of the heart. If you don't know where you are going, how would you know when you arrived? And how long would it take you to get there? As we confess God's Word, we establish God's goals by His principles.

Let me share some examples of confessions that are in a little book called *God's Creative Power Will Work For You.* I assembled these confessions in a booklet because the Lord told me to start confessing what God said about me. For I had been confessing what the devil said. So I wrote some scriptural confessions.

I was farming at the time, and I would get on the *'turn-row'* at the back side of the farm and walk up and down that turn-row confessing what God said about me. I spoke it aloud. These confessions changed my life.

Some people say, *"I bought this book, **God's Creative Power Will Work For You** and read it."* **But reading it is not the answer.** You must confess it aloud where you can hear your own voice; that brings faith, because faith cometh by hearing.

Faith does not come by reading. We have assumed that. But the Bible does not say that faith comes by reading. It says that **faith cometh by hearing** the Word of God.

I continued this confession of God's Word for months and months and months. The Word totally changed my life. When I started confessing the Word, I was probably one of the most negative people that you have ever met. But over several month's God's Word changed me, and God's Word will change you.

## DISCIPLINE YOURSELF

I want to show you how to discipline yourself to say what God said about you. You may feel like it's the biggest lie that you have ever let out of your mouth when you say some of these things God said about you. God said it the way He believes you will be. He doesn't see you the way you are, but the way the Word says you are.

Let's go through some of the confessions. All of the confessions from that booklet are included at the end of this book. It would take hours to go through every scripture that is the basis for those confessions and prove to you that they are Biblically sound. So we will only deal with a few of them at this point. These are selected to make you think the way God thinks about you. I like what Paul said in Romans 3.

*For what if some did not believe? shall their unbelief make the faith of God without effect?*

*God forbid: yea, let God be true, but every man a liar.*                    *(Romans 3:3-4)*

Some people do not believe these principles. You may look at your own situation or circumstances and

239

say, *"I do not believe that my needs are met according to His riches in glory by Christ Jesus."*

Whether you believe it or not, God's Word said it. You need to be obedient to God's Word. Therefore, why don't you just line up with what God said? It will not happen in your life just because it's in the Bible. It happens only when you get in agreement with what God said about you.

## CONFESSION
## ACCORDING TO YOUR SITUATION

These confessions are not cut and dried. Don't take these and say, *"That's the only thing you can confess."* You can tailor-make your confessions according to the direction the Lord is giving you for your particular situation. These are only examples. You can use them in different ways.

Let's begin with this one.

*I am the body of Christ and Satan hath no power over me. For I overcome evil with good.*
*(I Corinthians 12:27, Romans 12:21)*

That is all based on scripture. I am the body of Christ. Paul said, *"Now you are the body of Christ."* You are the only body that Christ has on the earth today. Confess it, for you are the body of Christ.

*I am of God and have overcome him (Satan). For greater is He that is in me, than he that is in the world.* *(1 John 4:4)*

That is renewing your mind.

*I will fear no evil, for thou art with me, Lord, your Word and your Spirit they comfort me.*
*(Psalms 23:4)*

240

You can word these as you wish, **so that they are a confession or a prayer.** It's hard to imagine what effect this has on the human spirit until you confess it every day for three or four weeks.

> *I am far from oppression, and fear does not come nigh me.*                              *(Isaiah 54:14)*

Someone may say, *"Yes, but I am not far from oppression, and I'm always afraid."*

That's all the more reason you should confess this Word from God. This is what God said about you. Fear brings oppression, so the confession is that *"I am far from oppression, and fear does not come nigh me."*

## CHANGE THE FACTS
## THAT DON'T AGREE WITH GOD'S WORD

A person who is in fear and has oppression will usually say, *"I am lying if I say that."*

But this is what God said. James 3:14 says, *". . . lie not against the truth."* There are many facts about your life that don't agree with God's Word. It might be true that you are fearful. It might be true that you are under oppression. Those may be facts in your life, but don't lie against the truth that God speaks about you. The Word of God is the truth. God says that you are far from oppression and fear does not come nigh you. God sees you that way. God's Word is truth before it happens.

There is a difference between a fact and a truth. There are some lying vanities. Jonah said,

> *They that observe lying vanities forsake their own mercy.*                              *(Jonah 2:8)*

So you need to confess, *"I am far from oppression; fear does not come nigh me."*

Someone said, *"You would be lying if you said that and you were fearful."*

241

No, I am speaking the truth. **It may not be true in my life yet, but that's the reason I'm saying it. I am calling the thing that is not manifest.** That is really what confession is all about. It is calling things that are not as though they were.

*No weapon formed against me shall prosper, for my righteousness is of the Lord. But whatever I do will prosper, for I am like a tree planted by the rivers of water.* *(Isaiah 54:17; Psalms 1:3)*

You may feel like that is the farthest thing from the truth, but it is the truth. **It may be that the facts in your life do not line up with that truth,** but that is all the more reason that you should confess it; because God said it.

*I am delivered from the evils of this present world, for it is the will of God.* *(Galatians 1:4)*

**That is the will of God concerning you.** That is what the Bible says. That scripture actually said,

*Jesus (Who) gave himself for our sins, that he might deliver us from this present evil world, according to the will of God and our Father.*
*(Galatians 1:4)*

It had to be the will of God, because that is what Jesus did.

*No evil will befall me. Neither shall any plague come nigh my dwelling. For the Lord has given His angels charge over me and they keep me in all my ways, and in my pathway is life and there is no death.* *(Psalms 91:10-11; Proverbs 12:28)*

Sometimes people get offended at that. They say, *"You are saying there is no death."*

I'm just quoting the Bible. That is a direct quote from Proverbs 12:28,

*In the way of righteousness is life: and in the pathway thereof there is no death.*

There is no spiritual death in the path of righteousness. We are not saying that you are not going to die physically, eventually, if Jesus tarries. But this is what God said about you. *"No evil shall befall me."* That's from Psalm 91. These things are in the scriptures, but they are not going to happen to you just because they are in the scriptures.

## MAKING SCRIPTURES VALID IN YOUR LIFE

**We must make the scriptures valid in our own lives.** That is what God told Joshua to do in Joshua 1:8. *"This book of the law shall not depart out of your mouth."* The book of the law was the Word of God that they had in that day. God told him to keep speaking the Word, and to speak in line with the Word of God. That's what we are doing here. And this is the way you will put confession to work for you. You must confess it when you feel like the very opposite is true. In fact, that's the time you need to confess it the most.

*I take the shield of faith and I quench every fiery dart that the wicked one brings against me.*

*(Ephesians 6:16)*

You take the shield of faith. **Some people take the shield of doubt and quench all the blessings of God.** You can do that, for that is the opposite end of this truth.

Somebody said, *"How can I say that? All the fiery darts of the devil are getting to me."*

That's all the more reason you should say it. You are calling this thing into manifestation.

*Christ has redeemed me from the curse of the law. Therefore, I forbid any sickness or disease to come upon this body. Every disease germ and*

243

*every virus that touches this body dies instantly in the name of Jesus. Every organ and every tissue of this body functions in the perfection in which God created it to function, and I forbid any malfunction in this body, in the name of Jesus.*
*(Galatians 3:13; Romans 8:11; Genesis 1:31; Matthew 16:19)*

They say, *"How in the world can you say that?"* It's easy. Just open your mouth and begin.

*"Well, yes, but I don't understand what scriptural basis you have."*

Mark 11:23 says that you can have what you say, if you believe and doubt not in your heart. **If I can have what I say, why not say what I need?** It is based on the scripture.

Some say, *"You cannot forbid anything. You are just trying to be God."*

But Jesus said that whatever you bind on earth will be bound in heaven, and whatever you loose on earth will be loosed in heaven. You can bind the principalities and the powers and the rulers of the darkness. So I choose to forbid any malfunction of my body.

But what if you are already sick?

Just keep saying it anyway. Confess God's Word in the face of every circumstance. If you need to, take your medicine. But confess with every dose, *"I believe I receive my healing."*

*I am submitted to God and the devil flees from me because I resist him in the name of Jesus."*
*(James 4:7)*

That is what God's Word said about you. You may not feel like the devil is fleeing from you. You may think he isn't, but the Word says he is. You need to get in line with the Word, and **confess it until your mind is renewed and your heart is changed.** You will wake up

244

some morning, and when you say, *"Satan, I resist you in the name of Jesus,"* you will think *"Wow! He did flee from me, didn't he!"*

I remember the day when that happened to me. I thought, *"Glory to God! There's power in the agreement with God's Word."* But it came weeks and months after I had started confessing it. It is not going to happen overnight. This is a process. Just speak God's Word over every situation.

## JESUS DEFEATED SATAN WITH THE WORD

Do you realize that this is what Jesus did to defeat Satan? On the Mount of Temptation, Jesus spoke only what God said. That is all He spoke. He defeated Satan with God's Words. **He shook Satan's kingdom beyond repair.** Satan was never able to get it back together against Him. If you will get hold of this principle, he won't get it together against you either. You have the authority to declare these things, because they are in the Word of God.

*For poverty He has given me wealth, for sickness He has given me health, for death He has given me eternal life.*
*(II Corinthians 8:9; Isaiah 53:5; John 10:10; John 5:24)*

You may be sick and poor, but confess this anyway. It is what God's Word says about you.

*There is no lack, for my God supplieth all my need according to His riches in glory by Christ Jesus.* *(Philippians 4:19)*

There may be lack all around you. But proclaim what God said about you, regardless of what appears to be fact. Take these confessions and get in your bedroom and walk up and down saying them aloud. Don't whisper them. Don't just read them to yourself. Quote them out loud. Speak them into your heart.

245

# CALLING THINGS THAT ARE NOT

The Bible principle on which you are operating by confessing the Word is the principle of calling things that are not. Let's look at what Paul said about it in First Corinthians.

*For ye see your calling, brethren, how that not many wise men after the flesh, not many mighty, not many noble are called:*

*But God hath chosen the foolish things of the world to confound the wise; and God hath chosen the weak things of the world to confound the things which are mighty;*

*And base things of the world, and things which are despised, hath God chosen, yea, and things which are not, to bring to nought things that are.*

*(I Corinthians 1:26-28)*

Notice that God has chosen this method. Some of you didn't know this scripture was in the Bible, even though you have read it many times. God chose this method of using things that are not manifest, things that you cannot see with the natural eye, **to bring to nought the things that are manifest.** Do you know what nought means? **It means zero or reduce to nothing the things that are manifest.**

This is a Bible principle. God chose it. I didn't choose it until after God chose it. God could have done it any way He wanted to, but He chose to do it this way. He chose to use things that are not manifest. He chose spiritual forces that you cannot see, feel, taste, smell, or hear to bring to nought the things that are manifest. He chose this to reduce to nought those things that you do not desire and are not in agreement with the Word of God. If you have a problem and you can see it, then it's in the natural realm. As long as you can see it, you can use your faith and the Word of God to change it.

# SAME SPIRIT OF FAITH

The apostle Paul gives some insight to this in Second Corinthians, chapter four.

*We having the same spirit of faith, according as it is written, I believed, and therefore have I spoken; we also believe, and therefore speak;*

*For our light affliction, which is but for a moment, worketh for us a far more exceeding and eternal weight of glory;*

*While we look not at the things which are seen, but at the things which are not seen: for the things which are seen are temporal; but the things which are not seen are eternal."*

*(II Corinthians 4:13, 17-18)*

The unseen realm is the powerful realm. The unseen is governed by eternal principles.

Here is the principle that God has ordained. God used this principle all through the Bible, from Genesis to Revelation. It's the principle that Jesus used in all of His ministry. It's the principle of calling things that are not as though they were. We find God doing this in Romans 4.

*(As it is written, I have made thee a father of many nations,) before him whom he believed, even God, who quickeneth the dead, and calleth those things which be not as though they were.*

*(Roman 4:17)*

God calls things that are not manifest as though they were manifest. This is God's method. Compare this with what the apostle Paul said: *"God has chosen the* ***things that are not to bring to nought things*** *that are."* (1st Corinthians 1:28) This is God's method. Call for eternal forces to put to nought things that are seen.

Call into manifestation the thing that is not, and it will do away with what is manifest.

Paul said that we should overcome evil with good. When you start talking about calling things that are not as though they were, some people get the idea you are denying what exists. Some believe that confessing the answer is to deny the things that exist. But confessing the answer is not denying what exists; it is the principle of calling things that are not as though they were.

## DON'T CALL THINGS THAT ARE

**There is a great difference between calling things that are not as though they were and calling things that are as though they are not.** God's method is to call things that are not. In other words, He calls them into manifestation. By doing that, He nullifies the problem that exists.

If the problem exists, you don't deny that the problem exists. If you are sick, you don't deny that you are sick. But you don't want to always be confessing your sickness, either. Sometimes those who misunderstand this message think, if they are sick, they should say, *"I'm not sick."* Just saying you are not sick doesn't make you well. In fact, it would be a lie. But there is a difference between a lie and a confession.

Confession is a method of calling things that are not as though they were. If I am sick, I will confess:

*I am healed by the stripes of Jesus. I am delivered from the authority of darkness. I am redeemed from the curse of the law. I am calling my body well and healthy in Jesus' Name.*

**I am not denying sickness, I am denying that it has a right to exist in my body.** I am calling for health and healing in my body. That is God's method. You will be criticized for it, but as long as you are doing what God says, they can go ahead and criticize you.

## DON'T ACT LIKE THE DEVIL

There are those who will say, *"You are just trying to act like God."*

And I appreciate that; I usually say, *"Thank you very much."*

I would rather act like God than the devil. **If I am acting like God, saying what God said about me, then those who are saying what the devil said are acting like the devil.**

They don't like that reply, but it's true anyway. If you are always quoting what the devil said, then you are falling right in line with the devil. The devil will tell you, *"You're sick, and you are going to die. You are never going to get any better."*

Well, it may look that way on the surface, but don't quote the devil — he is a liar. Even when there is no hope, don't confess no hope, but go to God's Word and get some hope.

## ABRAHAM ACTED AS GOD ACTED

When there was no hope, Abraham believed in hope. He went to the Word of God and got some hope. Then he said what God said about him. *"I am the father of many nations."* God forced him into it by changing his name. He had to say, *"My name is Abraham,"* and Abraham meant *"father of many nations."*

Faith cometh by hearing the Word of God. That was the Word of God concerning Abraham: **"You are the father of nations."** But he wasn't the father of nations at that point. But God said he was. What was God doing? He was calling it into manifestation. God taught Abraham how to develop his faith in God's Word. He taught Abraham to say what God said by changing his name.

## ZACHARIAS FAILED TO ACT

There is another Bible instance in Luke, chapter one where God spoke to Zacharias.

> *But the angel said unto him, Fear not, Zacharias; for thy prayer is heard; and thy wife Elisabeth shall bear thee a son, and thou shalt call his name John.*
>
> *And Zacharias said unto the angel, Whereby shall I know this? for I am an old man and my wife well stricken in years.*
>
> *And the angel answering said unto him, I am Gabriel, that stand in the presence of God; and am sent to speak unto thee, and to show thee these glad tidings.*
>
> *And, behold, thou shalt be dumb, and not able to speak, until the day that these things shall be performed, because thou believest not my words, which shall be fulfilled in their season.*
>
> *(Luke 1:13, 18-20)*

Allow me to paraphrase this. God sent an angel to him to tell him that his prayers were answered, and his wife was going to have a child. Zacharias said, *"How do I know you're telling the truth? You are going to have to give me a sign."*

The angel replied, *"I'll give you a sign all right. You won't be able to speak until the day it comes to pass."*

Notice how God dealt with these two individuals. Here was a man who was walking in doubt concerning what God said to him. So God said, *"If we don't get his mouth shut, this will never work."*

So the angel stopped Zacharias from talking for nine months. But God just renamed Abraham, so he would have to say what God said about him.

Remember that God chose this method of calling things that are not as though they were. But so many misunderstand, and just deny what exists. For instance, someone might say, *"I'm going to deny that I have emphysema,"* and continue to confess that they don't have emphysema.

If they could get rid of it by denying it, they might die with cancer. So that's not the answer. **God's method is to call the thing that is not. That does not mean to deny what exists.** You don't call things that are as though they are not. God's method is to call the thing that is not manifest as though it were manifest.

## CONFESSION IS NOT A LIE

If you were going to apply God's principles concerning sickness, you would say,

> *Thank God, the Bible says that I am healed by the stripes of Jesus. I am redeemed from the curse of the law. The curse of the law was poverty, sickness and spiritual death. First Peter 2:24 said that I was healed by the stripes of Jesus, and I am confessing these things and saying them in the name of Jesus. It is causing faith to come, and I am calling my body well. Body, are you listening to me? I am telling you that you are well in the name of Jesus.*

Then someone will say, *"I know that you are just lying, because you are hurting."* I may be hurting, but I am calling for the thing that is not manifest. They say, *"How can you say your body is well when you are sick?"* That's all the more reason that you should say it. You are calling for the thing that is not. You are calling it into manifestation. There would be no need to call for something that was already manifest.

I am not trying to convince you that I am not sick, or that I do not hurt. If I am, I am lying. That is the difference between lying and confession, or calling

251

things that are not. **If I am trying to convince you that I already have something that I don't literally have, then that's a lie.** But if you hear me saying, *"Thank God, my body is well, I am healed, I am delivered, I am free from sickness and disease, and I am calling my body well,"* and you say, *"That old boy doesn't have a pain in his body,"* you just heard me calling things that are not. I did not lie to you. I wasn't talking to you. I didn't say it for your benefit; I said it for my benefit. I would almost rather that you had not heard me, because you are likely to misunderstand me. I am calling for the thing that is not manifest.

## DON'T GET INTO BONDAGE; USE COMMON SENSE

Someone might say, *"Thank God, I am going to confess that I don't have any debts,"* when in fact, they owe everybody in the county. There are many people who are hung up on this scripture in Romans 13:8, *"Owe no man anything, but to love one another."* They say, *"Glory to God, that's what I'm going to do. I am going to owe no man anything."* They won't borrow any money at the bank to meet their bills when they are due, even though they don't have the money to meet them. They lose their credit and get kicked out of their apartment.

That is not a very good testimony is it? They are confessing, *"My God meets my needs according to His riches in glory."* The other people are wondering, *"Who is his God Who can't meet his needs?"*

You can't owe no many nothing when you owe everybody everything. You have to start where you are. You cannot operate in that until you get out of debt. Don't get into bondage over that. God told Israel in Deuteronomy 15:6, *"Thou shalt lend unto many nations, but thou shalt not borrow."* If it were wrong to

252

borrow money, it would be wrong to lend money. And they wouldn't have borrowed if there had not been someone to lend it.

If God has told you not to borrow money, then it would be wrong for you to do it. But don't get into bondage over that one verse of scripture. Quite frankly, this scripture in Romans 13:8 is talking about paying your taxes.

> *For this cause pay ye tribute also: for they are God's ministers, attending continually upon this very thing.*
>
> *Render therefore to all their dues: tribute to whom tribute is due; custom to whom custom; fear to whom fear; honour to whom honour.*
>
> *Owe no man any thing, but to love one another: for he that loveth another hath fulfilled the law.*
>
> *(Romans 13:6-8)*

Don't let a scripture quoted out of context hold you in bondage. What if someone said, *"I don't have any debts. Glory to God, I don't have any debts, thank God. I am confessing that every bill is paid. I don't have any debts."* But in fact, they owe many people. They are denying what exists. That is not God's method. God's method is to call the thing that is not manifest. If they could eliminate the debt by denying its existence, they could still starve to death. Most people who starve to death don't owe anybody anything. Just being out of debt is not the answer.

What is the answer? God's method is to call the thing that is not manifest. The thing that is not manifest in that individual's life is that they do not have an abundant supply. So they should go to the Word of God and find the promise of abundant supply. Then be obedient to what the Word said to do. Then proclaim,

*Because I have given, it is given unto me good measure, pressed down, shaken together, and running over. My God supplies all my need according to His riches in glory by Christ Jesus. Because I am a giver, because I operate on the principles of the Word of God, I sow bountifully, and I reap bountifully. My God has made all grace abound toward me. I am saying in the name of Jesus that I have abundance and all the good deals come my way. I am blessed going in and coming out, I am blessed in the basket and in the store. By the end of the year I will have abundance to pay every debt and give ten thousand dollars to missions.*

If someone heard you say that, they would say, *"I know you are lying, because I happen to know that you haven't made your car payment."*

That's all the more reason for saying it. You are calling the thing that is not.

## APPLY PRINCIPLE AND BE PATIENT

It may take weeks, months, or years to bring the fulfillment of that promise. But then you will be able to pay your debts off, buy the groceries, and give ten thousand dollars a year to missions. That is God's method, and it is the answer.

Let's say it another way. There is a backlash of denying what exists. A man says, *"I found the car I want to buy. If I sell my car, I will have enough money to buy this new car."* He has misunderstood the faith message. So he begins to deny that he has a car. He says, *"I believe I have sold my car, so I am going to deny that I have a car."* So he starts saying, *"I don't have a car."* He says, *"I don't have a car."* Somebody asks him about his car and he says, *"I don't have a car."*

Now, that is not God's method. He may wake up some morning and find that someone has stolen his car, and he really doesn't have a car. So that is not the answer. There is a backlash in denying things that exist. That is not faith, neither is it God's method.

God's method would be to say something like this.

*Father, in the name of Jesus, I ask you for a buyer for this car. Send someone to buy this car. Someone wants this car. This car will fill the need in someone's life, and they want it as badly as I want to sell it. Send them to me Father. Have the angels guide them here. I thank you Father, I believe that I have received a buyer for this car. Thank you, Father that my car is sold.*

Then go out and talk to your car. Say, *"Car, I am calling you sold. Thank God, someone just loves your paint job. They are impressed with you. By faith I call you sold, in Jesus' Name."*

*"How do I know that I'm not lying?"*

Because I am calling things that are not. Although the car is still in my possession, I am taking the spiritual force of faith and calling into manifestation the thing that will nullify what exists. This is God's method. **If you call health into your body, it will nullify sickness and disease. Call abundance into your finances, and it will nullify the lack.** It will nullify the thing that exists.

There is probably no other principle in the Bible that will cause you to be criticized more than this one. But yet it is God's method. There are so many Christians who simply don't understand this principle. That's why we take this much time teaching the faith and confession principle.

## ACTING AS GOD WOULD ACT

Some will accuse you of trying to be God. They say, *"You are trying to act like God."*

But you are trying to **act as God would act** in that situation. **You are not trying to be God.** If God had a car to sell, He would call it sold. For when He looked out and saw darkness, He said, *"Light."* God speaks the thing desired. He takes the thing that is not manifest and brings to nothing the thing that is manifest. I didn't invent this method. But I found out about it and I have proven it in my own life.

Let's consider how this principle would work regarding everyday things. I heard one lady say, *"Pray for my husband. I've been praying for him for twenty-five years, and he's getting meaner, and he won't go to church with me."*

The Spirit of God said, *"That woman has been praying that way all these years."* She has been telling me, *"my husband is getting meaner. He won't go to church with me. Lord, he is just a no-good."* She has been praying the problem for twenty-five years. If she had prayed the answer and called for the thing that was not, her husband would have been saved more than twenty years ago.

She was calling things that are as though they were. **This is another mistake many Christians make. They call things that are as though they are.** Why would you want to call something that is already manifest? It's amazing how you can understand things when you get it down to apples and oranges or cats and dogs. People do foolish things sometimes, thinking they are being spiritually minded. They say, *"I'm just telling it like it is. You have to say it like it is."*

But calling things that are manifest is unscriptural. The Bible method is to call the things that are not manifest.

# DON'T MAKE A HABIT
## OF CONFESSING YOUR WEAKNESS

*Say unto wisdom, Thou art my sister; and call*
*understanding thy kinswoman.* (Proverbs 7:4)

Someone might say, *"Wisdom is far from me."* They
are probably right. They have been saying that for
twenty years. They have shut off the wisdom of God
right from their spirit by the words of their mouth. In
this scripture **God is telling you to call wisdom and
understanding.** If you want wisdom, call for wisdom.
Proclaim that you have the wisdom of God.

If you made a dumb decision, begin to confess you
have the wisdom of God. Don't say it like it is. Say it the
way you want it to be.

Wouldn't it be foolish to always confess, *"I make
dumb decisions, I make dumb decisions, I always make
dumb decisions."* Many do it just that way, thinking
they are being honest. People will tell you that you have
to say it like it is. Some say,

*I'm just saying it like it is. We don't ever have*
*enough money to give in the offering. We aren't*
*ever able to give to missions because money gets*
*away from us so quickly that we don't ever know*
*where it went. We just can't keep money.*

Isn't that amazing! You have been saying that for
twenty-nine years. And money just flees from you and
seems to disappear.

Start confessing this instead.

*We always have enough money for every good*
*work. There is abundance and no lack. My money*
*just seems to multiply every month. It just seems*
*to stay with me. I always have sufficient money.*

But don't go tell your neighbors that, because they
will call you a liar. You are renewing your mind and
causing faith to come.

There is a fine line here. This is between you and God. **You proclaim these things based on the scriptures.** It is not a matter of whether or not it exists now. It's a matter of what you can call into existence by the Word of God and by your confession of faith.

I saw a lady get hold of this in one of my prayer seminars. She said, *"I want to pray, and I want to confess the Word of God."* She jumped up and started confessing, *"My husband is saved. He is filled with the Holy Ghost. My children are saved, and we have a Christian home."* She continued by praising God for a Christian home. She even got happy about it. She sat down and the woman next to her leaned over and said, *"I didn't know your husband was saved."*

What she was saying was not true in the natural at that time. She was calling for things that were not manifest. The woman next to her misunderstood what she was saying. She thought she was stating what was already true in the natural. **That's the reason you shouldn't make all these confessions in public. You will be misunderstood.**

A year later the woman's husband was saved and filled with the Holy Ghost. She called it by God's method, and the manifestation came within a year.

These things won't happen overnight. But when you continue to apply God's method, they will happen.

Confession is just the beginning of putting God's Word to work for you.

# Chapter Thirteen

# CALLING THINGS THAT ARE NOT — A DIVINE PRINCIPLE

Calling things that are not is a Bible method. It is a profound Bible principle.

Notice that this is not calling things that **are as though they are not,** for that would be denying what exists. Denying what exists is not a principle of God.

God's method is to call for the manifestation of the things that are not manifest; call for the things that are promised.

## WORRY IS CALLING THINGS THAT ARE NOT, ON THE NEGATIVE SIDE

There are some who will say, *"I don't believe in calling things that are not."* But if you follow that individual around, you will find they are doing it almost every day. They will say, *"You watch and see. That car is going to pull right out in front of us." "I can already tell you that we are not going to have the money to make that payment on our house at the end of the year." "If you buy that car, sure as the world you'll lose your job."*

These are the people who will criticize you for calling things that are not as though they were, on the positive side.

Worry is simply calling things that are not as though they were, on the negative side. When we start doing this on the positive side, many religious people get upset about it. They say, *"Why, you're just trying to live in a world of fantasy."* But yet they will stand there

259

and call things that are not, on the negative side, and then say, *"Well, I'm just saying it like it is, I'm being truthful."*

It may be true all right, but we are not required to call something that is already there. That is not God's method. They are calling the bad things that are not as though they were. If they continue to do that, they will call those bad things into manifestation. The thing they greatly feared will come upon them, just as it happened to Job.

## ACTING ON SCRIPTURE

Calling things that are not is actually acting on Mark 11:23: *"Whosoever shall say unto this mountain, Be thou removed, and be thou cast into the sea."* If you are saying to the mountain, *"be thou removed,"* you are doing it on the positive side. You will probably be criticized. The same people who criticize you **are talking to the same mountain and saying, *"Whooooo, mountain you're getting bigger every day. I'll never get over you.*** *You are always there to hinder me."*

They will criticize you, and they are using the same principle, only they are using it in reverse.

## NOT DENYING WHAT EXISTS

There are some who say, *"You are denying what exists if you call things that are not."*

No, we are not denying the things that exist. We are doing something about what exists by calling something in its place. You notice in the scriptures that God taught Abraham **His** method of calling things that are not as though they were. And Abraham did not deny what existed, but rather gave affirmation to what God said about him.

Abraham did not say, *"I am not old, I am not old, I am not old."* He didn't deny that he was old. He was seventy-five years old when God told him that he would make of him a great nation. (Genesis 12:2-4) It was twenty-five years later when he became the father of nations in the natural. **He held fast to that confession for twenty-five years,** and he was getting older all the time. He was already too old to father a child when God told him he was the father of many nations. He did not deny that he was old, but rather gave the positive affirmation in agreement with God. When he said, *"I am Abraham,"* he was saying, *"I am the father of nations."* And faith cometh by hearing.

## SARAH RECEIVED STRENGTH TO CONCEIVE

The Bible specifically speaks about Sarah in Hebrews.

> *Through faith also Sara herself received strength to conceive seed, and was delivered of a child when she was past age, because she judged him faithful who had promised.* (Hebrews 11:11)

She received strength to conceive seed through faith. The same principle worked for her that worked for Abraham. In Genesis 17 God changed her name.

> *And God said unto Abraham, As for Sarai thy wife, thou shalt not call her name Sarai, but Sarah shall her name be.*
>
> *And I will bless her, and give thee a son also of her; yea, I will bless her, and she shall be a mother of nations; kings of people shall be of her.* (Genesis 17:15-16)

Every time she said, *"I am Sarah,"* she was saying, *"I am the mother of nations."* Every time somebody called, *"Sarah,"* she didn't hear 'Sarah,' she heard

261

what God said, *"Mother of Nations."* And faith cometh by hearing. God used the principle of confession on Abraham and Sarah. He made them confess it by changing their names. Their confession became a way to possession of the promise.

## NEW COVENANT REVEALS
## MORE OF THE PRINCIPLE

God has revealed some things to us in the new covenant about faith that He did not reveal to Abraham. It is important to know how to operate in these principles. If we don't know and understand these principles, we are likely to deny what exists. Through this principle we don't deny what exists, we just don't give it first place. Don't continually talk much about what exists, especially if it doesn't agree with God's Word. For the more we talk it, the more we will believe it. The more we believe it, the more we will talk it. Faith and fear both come by hearing.

The principle that God has chosen uses things that are not manifest **to bring to nought things that are manifest.** But yet you hear some say, *"I'm going to say it like it is; that's the way you have to do it. If I say it any other way, I would be lying, so I always just say it like it is."*

## WHEN IT COMES TO CATS AND DOGS
## THEY DO IT DIFFERENTLY

Let's see if that is really true in their life. Let's suppose that person has a dog, and it's time to feed him. They take the food out some morning, and the dog isn't there. If they really practice what they say they believe — that you have to say it like it is — here is what they will do. They will sit down on the doorstep and start saying, *"My dog isn't here, my dog isn't here. Oh Lord, my dog isn't here. Oh, it's true, the dog isn't here."*

They moan and groan all morning saying, *"The dog isn't here."*

Finally, their neighbor comes over and says, *"What are you doing?"*

They reply, *"Well, I'm just saying it like it is. The dog isn't here. The dog isn't here."*

The neighbor says, **"Have you tried calling the dog?"**

They reply, **"No! You can't do that. You have to say it like it is, and dog isn't here.** *The dog isn't here."*

It is true that the dog is not there. That person is not that foolish. They know the dog may never be there, unless they call him. No one would even think of doing such a thing. It's ridiculous to even talk about it, because no one would do that in natural things.

## ARE THEY LYING ABOUT POOCH?

Do you know what they would do if they went out to feed the dog and the dog wasn't there? They would say, *"Here pooch! Here pooch!"* — even though pooch is not there.

Are they lying about it when they say, *"Here pooch! Here pooch!"* and the pooch is not there? They say that they always say it like it is, but if they are going to say it like it is, they should say, *"Yonder pooch! Yonder pooch! Somewhere else pooch!"* For if the dog was gone, that would be the dog-gone truth. But no one would do it that way when it comes to natural things such as cats and dogs.

## DON'T TOTALLY SEPARATE NATURAL THINGS FROM SPIRITUAL THINGS

Why is it, when we get into the Bible in regard to these principles, we forget about cats and dogs and the natural things? For the simple reason that **we have totally separated natural principles from spiritual**

**principles.** We shouldn't do that, because there are parallels between the two. Whatever you call in the natural will come. When you plant a seed you are calling for more seed. Seedtime and harvest is God's method. Planting a seed calls for the things that are not there at the time you plant.

## SAYING IT LIKE IT IS, OR SAYING IT LIKE IT IS NOT

So, you call the dog, *"Here pooch! Here pooch!,"* until pooch comes. Remember, when it comes to dogs and cats, even the person who says he believes in calling it like it is calls the thing that is not there. Suppose he goes out to feed the dog, and the dog is there. He sits down and says, *"Here pooch! Here pooch! Pooch is here; here pooch!"*

His neighbor comes over and says, *"What are you doing?"*

He replies, *"I'm just saying it like it is. Pooch is here, so I am calling pooch here."*

No one would do that, for there is no need to call the dog, if the dog is already there. Everybody knows the dog is there.

Here is the point I want to make. Some people say, *"We are so financially strapped we will never be able to buy anything that we need. We always have month left at the end of our money. We can never keep money. Every time we save up any money, our kids get sick and we have to spend every dime on doctor bills."*

## WHY CALL THINGS THAT ARE HERE?

What are they doing? They are calling things that are already there.

**They wouldn't do that to their dog.** They wouldn't do that to their cat. Why are they doing it to the things they don't want? They don't want lack in their house.

264

They don't want poverty on their doorstep. They don't want sickness in their family. So why would they continue to call it the way it is? Why not **call it the way the Bible says it should be?** Call for the thing desired, the thing God promised. Use God's method to change what exists.

God chose this method. You can choose whatever method you want to in life. But you will have success if you go with God's method.

There are many who will disagree with you. They will say you are lying. But if you bring it back to cats and dogs, you will find they are using God's principles in natural things, such as calling cats and dogs. But when they get into spiritual things, they get so heavenly minded that they are no earthly good. They get confused because they haven't studied and meditated on these Bible principles.

In natural things, you wouldn't call something that was already manifest. If the cat was there, and you didn't want the cat but you wanted the dog, **you would stomp your foot and say, *"Scat!"* and then call the dog.** If lack is on your doorstep, if lack has come home with you and prosperity hasn't come to your house, tell lack to *"Go! in the name of Jesus."* And call for abundance by confessing the Word of God. **Don't sit there and call it like it is.** Call it the way God promised it would be. **Call the promise into manifestation.** God has chosen this method.

## CALL THINGS DESIRED

In the area of sickness and disease, **you call the thing that is desired.**

> . . .*What things soever ye desire, when ye pray, believe that ye receive them, and ye shall have them.*                                    (Mark 11:24)

**You shall have them.** It's foolish in the natural realm to call something that you already have. You would call the thing that was not there. That is very simple. It's a simple principle. It is so simple that we have missed it. This principle is used throughout the Bible. Jesus operated in it during all of His earthly ministry. God operated in it. It is one of the most tremendous truths in the whole Bible. But because we have been taught wrong, the devil has blinded our minds to some of these principles. The enemy has convinced so many that they are lying when they call things that are not as though they were.

## YOUR BODY IS AS SMART AS THE DOG

If you call the cat or dog that is not there, they will obey you and come. Someone may say, *"I can understand that cat and dog business, but talking to your body and calling it well, that's just too far out."* Do you mean to tell me that the cat and the dog are smarter than your body?

## THE MOUNTAIN HAS NO CHOICE

Jesus said in Mark 11:23 that a man shall have whatever he says if he believes and doubts not in his heart, but shall believe what he is saying will come to pass. He shall have whatever he says. (Paraphrased)

That is God's Word. He is telling you how to call the thing that is not. You say to the mountain while it is still standing there, *"Be removed, be cast into the sea."* You say to the sycamine tree, *"Be plucked up by the root, be planted in the sea."* You are calling it the way you want it, according to the scriptures. The mountain of problem must obey. It has no other choice. You have scriptural basis for it.

# CHECK UP ON YOURSELF

The promises in the Bible are God's will for you. But they will not come to you just because they are in the Bible. You must call them. Check up on yourself. You have been calling things for years, and that is the reason some of you are in the mess you are in. You have been calling the wrong things. You have been calling things that are not, but doing it on the negative side. To change your situation, all you have to do is switch over to the positive side of the same principle.

# GOD'S WORD OVER ALL MATTER

Some may say, *"That's just positive thinking or mind over matter."*

No. **It's the principle of God and the power of His Word over all matter.** It's God's method. We are created in the image of God and we can operate in His principles.

You must have some understanding to operate in these principles. If you don't have a good understanding, people will talk you out of it. They will tell you that *"you are not operating in Bible principles, you're just lying."*

They don't know this is God's principle, or God's way. **If they could just live a few days in it, they would never go back to the old way.** But their eyes have been blinded, and their words have deceived their heart. Learn to call things that are not as though they were. This is God's method to nullify what exists, and to call into manifestation the thing that the Bible promised.

We are talking about calling into manifestation the promises of God. It is not something that God doesn't want you to have, **but things that God has already given to you.**

267

## JESUS OPERATED IN THIS PRINCIPLE

Jesus operated in this principle of calling things that are not. In the second chapter of the book of John is the account of the marriage in Cana of Galilee where they ran out of wine.

*His mother saith unto the servants, Whatsoever he saith to you, do it.*

*And there were set there six water pots of stone, after the manner of the purifying of the Jews, containing two or three firkins apiece.*

*Jesus saith unto them, Fill the water pots with water. And they filled them up to the brim.*

*And he saith unto them, Draw out now, and bear unto the governor of the feast. And they bare it.*

*(John 2:5-8)*

They filled the water pots to the brim with water. It was water. It wasn't root beer, it wasn't coffee, it wasn't grape juice, it was water. They knew it was water, John knew it was water, Peter knew it was water, Jesus knew it was water.

## THE WATER WAS CALLED WINE

But Jesus called it wine. You need to understand that Jesus was more highly developed in this than you. Jesus spoke only what His Father said. You can see the principle here. I am not telling you to go out and try to turn water into gasoline.

The point that I am making is that this is a principle. It works in everything in life. He is not telling you to go turn water into wine, or wine into water. But this Bible principle can be used to supply your need.

Jesus said,

*Draw out now, and bear unto the governor of the feast. And they bare it.*

*(John 2:8)*

# SOME BELIEVE IT'S MAKE-BELIEVE

Some will tell you, *"You are just playing make-believe, confessing all these things. You're just living in a world of make-believe."*

What did the scripture say? Did it say, *"this is the beginning of make-believe which Jesus did?"* No, it doesn't say that. It says,

> *This beginning of miracles did Jesus in Cana of Galilee.*       *(John 2:11)*

People may tell you that you are playing make-believe, and they may tell you that you are in a cult. They may tell you all sorts of things. Religious people who are dogmatic about their own little doctrines are the most vicious people in the world.

## THIS IS A PRINCIPLE, NOT A MEANS TO AN END

Obey the principle. Don't try to turn water into gasoline or wine. Jesus didn't just sit there and say, *"We can't have wine. We don't have wine."* He called for some water, and it came. Then He called it wine. This is a principle. **He used what was available to call the thing that was needed.** Water which was not wine brought to nought the need, which was wine.

In Luke 13 Jesus was in the synagogue.

> *And, behold, there was a woman which had a spirit of infirmity eighteen years, and was bowed together, and could in no wise lift up herself.*
>
> *And when Jesus saw her, he called her to him, and said unto her, Woman, thou art loosed from thine infirmity.*       *(Luke 13:11-12)*

But she wasn't loosed. She was still as bent over as she ever was. What was Jesus doing? Was He trying to play make-believe again? No. He was calling for the thing that was not manifest.

## GOD SAYS BEFORE HE DOES

As you study the Bible, you will notice God never does anything until He says it. That's the way He works. God has done nothing in the earth without first speaking it. Even now, it seems that God will do nothing in the earth unless it it spoken, prophesied, or called for by the prayer of faith. You see these bumper stickers that say, *"God has everything under control."* But God doesn't have everything in this earth under control. If He is controlling everything in this earth, He really has it in a mess.

God is not controlling everything in the earth today. But He has an overall control through His Word. There are certain things that God will do, and there are certain things that won't be done, unless you do them by acting on His Word.

## JESUS CALLED THE CROOKED STRAIGHT

When Isaiah prophesied that a virgin would conceive and bear a child, it was 750 years before Jesus was born in the earth. It was prophesied. God always prophesies it before it happens. Jesus operated in the same principle. He walked up to that little woman and said, *"You are loosed from your infirmity."* But she wasn't, at that point. He was calling for the thing that was not manifest.

*And he laid his hands on her; and immediately she was made straight, and glorified God.*

*(Luke 13:13)*

First, Jesus called it the way it was going to be. Faith always looks through the storm. Faith always sees the end results. When Jesus walked up to the woman, He could see the end results by His faith, so He just called for it. That is God's method.

Let's look at the story of Lazarus of Bethany in John eleven.

*Therefore his sisters sent unto him, saying, Lord, behold, he whom thou lovest is sick.*

*When Jesus heard that, he said, This sickness is not unto death, but for the glory of God that the Son of God might be glorified thereby.* (John 11:3-4)

Jesus said, *"This sickness is not unto death."* What are you going to do with that statement? For as you read further, you find that Lazarus died.

## JESUS CALLED THE DEAD LIVING

Jesus said this sickness is not unto death, but for the glory of God, that the Son of God might be glorified thereby. Some say, *"Jesus said that Lazarus was sick and died so God would be glorified."*

It wasn't God's will for Lazarus to be sick. Neither was it God's will for Lazarus to die.

Let me show you why you cannot interpret this scripture to mean the sickness or death was for God's glory. The rule of thumb is to always take a scripture literally if you can. But you cannot take verse four literally. If you do, you make Jesus a liar. There is a difference between a lie and a confession, or calling things that are not. If you interpret this verse literally, then you would have to say Jesus lied. But a lie is sin, and the Bible said there was no sin in Him. So we have to look at it from a different angle.

## HE CALLED END RESULTS

**Jesus is calling the end results of the matter.** He said the end result will not be death; but **the end results of this whole matter will bring glory to God.** The glory that God received came when Lazarus was raised from the dead. Not when he was sick, nor when he died.

271

Neither the sickness nor the death glorified God. **The resurrection glorified God.** God raised him from the dead. If it was God's will for him to die, then Jesus destroyed the work of His Father when He raised Him from the dead. It wasn't God's will for him to be sick or die. Jesus was sent *"that he might destroy the works of the devil."* (I John 3:8)

If you follow Jesus, you will learn something, as he starts toward Bethany.

## JESUS WAS MISUNDERSTOOD BECAUSE OF HIS CONFESSION

> *These things said he; and after that he saith unto them, Our friend Lazarus sleepeth; but I go, that I may awake him out of sleep.*
>
> *Then said his disciples, Lord, if he sleep, he shall do well.*
>
> *Howbeit Jesus spake of his death: but they thought that he had spoken of taking of rest in sleep.* (John 11:11-13)

Jesus realized they had misunderstood Him when the disciples said, *"if Lazarus is asleep, he is doing well."* Jesus was calling the thing that was not. Lazarus wasn't asleep, he was dead, and Jesus knew he was dead. After Jesus heard the bad news, He stayed two more days in the same place. It took the runner about a day to get down there with the news. Then Jesus stayed there two more days, and then walked to Bethany, which took about one day. On the way to Bethany, Jesus said, *"Lazarus sleepeth."*

## JESUS GUARDED HIS DECLARATION

What was He doing? He was guarding His conversation so He wouldn't undo what He already declared in the beginning. But His disciples misunderstood Him.

272

## JESUS EXPLAINED WHAT WAS
## BUT CALLED WHAT WAS NOT

Jesus stopped and gave His followers an explanation. *"Lazarus is dead."* That's the way the King James version states it. But if you read the interlinear Greek, the word translated *"dead"* in the King James version is translated *"died."* One is present tense; the other is past tense. Jesus said, *"Lazarus died."* There is a difference between someone who died and someone who is dead. If you don't understand that, look at Jesus. He died, **but He is not dead.**

Jesus called the thing that was not manifest. Lazarus was not asleep. He was dead. But Jesus called him *"asleep."* Jesus would not admit death. That didn't mean that He denied it. He just would not establish anything but what He declared when He heard the bad news.

Again, in this principle, Jesus is not teaching you to go raise all the dead. He is teaching you how the principles of calling things that are not works.

When Jesus came to Bethany, He said,

*. . .Take ye away the stone. Martha, the sister of him that was dead, saith unto him, Lord, by this time he stinketh: for he hath been dead four days.*

*(John 11:39)*

This fact that he has been dead for four days proves that he was either dead when the messenger got to Jesus, or immediately after.

For when Jesus arrived, they said that Lazarus had been dead four days. So Jesus knew Lazarus was dead. Jesus was calling the thing that was not manifest. This is God's method.

Jesus finally talked them into rolling away the stone.

*Then they took away the stone from the place where the dead was laid. And Jesus lifted up his*

*eyes, and said, Father, I thank thee that thou hast
heard me.*                                     *(John 11:41)*

Notice at this point, Jesus hasn't said anything yet,
but He is thanking God that He has heard Him. Jesus is
referring to what He said four days ago. In effect, He
was saying, *"Father, I thank You that You heard what I
decreed by faith four days ago; that the end results will
not end in death but bring glory to You."*

## OBEYING THE PRINCIPLE

We must learn to obey this principle.

If someone calls and says, *"Aunt Susie is in the
hospital, and she's going to die for sure,"* use your faith
to the limit. Dare to say some things in faith. Say, *"In
the name of Jesus, she will live and not die. I decree it in
Jesus' Name."*

*"But what if she dies?"*

Well, you used your faith to the limit. That's what is
required of you.

There are some things you can't control by your
faith. Aunt Susie might have wanted to go on to
heaven, and you couldn't stop her. If she wants to go,
you shouldn't stop her.

These are some things we need to understand. Don't
get under condemnation for using your faith. Someone
might say, *"But I prayed for somebody, and they died."*

What does that have to do with it? You are required
to use your faith, but you can't control every situation
or every circumstance.

You should use your faith to the limit in these things.
Don't get under condemnation if it doesn't turn out the
way you decreed it. Someone may say you are a *"false
prophet."* But you weren't prophesying, **you were
decreeing something by faith.** You were using your
faith to the limit. Wouldn't you rather do that than just
say, *"Yes, she'll probably die. She almost died last time;
I guess she is going to die this time for sure."*

I'd hate to be a partner to anyone dying before their time. But if an individual wants to go, you shouldn't always try to stop them. They should have the right to go home.

## JESUS ESTABLISHED END RESULTS

At the tomb of Lazarus, Jesus said to the Father, *"I thank thee that thou hast heard me."* He has established something.

> *And I knew that thou hearest me always: but because of the people which stand by I said it, that they may believe that thou hast sent me.*
>
> *(John 11:42)*

He said, *"I knew You would hear Me. That's the reason I said it. I wanted to establish this on earth."*
Psalm 119:89 says,
*For ever, O Lord, thy word is settled in heaven.*

God's Word is already established in heaven; but on earth is where it needs to be established now. Look at what Jesus said, to Peter.

> *And I will give unto thee the keys of the kingdom of heaven: and whatsoever thou shalt bind on earth shall be bound in heaven: and whatsoever thou shalt loose on earth shall be loosed in heaven.*
>
> *(Matthew 16:19)*

**Jesus said the power of binding and loosing is on earth.** You have authority to bind on earth those things which have been bound out of heaven. You can loose some things and they will be loosed — not only by you, but God in heaven will loose some things, if you will loose them. But you must do something first on earth.

> *And when he thus had spoken, he cried with a loud voice, Lazarus, come forth.*    *(John 11:43)*

I can just see Peter and John. Peter punches John and says, *"now He's talking to the dead."*

## JESUS SPOKE TO THINGS AND THEY OBEYED

Notice that in Jesus' ministry, He talked to trees. He talked to the wind. He talked to the sea. He talked to dead people. And they all obeyed Him. In every instance, He was calling for things that were not manifest.

When Lazarus came forth, I can see John nudging Peter and saying, *"Hey, look, Peter! There is Lazarus standing in the door of the tomb!"*

Then all the embarrassment was gone. You may be embarrassed sometimes about some of the things you are saying, because it took so long for them to happen. But when you call the promise of God into manifestation in your life, all the embarrassment will leave.

## JESUS CALLED FOR PEACE IN THE STORM

Then again in Mark, chapter four we find Jesus calling things that are not manifest.

*And the same day, when the even was come, he saith unto them, Let us pass over unto the other side.*

*And there arose a great storm of wind, and the waves beat into the ship, so that it was now full.*

*And he was in the hinder part of the ship, asleep on a pillow: and they awake him, and say unto him, Master, carest thou not that we perish?*

*And he arose, and **rebuked the wind, and said unto the sea, Peace, be still.** And the wind ceased, and there was a great calm,*

*(Mark 4:35, 37-39)*

276

Notice, Jesus spoke to the wind and the waves. He stood up in the boat and saw the wind boisterous and the waves coming into the boat. There was a real storm on the sea. He looked out there at the storm and said, *"Peace, be still."*

There wasn't any peace when he said that. But He was calling the thing that was not manifest. *"Peace be still!"* sounds like a lie, doesn't it? There was no peace and nothing out there was still. **But He called it.**

I'm glad some of the people I know weren't in that boat. They would have said, *"But, Jesus, You can't do that. You have to say it like it is."* Wouldn't that have been foolish to stand up in the boat and say, *"Big waves and strong winds! We're sinking!"* They would have gone straight to the bottom.

Some people operate this principle Jesus used in reverse to **prophesy their own doom.** There are many people who don't operate in these principles because they don't know these are Bible principles.

## CALLING THE LEPERS CLEAN

Jesus called things that were not, in all of His ministry. He taught us to do the same. In Luke seventeen we find the story of the ten lepers who cried out for Jesus to have mercy on them.

*And as he entered into a certain village, there met him ten men that were lepers, which stood afar off:*

*And they lifted up their voices, and said, Jesus, Master, have mercy on us.*

*And when he saw them, he said unto them, Go shew yourselves unto the priests. And it came to pass that, as they went, they were cleansed.*

*(Luke 17:12-14)*

277

Notice that Jesus said, *"Go show yourself to the priest."*

What is He talking about? Doesn't He know they are lepers?

Yes, Jesus knows they are lepers. But He is calling them clean. The only scriptural reason they would show themselves to the priest was if they were cleansed. So Jesus was calling them clean. They could have said, *"But Jesus, we don't believe in this calling things that are not. We don't believe in confessing something that is not already true. We just believe in saying it like it is. We call things as they are."*

Had they said that, they probably would have been lepers for the rest of their lives, and would have felt very religious about it. But the Bible says, **as they went, they were cleansed.** They acted on the words of Jesus, as He was calling things that were not. As they went, they were calling things that were not, by their actions.

Every time Jesus told a cripple to take up his bed and walk, He was calling things that were not, as though they were. (John 5:8; Luke 5:24)

We know a cripple can't walk, and Jesus knew a cripple couldn't walk and carry his bed. **Jesus called them healed when they were bedfast.** The individuals called themselves healed by their actions.

Again in Luke 6:10, Jesus tells a man with a withered hand to stretch forth his hand. A withered hand can't be stretched forth unless it is healed. When the man acted on Jesus' Words, he was calling his hand normal. This was God's method, and Jesus used it.

## THREE METHODS

There are three main methods of calling things that are not. You can call things that are not **by praying the answer.** You can call things that are not **by confession of the Word of God.** You can call things that are not **by**

**your actions.** These people were actually calling things that were not by their actions.

**Speaking the end results is a method of calling things that are not.** Jesus continually operated in this principle.

**You must continue to practice this principle if you are to develop in it.** It takes time to get developed in this — it doesn't come overnight. You have to discipline yourself to believe the things that you say will come to pass. You can't talk all kinds of foolishness day after day and develop in this principle.

## A NEW WAY OF LIFE

Let your Yea be Yea, and your Nay be Nay. Speak what you mean, and mean what you speak. Develop faith in your words. Learn to release faith in every word you speak.

**The Word of promise is near you. First it's in your mouth, and then it's in your heart.**

Because it is so important for you who have read this book to begin **now** to call things that are not, I have included the confession from the book, *God's Creative Power Will Work For You.* Use them as a guide to begin scriptural confession. This is not a fad. It is a way of life. Be diligent to call daily the promises of God that are not in manifestation in your life.

**This is the beginning of a new way of life.**

**You can develop into what God desires in your life.**

**Confess these aloud several times a day.**

**Don't just read them.**

**With a loud voice, decree them to be true.**

**Faith cometh by hearing.**

# CONFESSIONS BASED ON GOD'S WORD

## To Defeat Worry and Fear Confess These Three Times a Day

*I am the body of Christ and Satan hath no power over me. For I overcome evil with good.*
*(I Corinthians 12:27; Romans 12:21)*

*I am of God and have overcome him. For greater is He that is in me, than he that is in the world.*
*(1st John 4:4)*

*I will fear no evil for thou art with me Lord, your Word and your Spirit they comfort me.* *(Psalms 23:4)*

*I am far from oppression, and fear does not come nigh me.* *(Isaiah 54:14)*

*No weapon formed against me shall prosper, for my righteousness is of the Lord. But whatever I do will prosper for I'm like a tree that's planted by the rivers of water.* *(Isaiah 54:17; Psalms 1:3)*

*I am delivered from the evils of this present world for it is the will of God concerning me.* *(Galatians 1:4)*

*No evil will befall me neither shall any plague come nigh my dwelling. For the Lord has given His angels charge over me and they keep me in all my ways, and in my pathway is life and there is no death.*
*(Psalms 91:10-11; Proverbs 12:28)*

*I am a doer of the Word of God and am blessed in my deeds. I am happy in those things which I do because I am a doer of the Word of God.* (James 1:22)

*I take the shield of faith and I quench every fiery dart that the wicked one brings against me.* (Ephesians 6:16)

*Christ has redeemed me from the curse of the law. Therefore, I forbid any sickness or disease to come upon this body. Every disease germ and every virus that touches this body dies instantly in the name of Jesus. Every organ and every tissue of this body functions in the perfection to which God created it to function, and I forbid any malfunction in this body, in the name of Jesus.* (Galatians 3:13; Romans 8:11, Genesis 1:31; Matthew 16:19)

*I am an overcomer and I overcome by the blood of the lamb and the word of my testimony.* (Revelation 12:11)

*I am submitted to God and the devil flees from me because I resist him in the name of Jesus.* (James 4:7)

*The Word of God is forever settled in heaven. Therefore, I establish His Word upon this earth.* (Psalms 119:89)

*Great is the peace of my children for they are taught of the Lord.* (Isaiah 54:13)

### Confess To Control Weight
### Three Times a Day Before Meals

*I don't desire to eat so much I become overweight. I present my body to God, my body is the temple of the Holy Ghost, which dwelleth in me. I am not my own, I am bought with a price therefore, in the name of Jesus I refuse to over-eat. Body settle down, in the name of Jesus and conform to the Word of God. I mortify the desires of this body and command it to come into line with the Word of God.* (Romans 12:1; I Corinthians 6:19)

## For Material Needs Confess These Three Times a Day Until They're Manifest

*Christ has redeemed me from the curse of the law. Christ has redeemed me from poverty, Christ has redeemed me from sickness, Christ has redeemed me from spiritual death.* (Galatians 3:13; Deuteronomy 28)

*For poverty He has given me wealth, for sickness He has given me health, for death He has given me eternal life.* (II Corinthians 8:9; Isaiah 53:5-6; John 10:10; John 5:24)

*It is true unto me according to the Word of God.* (Psalms 119:25)

*I delight myself in the Lord and He gives me the desires of my heart.* (Psalms 37:4)

*I have given and it is given unto me good measure, pressed down, shaken together, running over, men give unto my bosom.* (Luke 6:38)

*With what measure I meet, it is measured unto me. I sow bountifully, therefore I reap bountifully. I give cheerfully, and My God has made all grace abound toward me and I having all sufficiency of all things — do abound to all good works.* (II Corinthians 9:6-8)

*There is no lack for my God supplieth all of my needs according to His riches in glory by Christ Jesus.* (Philippians 4:19)

*The Lord is my shepherd and I DO NOT WANT because Jesus was made poor, that I through His poverty might have abundance. For He came that I might have life and have it more abundantly.*

*(Psalms 23:1; II Corinthians 8:9; John 10:10)*

*And I, having received abundance of grace and the gift of righteousness to reign as a king in life by — Jesus Christ.*
*(Romans 5:17)*

*The Lord has pleasure in the prosperity of His servant, and Abraham's blessings are mine.*

*(Psalms 35:27; Galatians 3:14)*

### For Wisdom and Guidance Confess These Three Times a Day

*The Spirit of truth abideth in me and teaches me all things, and He guides me into all truths. Therefore I confess I have perfect knowledge of every situation and every circumstance that I come up against. For I have the wisdom of God.* *(John 16:13; James 1:5)*

*I trust in the Lord with all my heart, and I lean not unto my own understanding.* *(Proverbs 3:5)*

*In all my ways I acknowledge Him and He directs my path.* *(Proverbs 3:6)*

*The Lord will perfect that which concerneth me.*
*(Psalms 138:8)*

*I let the Word of Christ dwell in me richly in all wisdom.*
*(Colossians 3:16)*

*I do follow the good shepherd and I know His voice and the voice of a stranger I will not follow.* (John 10:4-5)

*Jesus is made unto me wisdom, righteousness, sanctification, and redemption. Therefore I confess I have the wisdom of God, and I am the righteousness of God in Christ Jesus.* (I Corinthians 1:30; II Corinthians 5:21)

*I am filled with the knowledge of the Lord's will in all wisdom and spiritual understanding.* (Colossians 1:9)

*I am a new creation in Christ, I am His workmanship created in Christ Jesus. Therefore I have the mind of Christ and the wisdom of God is formed within me.*
(II Corinthians 5:17; Ephesians 2:10; I Corinthians 2:16)

*I have put off the old man and have put on the new man, which is renewed in the knowledge after the image of Him that created me.* (Colossians 3:10)

*I have received the Spirit of wisdom and revelation in the knowledge of Him, the eyes of my understanding being enlightened. And I am not conformed to this world but am transformed by the renewing of my mind. My mind is renewed by the Word of God.*
(Ephesians 1:17-18; Romans 12:2)

### For Comfort and Strength Confess These as Often as Necessary

*I am increasing in the knowledge of God. I am strengthened with all might according to His glorious power.* (Colossians 1:10-11)

*I am delivered from the power of darkness and I am translated into the kingdom of His dear Son.*

*(Colossians 1:13)*

*I am born of God and I have world overcoming faith residing on the inside of me. For greater is He that is in me, than he that is in the world.*  *(I John 5:4-5; I John 4:4)*

*I will do all things through Christ which strengtheneth me.*  *(Philippians 4:13)*

*The joy of the Lord is my strength. The Lord is the strength of my life.*  *(Nehemiah 8:10; Psalms 27:1)*

*The peace of God which passeth all understanding keeps my heart and my mind through Christ Jesus. And things which are good, and pure, and perfect, and lovely, and of good report, I think on these things.*

*(Philippians 4:7-8)*

*I let no corrupt communication proceed out of my mouth, but that which is good to edifying, that it may minister grace to the hearer. I grieve not the Holy Spirit of God, whereby I'm sealed unto the day of redemption.*

*(Ephesians 4:29)*

*I speak the truth of the Word of God in love and I grow up into the Lord Jesus Christ in all things.*  *(Ephesians 4:15)*

*No man shall take me out of his hand for I have eternal life.*  *(John 10:29)*

*I let the peace of God rule in my heart and I refuse to worry about anything.*  *(Colossians 3:15)*

*I will not let the Word of God depart from before my eyes for it is life to me for I have found it and it is health and healing to all my flesh.* (Proverbs 4:21-22)

*God is on my side. God is in me now, who can be against me? He has given unto me all things that pertain unto life and godliness. Therefore I am a partaker of His divine nature.*
(II Corinthians 6:16; John 10:10; II Peter 1:3-4; Romans 8:31)

*I am a believer and these signs do follow me. In the name of Jesus I cast out demons, I speak with new tongues, I lay hands on the sick and they do recover.* (Mark 16:17-18)

*Jesus gave me the authority to use His name. And that which I bind on earth is bound in heaven. And that which I loose on earth is loosed in heaven. Therefore in the name of the Lord Jesus Christ I bind the principalities, the powers, the rulers of the darkness of this world. I bind and cast down spiritual wickedness in high places and render them harmless and ineffective against me in the name of Jesus.*
(Matthew 16:19; John 16:23-24; Ephesians 6:12)

*I am complete in Jesus who is the head of all principality and power. For I am His workmanship, created in Christ Jesus unto good works which God has before ordained that I should walk therein.*
(Colossians 2:10; Ephesians 2:10)

These confessions call the things that are promised. They also renew your mind **and cause faith to come. Be positive. Don't give up. God is on your side.**

287